AN
INTRODUCTION TO
THE HISTORY OF
EAST AFRICA

AN INTRODUCTION TO THE HISTORY OF EAST AFRICA

BY

ZOË MARSH

&

G. W. KINGSNORTH

CAMBRIDGE

AT THE UNIVERSITY PRESS

1957

PUBLISHED BY
THE SYNDICS OF THE CAMBRIDGE UNIVERSITY PRESS

London Office: Bentley House, N.W.1
American Branch: New York

Agents for Canada, India, and Pakistan: Macmillan

Printed in Great Britain at the University Press, Cambridge
(Brooke Crutchley, University Printer)

CONTENTS

v

CONTENTS

CONTENTS

CHAPTER IV. THE ABOLITION MOVEMENT IN THE EMPIRE AND IN EAST AFRICA (*page* 40)

I. *Abolition in the British Empire*

II. *Abolition in East Africa*

CONTENTS

CHAPTER V. EXPLORATION (*page 55*)

CONTENTS

CHAPTER VI. MISSIONARY SOCIETIES AND THE
EARLY DEVELOPMENT OF EAST AFRICA (*page* 77)

CONTENTS

CHAPTER VII. THE SCRAMBLE FOR AFRICA AND THE FIRST PARTITION OF EAST AFRICA (*page* 91)

I. *The scramble for Africa*

II. *The partition of East Africa*

CHAPTER VIII. THE HISTORY OF UGANDA
UP TO 1890 (*page* 115)

CONTENTS

CHAPTER IX. LORD LUGARD (*page* 135)

CONTENTS

CHAPTER X. LATER ZANZIBAR (*page* 154)

CHAPTER XI. THE RAILWAY AND THE ECONOMIC DEVELOPMENT OF KENYA (*page* 168)

CHAPTER XII. THE CONSTITUTIONAL DEVELOPMENT OF KENYA (*page* 191)

CONTENTS

CHAPTER XIII. THE LATER HISTORY OF
UGANDA (*page* 203)

CHAPTER XIV. THE LATER HISTORY OF
TANGANYIKA (*page* 221)

CONTENTS

LIST OF MAPS

PREFACE

While books of various sizes have been written on Uganda alone, Tanganyika alone, Zanzibar alone, and Kenya alone, to the best of our knowledge no book has previously been written which deals specifically with the history of East Africa as a whole, giving roughly equal weight to each territory. The purpose of this book is to fill that gap by supplying an outline of the history of all the East African countries.

As Uganda, Tanganyika, Zanzibar, and Kenya each have their own clear characteristics as a result of their widely differing processes of development, we have been at pains to stress the separate histories of all four countries. On the other hand, the story of their development is so much of a unity that at some points in their history it seemed necessary to pursue a theme in relation to East Africa as a whole. The chapters on Exploration and Partition may be taken as examples of this. But East Africa is not an isolated unit unconnected with other countries of the world or separated from the rest of the African continent by some magic barrier, and the significance of its development cannot be gauged unless it is seen in a wider frame, especially in its relation to the rest of Africa. Therefore, in the chapters on Slavery, Partition, and Lord Lugard, we have tried to present the picture in its true perspective by exploring beyond the boundaries of East Africa.

Most of us have disagreeable associations with the words 'school text-book', and it is hoped that the general reader will not be repelled by the fact that this book was primarily designed for students in connexion with the Cambridge School Certificate syllabus on 'The Development of Tropical Africa'. It was written with the hope also that the story of East Africa's growth would prove sufficiently interesting and readable to be of interest to all. But because we were thinking especially of schools, emphasis has been laid on the biographical presentation of material, and because the book is meant to be used for School Certificate purposes in conjunction with the companion volume by W. D. Hussey (*Discovery*, *Expansion*, *and*

Empire, also published by the Cambridge University Press), an effort has been made not to duplicate material given there. As a general history of East Africa, however, this book stands as a self-contained volume.

Since adequate information about the constitutional development of Kenya is not readily available, we have included in the chapter on that subject more detail than would be required by the School Certificate candidate. It is hoped that this will have some value, however, for the general reader and for the teacher.

We have worked closely together throughout the writing of the book, and share responsibility for the work equally. Authorship of particular chapters is as follows: by Z.M., 1, 2, 5, 6, 10, 11, 12, appendix 1; by G.W.K., 3, 4, 7, 8, 9, 13 and 14.

Specialist checking and criticism of parts of the draft have been most kindly given by Mr H. B. Thomas, O.B.E., Miss M. Perham, C.B.E., Dr R. Oliver, Mr J. R. Moffett, Miss D. Middleton, Mr J. Smart, M.B.E., D.P.A., and Sheikh Mubarak Ahmad. We should also like to thank Mr C. G. Richards of the East African Literature Bureau, and Mr G. Kemp of the Macmillan Library for their invaluable co-operation throughout. So many people have helped us that it would be impossible to thank them all here, but special thanks are due to the Principal of the Aga Khan School, Nairobi, Mr F. H. Goldsmith of the Prince of Wales School, Nairobi, and our colleagues on the staffs of the Kenya High School, Nairobi, and the Alliance High School, Kikuyu. Mrs B. M. Weller and Mr J. A. Boxhall have also given us special help. Particular thanks are due to Miss S. White of the African Girls High School, Kikuyu, who not only gave us much valuable criticism but also drew some of the maps.

Z.M.
G.W.K.

NAIROBI
31 March 1956

CHAPTER I

EARLY HISTORY OF EAST AFRICA

Link with geography. The study of history is closely linked with that of geography. Hence a map is helpful in explaining why the north and south of Africa have been more closely linked with Europe than either the west or east. It also indicates why the early invaders of West Africa came from Europe, and those of East Africa from Asia. The map shows that the close link between Europe and North and South Africa is partly due to the climate, which in both these latter areas is sub-tropical and therefore attractive to Europeans. It also makes it clear that the Sahara Desert was an obstacle in the way of an overland route from Europe to any part of Africa except the north. One can see too that before the Suez Canal was cut the shortest sea route from Europe to East Africa was over 8,000 miles. By contrast the distance from Zanzibar to Bombay is only 2500 miles, or about the length of the Mediterranean. Therefore, while early visitors to West Africa came mostly from Europe, those to East Africa came from Asia.

Dhows and the monsoons. These visitors to East Africa were helped by the fortunate direction of the monsoon winds, which start to blow from the north-east in December and from the south-west in March. Very early on the Arabs realized that this meant that their dhows could be blown south to East Africa by the monsoon in December; and a few months later driven back by the same wind, when it had changed direction. The dhows were similar to those which today still use the monsoons to sail up and down the east coast of Africa.

Early visitors. The monsoon also helped the Hindus, the Phoenicians, and possibly the Assyrians and the Jews to reach East Africa. As these traders were coming long before the birth of Christ, we do not know much about their early voyages; we do not even know enough to be sure that the last two peoples came to the shores of East Africa; although we are certain that the Hindus, Arabs and

Phoenicians did. And we do not know for certain whether the land of Punt, to which the Egyptian books say Egypt was sending traders in 5000 B.C., really was Somaliland or not. We know that the ancient Assyrians, who lived on the Persian Gulf, in the country which is now called Iraq, are said to have believed in a form of magic which is like that used among the coastal people of East Africa.

The Assyrians. Another link between Assyria and East Africa is the symbol of the horn. This was used by the Assyrians as a sign of power, and it is still so used in parts of East Africa; in Wachagga country, for instance, the chief still calls his meetings by blowing a horn. These resemblances make us think it possible that the Assyrians came to East Africa, especially as they knew how to use ships, and could have been blown there by the monsoon from their homes near the Persian Gulf. The Jews in Palestine were also well placed for visiting East Africa, and the use of Jewish names and Jewish customs in Madagascar makes us conclude that they probably sailed there, down the east coast.

The Chinese. By the beginning of the Middle Ages we know that the Chinese also were visiting the coast. Their writers tell of the annual visit, paid when the monsoon blew; and so many pieces of Chinese pottery have been found on the east coast that a famous archaeologist has said that 'the history of East Africa in the Middle Ages is written in Chinese porcelain'.

Early trade. All these visitors came for the sake of trade. They hoped to get from East Africa spices, ivory and slaves, for which they would usually trade beads and cloth. In those days spices were valued as preservatives, as well as for the flavour they gave to food: and these spices were obtained from the area round Cape Guardafui. Africa has always been the chief source of ivory, because the elephants there are not used for work and are, therefore, hunted for their tusks. Unfortunately Africa was also for centuries the centre of the slave trade.

Invaders of the interior. Before these traders saw the coast of East Africa for the first time, there were invasions of the interior by people speaking an Hamitic language who came from north-west Asia and who pushed down from the Nile Valley and Abyssinia into what Professor Coupland calls: 'Negroland, the mid-African home of the black-skinned, fuzzy-haired, thick-lipped Negroes.' These invading Hamites brought with them the goat, the dog and certain grains, all of which were until then unknown in East Africa. In the north of Africa one group of them settled in the country between Abyssinia and the Gulf of Aden. These were the Galla. Later they in their turn were pushed out by the Somali, with the result that today the Galla are scattered across the northern part of Kenya, while Somaliland shows where the Somali settled.

The Bantu. Another group of the Hamitic people drifted further south and intermarried with the Negroes, thus producing a race often called Bantu. One link between the Bantu people is that of language, for while they speak several hundred languages these are all closely related. In the same way, Portuguese, Spanish, Italian and French are akin and together make up what Europeans often call the Latin or Romance languages. In all Bantu languages, for instance, the use of the suffix and prefix is similar and has an important effect on the meaning of the word. The Negroes, on the other hand, speak languages which are not only different from those of the Bantu, but are also distinct from each other. They live today in the Sudan and in West Africa south of the Sahara desert.

The tribes of East Africa. A map on p. 4 gives the present position of the chief tribes in East Africa; and in the appendix titles are given of several books dealing with the histories of these tribes. We know few details of the past of these tribes, unfortunately, for they have no written records of their history. This is a gap which will have to be filled by the research of students, but the brief list of books we have given, which does not claim to be complete, may encourage readers to find out what is at present known about the history of local tribes.

Population. In studying East African tribal history, however, it is possible to make a few generalizations. First of all it is important to notice that there are comparatively few inhabitants. Kenya, Uganda and Tanganyika cover an area of over 600,000 square miles (though it should be noted that large parts of this are semi-desert). The native

I-2

inhabitants of this area number roughly 18,500,000. This gives a density of twenty-six to the square mile, compared to a density of forty-eight for the world as a whole. Even today, therefore, East Africa has

Map 1. The Tribes of East Africa.

comparatively few people to the square mile; and there are good reasons to think that there were still fewer at the end of the nineteenth century. This may well have been due, not only to disease but also to the slave trade, and the war between tribes that often went with it. One must also remember that vegetation in East Africa is unevenly distributed. In parts of the country there is an excessive tropical growth, yet in other areas there are semi-desert conditions. These difficulties may also be the reason why East African society, before the penetration of the interior by Europeans, was described by Coupland as 'simple in character and limited in scope'.

Usambara. This description, of course, did not apply to Uganda, and possibly not to Usambara either. Pp. 118–20 in ch. VIII describe the feudal state which Buganda had reached before the coming of the Europeans, while in the first half of the nineteenth century the kingdom of Usambara was ruled by one of the greatest of its kings. This was Kimweri who, by 1840, had conquered the greater part of the Pare Mountains and also the plain between Usambara and the sea; by the time the first European missionary, Krapf, visited him in 1848, he considered he ruled over at least half a million people, whose land stretched sixty miles from north to south and about 140 miles from north-west to south-east. This area was divided into districts, each of which was placed under a governor, who had to send a representative to the court of Kimweri. All state business was done by Kimweri through these representatives. Direct taxes were also levied from time to time by Kimweri on this or that district. The kingdoms of Usambara and Buganda were the only states or empires which could be compared with those in West Africa. In the rest of the interior of East Africa the government was far more primitive and limited in extent. There were tribal wars, of course, but they only resulted in cattle and slaves being carried off. They did not lead to the conquest or government of larger areas of land.

Mohammed. The next stage in the history of East Africa, the Arab and Persian settlement of the coast, derives from an event of great importance in the history of civilization. This was the birth of Mohammed in Mecca in A.D. 570. He taught the Arabs to turn from heathen gods to the worship of one God. 'There is one God (Allah), and Mohammed is his Prophet.' Mohammed's teaching angered the rulers of Mecca, and in 622 he was forced to flee to Medina. His power and influence, however, continued to spread, and eight years later he was able to conquer Mecca. When Mohammed died in 632, practically the whole of Arabia had accepted the faith of Islam.

Effect of Islam. The chief political effect of Islam was that it united the tribes of Arabia, who were now determined to use their strength to convert as many people as possible to their new religion of Islam, which was the word they used for submission to the will of Allah. The Muslims believed that those who died fighting for their religion went straight to Paradise, and they fought bravely and with strict discipline; and in the first eighty years after the death of the Prophet they conquered Syria, Mesopotamia, Persia and Egypt, and had spread their empire through North Africa as far as Spain. At the head of this empire was the Caliph (or successor) of the Prophet, and it was not long before disputes broke out as to who was the rightful Caliph. These disputes divided the Arab empire, and caused some of those who had been on the losing side to take refuge on the pleasant coast of East Africa, with which trade had already made them familiar. Among those who knew the coast well were the traders of Oman. Their land is in the south-east corner of Arabia and juts out into the Indian Ocean with the Arabian desert behind it. Those who lived in Oman were therefore in a very good position for trade, and were quick to seize any chance to win independence. Among the lovers of independence were Suleiman and Said, who led a rebellion against the Caliph towards the end of the seventh century A.D. When this failed they had to flee to Zenjibar (Zenj is a Persian word for black, and Bar means coast), or the land of the Blacks. They finally settled on the Lamu archipelago where they lived by hunting, fishing and farming. After a time they became traders, and it is said that they eventually became the first slave hunters to operate on a large scale in East Africa. Two other groups of refugees followed: the people of Zaid, who left Yemen because they hated the Caliph, and the Seven Brothers of El Hasa. The Seven Brothers were probably the seven leaders of a large group of warriors who left El Hasa, which at that time was the capital of a state in southern Mesopotamia. They conquered the whole coastal strip down as far as Mombasa. Finally Hasan bin Ali and

6

his six sons set sail from southern Persia in A.D. 975, in seven ships, and each shipload founded a settlement. Four of these settlements are known: Mombasa, Pemba, Johanna in the Comoro Isles, and Kilwa. It was at Kilwa that Hasan bin Ali himself settled.

The Zenj empire. Thus the Persians and the Arabs settled on the east coast of Africa, and the period from 975 (when Hasan bin Ali and his sons took refuge there) to 1498, when Vasco da Gama sailed to Mombasa, is often called the time of the Zenj empire. The word 'empire' is used because the state of Kilwa took the lead among the coastal settlements. These were Sofala, Mozambique, Kilwa, Tumbatu, Pemba, Zanzibar, Vumba, the Lamu Archipelago and Mogadishu.

Map 2, page 10, shows that most of these places were on islands, although some of them, like Mombasa, were only separated from the mainland by a narrow stretch of water. This was because their Arab or Persian settlers were people who were used to making their living as traders on the sea. As they were settlements in a strange land they were also all fortified, and gradually towns grew up behind these defences. From the ruins left behind by these settlers we know that many of them carried with them memories of their homes in Persia. To Kilwa, for instance, they brought the knowledge of how to build in stone, carve wood and weave cotton. But as the years went on, these settlements became more and more Arab in character. That is why these 500 years of the Zenj Empire are thought of nowadays as the period of Arab settlement. True to their Arab character the groups were always quarrelling among themselves; now one town, now another, took the lead, although Kilwa always had an important position from the time when it was bought by Hasan bin Ali from the Africans (on condition that it was fenced round with coloured cloth); guessing that the Africans meant to come back later and recapture it, Hasan dug a channel between the town and the mainland, thus making Kilwa an island, not only at high tide, but at all times. When he had also added fortifications, Kilwa became a strong point from which Hasan went on to control the coast from Sofala to Pemba. The leading position of Kilwa at this time is illustrated by the fact that, in

7

the reign of Hasan's son Ali, it was possible for Ali to appoint his son Muhammad as governor of Mombasa.

Decline in Arab trade. From earliest times Southern Arabia was the market for goods from the East, and the north-eastern monsoon brought Arabian dhows to the coast of East Africa. In the second century A.D. this trade decreased. First, the irrigation of south-west Arabia was seriously disturbed by the bursting of a large reservoir which reduced the prosperity of the whole of the area. Second, the Bantu people had begun to appear on the coast and, as they were fiercer and better armed than the original peoples, the Arab traders were further discouraged. Trade revived with the rise of Islam and the arrival of Arab settlers on the coast.

Trade in the Zenj Empire. During the period of the Zenj empire southern Arabia was the centre of the valuable maritime trade between the Far East, Mesopotamia and Persia and the countries bordering the Mediterranean Sea. Chinese silks, Indian cotton cloth, rhubarb from China (valued for its medicinal properties), precious stones, pepper, nutmeg, mace, ginger and cloves were brought there by sea and sent thence by caravan across the desert, or transhipped up the Red Sea by the Arabs, who monopolized its navigation. To the East went copper from Arabia and horses from Mesopotamia.

As well as being an important market-place for the traffic between East and West, Arabia also annually sent a fleet of ships down the east coast of Africa to carry on the trade in ivory, slaves and spices which had originally attracted the Arabs to the coast. While Africa was the chief source of the first two, the only spices that were then obtained from East Africa were frankincense and cinnamon. Other spices, such as cloves, which came from the Molucca islands, and pepper, from India, were obtained in the Far East, where the merchants of East Africa and Arabia paid the local rulers for the right to have factories and agents. There was also a fair amount of East African trade in ambergris and gold. This last had its centre at Sofala, the nearest port to Zimbabwe. The Indians, also, who owned a good deal of the ocean shipping, shared in this trade. They were probably the experts who dealt with finance and with the retail trade, for this is work for which they, unlike the Arabs, have long shown ability. Neither Indian nor Arab showed any desire to explore the vast continent which lay behind the coast. They were content to exchange the goods they brought, their beads, glass, metal-work and cloth, for the ivory, ambergris, slaves and gold. This exchange involved sending caravans into the interior and sometimes fighting to keep a trade-route open. But unless it served the interests of trade, the Arabs were not to be found in the interior.

Life on the coast. On the coast the Arabs intermarried with the Africans. The result was the birth of the Swahili people, who shared the faith of Islam and much of the Arab way of life. This life on the coast was dependent on slaves who had marched down from the interior. Those who survived this journey to serve Arab masters in their plantations and homes were relatively fortunate, for the Koran taught Muslims that kindliness to slaves was a virtue, and many were as well treated as slaves can be. The more unfortunate were those who had still to face the horrors of a sea-passage in which they were packed so closely together that they could hardly turn round. These included those who were shipped to Oman (where the slaves made up a large portion of the population), to India and probably to China.

The 'Periplus'. Although it is thousands of years since the monsoon blew the first Arab dhow into an East African harbour, we are able to get a picture of life on the coast before the Arabs had made their first settlement there. We owe this to Hippalus, a Roman sailor who sailed down the Red Sea in A.D. 45 and discovered the regularity of the monsoon winds. Soon this knowledge spread, and books were written in Greek and Latin telling of the Indian Ocean and its ports. One of these books was a guide-book to the Indian Ocean. Its title was the *Periplus* (circumnavigation or sailing round) *of the Erythraean Sea*, as the Greeks and Romans called the Indian Ocean. This book still exists today, and in it we find references to East Africa, where there lived along the coast 'men of piratical habits, very great in stature, and under separate chiefs for each place'. To the coast there came 'Arab captains and agents, who are familiar with the natives and intermarry with them and who know the whole coast and

9

understand the language. There are imported into these markets the lances made at Muza especially for this trade, and hatchets and daggers and awls, and various kinds of glass.' The *Periplus* tells us

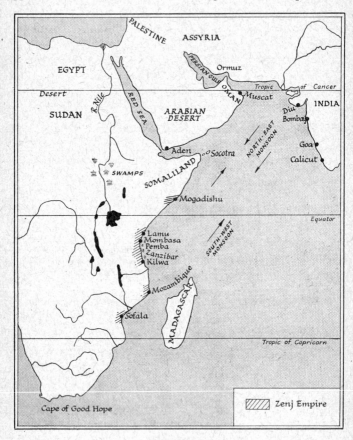

Map 2. The Indian Ocean.

that the Arabs also imported a little wheat, not so much for trading purposes as to secure the good will of the native inhabitants of the coast, for 'there are exported from these places a great quantity of ivory...and rhinoceros horn and tortoiseshell...and a little palm oil'; while from just below Cape Guardafui there were exported 'slaves of the better sort which are brought to Egypt in increasing numbers'.

Early Mombasa. There is another very interesting description of parts of the East African coast which was written much later, at the beginning of the sixteenth century, by Duarte Barbosa, who writes:

There is a city of the Moors, called Bombaza (Mombasa) very large and beautiful, and built of high and handsome houses of stone and whitewash, and with very good streets, in the manner of those of Quiboa. And it also had a king over it. The people are of dusky white and brown complexions, and likewise the women, who are much adorned with silk and gold stuffs. It is a town of great trade in goods, and has a good port, where there are always many ships, both of those that sail for Sofala and those that come from Cambray and Melinde, and others which sail to the islands of Zanzibar, Manfia and Pemba, which will be spoken of further on. This Mombasa is a country well supplied with plenty of provisions, very fine sheep, which have round tails, and many cows, chickens and very large goats, much rice and millet, and plenty of oranges, sweet and bitter, and lemons, cedrats, pomegranates, Indian figs, and all sorts of vegetables, and very good water. The inhabitants at times are at war with the people of the continent (Mombasa itself is an island) and at other times at peace, and trade with them and obtain much honey and wax, and ivory.

Arrival of Vasco da Gama. Such was the life lived in East Africa when Vasco da Gama rounded the Cape of Good Hope on his search for a new route to the spice islands of the East, the old overland routes having been blocked by the Turks, who had captured Constantinople in 1453. In 1498 da Gama saw the prosperous town of Malindi and was greeted by a king, 'wearing a robe of damask trimmed with green satin, and seated on two cushioned chairs of bronze'. He proved helpful and supplied Vasco da Gama with a good pilot to guide him across the Indian Ocean to Calicut. This reception was the beginning of a long friendship between the Portuguese and Malindi, and was partly due to the bad feeling that existed between Mombasa and Malindi. Once it was known at Malindi that Vasco da Gama had been received badly in Mombasa, the king was eager to welcome him.

D'Albuquerque's plan for the Portuguese conquest. In 1499 Vasco da Gama returned to Portugal and told of his great discoveries. Portugal was quick to see the importance of these, and ten years later she had conquered the east coast of Africa and was able to appoint Dom Duarte de Lemos as governor of all the Portuguese possessions in Africa and Arabia. This conquest of the East African coast was part of the great plan of the ambitious Portuguese d'Albuquerque, who had worked out his ideas before he became viceroy of India in 1509. At that time the Portuguese merchants were dependent for their share of the valuable spice trade on the good will of the local rulers in India, who allowed them to maintain warehouses and agents on their soil. D'Albuquerque realized that this precarious foothold could be converted into a maritime and Christian empire only if Portugal had a permanent fleet in the Indian Ocean. This meant that Portugal must have fortresses which would command the chief routes of the Indian Ocean trade. Once these had been conquered, she would cease to be dependent on an interloping commerce with a far distant base in Lisbon and would rule a secure commercial empire covering the whole of the Middle East. Its centre was to be at Goa in India, where the chief representative of Portugal, called the viceroy of India, would have his headquarters and control the trade of the west coast of India. To guard the routes to India, Albuquerque reckoned that he must gain control of three places: Socotra, which was to be a base for ventures into the Red Sea and so useful for the interception of spice cargoes (he would have preferred Aden, but it proved impossible to capture); Ormuz, which controlled the entry to the Persian Gulf and was one of the most important markets in the world for Eastern products; and Malacca, which was the western end of the Chinese trade and the only place from which the Portuguese could control all the trade, mostly in spices, across the Bay of Bengal. But it was not enough for Portugal to conquer these places only; she had to think also of supplying her sailing ships on their long voyages to the East. For this it was essential for Portugal to conquer the East African coast, and between 1500 and 1509 this was done with great savagery.

Beginning of the Portuguese conquest. The first step was taken by Vasco da Gama on his second voyage to India in 1502. He called at Kilwa and forced the sultan to pay a yearly tribute to the king of Portugal. This was typical of Portugal's dealings with the coast. Tribute was demanded and unless it was paid the town was destroyed. If it was paid the local sultan was usually left in peace, provided he carried out the wishes of the Portuguese. After Kilwa, Zanzibar was the next place to suffer from the Portuguese. In 1503 a Portuguese commander called Ravasco showed the power of guns by using two boats with cannon to defeat canoes carrying four thousand men. These canoes had been manned by the ruler of Zanzibar in protest against Ravasco's unprovoked attack on a number of small local ships carrying goods that Ravasco wanted.

D'Almeida. This was only the beginning. In 1505 a fleet of more than twenty ships set sail from Portugal for India. The newly appointed viceroy of India, d'Almeida, was in command, and his first task was to gain control of three key places on the coast of East Africa: Sofala, Kilwa and Mombasa. Sofala was important to the Portuguese because it would give them control of the gold supply. It offered hardly any resistance, and a fort was built to protect the Portuguese colony that now replaced the old Arab settlement. The same fate was shared by Kilwa, which once claimed to rule the coast. D'Almeida's fleet then sailed away to deal with Mombasa, which of late had secured a larger share of trade than Kilwa; so that by 1505 Kilwa had only 4000 inhabitants, compared to Mombasa's 10,000. Unlike Sofala and Kilwa, Mombasa did not yield without a fight, and throughout the two hundred years during which the Portuguese ruled in East Africa, she was to be a thorn in their side, an island well named the 'Island of War'. But the bowmen of Mombasa could not long resist guns and armour, and Mombasa too was conquered and set on fire.

Not one of these three places, Sofala, Kilwa and Mombasa, however, was to be the headquarters of the Portuguese on the East coast. They found it more convenient to rule from Mozambique, which was 'colonized' in 1507.

Bases of the Portuguese Empire. When d'Albuquerque died in 1515, six years after the first Portuguese governor-general of the coast had been appointed, he left his country ruling an empire in the Indian Ocean which had its supply bases on the east coast of Africa, the chief of which was Mozambique. The headquarters of this empire was at Goa, the most important of the Portuguese trading stations on the west coast of India. It included Malacca, parts of Ceylon, a number of places in the Malay Archipelago, Socotra, Muscat in Oman and Ormuz, which guards the entry to the Persian Gulf. Aden alone had successfully resisted the Portuguese. The importance of their conquests either as trading centres or as forts guarding their empire is shown by the map on p. 10.

Results of the Portuguese conquest. From the beginning the Portuguese found the East African part of their empire disappointing, because it never brought them the wealth they had expected. They had hoped to secure this by cutting off Arab trade with India, and by attacking the Arab coastal trade, both on sea and land. They intended to deal direct with the Africans themselves, and no share of their profits was to be taken by Arab or Indian middlemen. So the Portuguese were content to fill their warehouses with calico and beads from India and wait for the Africans to bring gold, ivory and slaves from the interior. The Arabs too had had their headquarters on the coast, but they had also sent out caravans into the interior to encourage trade. The Portuguese under-estimated the part played by these caravans, and in the event lacked the men to staff them. So the supply of gold, ivory and slaves dried up, and the old Arab settlements, which had been taken over by the Portuguese, became poorer and weaker. This was most marked in the south where Mozambique, Kilwa and Sofala had their Portuguese garrisons and forts. Things were a little easier in the north where local sultans were still allowed to rule, provided they paid the annual tribute, but even here the conquerors were hated, and the Africans called the chief of the Portuguese 'Afriti' or devil.

Unrest in Mombasa. Mombasa was the leader in most of the trouble that arose from this hatred, and as she was unpopular with some of her neighbours, for example, Malindi and Zanzibar, they sometimes helped the Portuguese to punish her. In 1528, for instance, both Malindi and Zanzibar helped Nuño da Cunha to attack Mombasa while he was on his way to India to take up his post as viceroy. The result was that Mombasa had to pay a large sum of gold as tribute every year, and when the town tried to avoid this it was burnt to the ground. After this the 'Island of War' gave no trouble until 1586, when a Turkish pirate called Mirale Bey came sailing down the coast looking for loot. He told the people of Mombasa that he had been sent by the sultan to rescue them, and he did in fact drive the Portuguese out of most of their settlements. He then sailed away, and it was not long before the viceroy at Goa heard from Malindi what had happened. Punishment followed swiftly, but the spirit of Mombasa was not crushed. Three years later the people again welcomed Mirale Bey on his return to the coast. The viceroy of India also heard the news, and sent a fleet of ships to prevent another rebellion. Although Mirale Bey had come fairly well equipped this time, leading five ships, he knew that it would be very difficult to hold Mombasa against the Portuguese, and therefore accepted help offered by the Wazima. This was a Bantu tribe which had been eating their way up Africa since they left their lands near Zululand (they were cannibals). They had captured Kilwa, and were certain that if they waited for their chance they would be able to cross to the island of Mombasa, and enjoy the feast that the fine town offered. Mirale Bey mistrusted them, but he could not resist accepting their offer of help against the Portuguese and allowed them to cross to the island. No sooner were they there than they turned on the inhabitants, many of whom flung themselves desperately into the sea, where sharks were waiting for them.

Fort Jesus. Although the Portuguese put down this rebellion of Mombasa, the island continued to give trouble, and so in 1592 they again attacked and largely destroyed the town. This time they deposed the sultan and put the sultan of Malindi in his place, because they hoped that, as Malindi had always been loyal to them, Mombasa under his rule would cease to give trouble. This they considered important, for there was no doubt that the town was in a very strong position, and with the change of rulers they decided to make it the capital of their East African lands. To guard their new capital Fort Jesus was built, looking out over the harbour.

The decline of Portuguese power. By the end of the sixteenth century the first English ships had begun to appear in the Indian Ocean. They were the forerunners of the British East India Company, and were disliked by the Portuguese, who dreaded any interference with their trade monopoly in this area, especially as they knew that their hold on the coast was weakening. There were several reasons for this. In the first place Portugal never had a large enough population to carry out all her colonial plans. Two million people were not sufficient to cultivate Portugal as well as control Brazil and their empire in the Indian Ocean. Such energy as they had was devoted to Brazil rather than East Africa, which was not a place where many Portuguese settled, even temporarily. In addition, many of the Portuguese settlers in East Africa died from tropical diseases. Others were killed in the continual fighting on the coast. In 1580 Philip II, King of Spain, inherited the throne of Portugal. Philip had already more lands to administer than he was capable of dealing with, and the affairs of Portugal took second place. Thus, by the end of the sixteenth century, Portugal's grasp on the east coast of Africa was feeble. She had long been hated in her empire, where the conquered people could not forgive her greed and cruelty. They were quick, therefore, to seize every chance of rebellion.

Serious revolts against the Portuguese. The first serious revolt to succeed was in Ormuz, where in 1622 the Persians drove out the Portuguese. When this news spread down the coast it encouraged a feeling of restlessness, and in 1631 Mombasa, as usual, was the first to rebel. The leader was the Sultan Yusuf, who had been brought up as a Catholic by the Portuguese and educated at Goa. In India he grew familiar with the Portuguese way of life, despising it. Soon after his appointment as Sultan of Mombasa Yusuf became a Muslim. In a few months he was complaining, with justice, of the way in which the Portuguese governor of Mombasa ruled. By 1631 he was plotting against the Portuguese, and then managed to lead three hundred of his followers into Fort Jesus, where he stabbed the governor.

Although Yusuf followed this up by behaviour as savage as that of the Portuguese at their worst, his lead was followed by Pemba and other places on the coast. When it looked as if the forces from Goa would be successful in reconquering Mombasa, Yusuf himself dismantled the fort and destroyed it before sailing away to Arabia. Thus Mombasa lost its last sultan. The years of the Portuguese Empire in the East were numbered.

The British and the Dutch East India Company were replacing the Portuguese traders on the eastern shores of the Indian Ocean, and one by one Portugal's strong places were taken from her. Oman too had followed Ormuz in driving out her Portuguese conquerors, who now had only East Africa left of their empire in the east. Even that was not to be theirs long; for Mombasa was quick to appeal to the Sultan bin Seif, who as Imam of Oman was the religious head of his country as well as its ruler, to come to the rescue of his fellow-Muslims. Sultan bin Seif answered this appeal by freeing Mombasa from the Portuguese. However, owing to revolts in Oman he had to leave the town to be recaptured, and it was his son, the Imam Seif bin Sultan, who finally captured Fort Jesus and became master of Mombasa in 1698. In 1699 he drove the Portuguese out of Kilwa and Pemba also, and this date is usually counted as marking the end of Portuguese rule in East Africa north of Mozambique, which they hold to this day.

Seif bin Sultan. Like his father, Seif bin Sultan was called back by one of the revolts which always seemed to break out when a ruler left Oman. He had, therefore, to leave various Omani Arabs to rule the different towns in East Africa. In Mombasa, for instance, he left the head of the Mazrui family.

The results of Portuguese rule. Considering that they ruled the coast of East Africa for 200 years the Portuguese had done very little for East Africa beyond introducing manioc, maize and the pineapple. This may have been due to the fact that there were never more than a hundred Portuguese living north of Lake Delgado. The hatred these inspired checked any impulse to imitate them. It may also have been because they were never really interested in the land except as a useful stopping place on the way to India. In fact the chief result of their rule was that it had crippled the old Arab settlements, which had lost their wide trade interests and become decaying towns off the main shipping routes, whose only political link with the outside world was that with the Imam of Muscat who ruled Zanzibar.

CHAPTER II

ZANZIBAR UNDER SEYYID SAID

Accession of Seyyid Said. The foundation of Zanzibar's prosperity was laid by Seyyid Said who in 1804, at the age of fifteen, became ruler of Oman, as a consequence of murdering his rival, this being a recognized Arab method of securing a throne. Power won by this means must be held firmly, and the young Seyyid saw the value of a British alliance in his struggle against both the warlike Wahabi of the desert and the Jawasmi pirates who had their headquarters in the Persian Gulf, where they attacked the shipping both of Oman and of the British East India Company.

Co-operation with Britain. These attacks finally became so serious that the British government of India co-operated with Said, and in 1810 it looked as if the power of the Jawasmi would be broken. They had recently accepted control by the Wahabi, who now came to their rescue; by 1814 Said had finally defeated the Wahabi. In this he had not been assisted by Britain, but he remembered with gratitude the assistance that Britain had given him earlier against the Jawasmi pirates, and, as the long war between Britain and Napoleon ended at much the same time, the danger that Oman would be seized by one of the two was also at an end. Its value to either would have been as a base for attack.

The Moresby treaty. Seyyid Said could now rejoice that he had the support of the victorious British. It was unfortunate, of course, from Said's point of view, that they were so determined to check the slave trade that he felt it only wise to sign the Moresby Treaty of 1822, thus limiting the profitable Arab slave trade. However, he was pleased to think that in exchange for this concession the British had recognized his claim to overlordship in East Africa. It was now time, he judged, to make good this claim.

Said's struggle with the Mazrui. This meant a struggle with the Mazrui of Mombasa, who had seized control of the town nearly a hundred years earlier, and were well aware that the Imam of Oman had ceased to have any real power on the coast, except in Pemba, Zanzibar, Mafia, and later Kilwa. In the early part of Seyyid Said's reign things had indeed become even worse; for the Mazrui family were no longer loyal followers of the ruler of Oman. They aimed at ruling themselves. When they seized Pemba it looked as if Oman's control of the coast was slipping away. So with the Treaty of Moresby signed, and Oman for once peaceful, Said thought that the time had come to attack the Mazrui and make good his claim to the overlordship of the east coast of Africa, which his ancestors had freed from the Portuguese. To do this he had to capture Mombasa, which, by reason of its good harbour, protected by Fort Jesus, was still the key to the coast. The Mazrui, however, made a last desperate bid to remain independent of Oman by offering the Protectorate of Mombasa to Britain. Captain Owen, to whom the offer was made in 1823, accepted it with a view to using the port as a base against the slave trade.

Protectorate of Mombasa declined by Britain. This was a bitter blow to Seyyid Said, who had so recently signed the Treaty of Moresby with the one object of keeping Britain's friendship. Britain, however, did not want land in East Africa, and when Seyyid Said's protest was followed by evidence that the Mazrui only wanted to shelter under the Union Jack, and were not eager to accept British control, orders were given that the flag was to be taken down and the small garrison removed. This did not end the ruler of Oman's difficulties. He still had to conquer Mombasa, which meant getting control of Fort Jesus. At first it seemed as though this was beyond his power. A split among the Mazrui as to who should be ruler of Mombasa gave him his chance.

He got control of Fort Jesus in 1837, and in a few months he was the unquestioned ruler of Mombasa.

Said moves his capital to Zanzibar. During the years in which Said had been concentrating on the capture of Mombasa he had grown very attached to the island of Zanzibar which had loyally supported all his efforts. By 1837 he was spending as much time at Zanzibar as at his capital, Muscat. It was, however, a serious matter to shift the capital from Muscat to the island of Zanzibar from which it was separated by 2500 miles, especially as the dhows could only reach Zanzibar from Oman at the time of the monsoon. Said, moreover, meant to keep control in his lifetime of both Oman and the East African coast.

Assets of Zanzibar. In making Zanzibar his real capital in 1832, Seyyid Said knew that he risked loosening his hold on Oman, but he was a man with great commercial insight, and saw the possibilities of obtaining more real power in Africa than he had inherited as Imam of Muscat. Besides, Zanzibar was a green and pleasant land, with a delightful climate; and Muscat reflected the fierce heat of a sun-baked soil. It was also true that, until Seyyid Said developed Zanzibar, it was only an unimportant little town at which ships called for water and provisions on their way to the big centres of trade. It had, however, four very important assets. First, a good harbour, seven to nine fathoms deep, in which ships could anchor. Secondly it had, in Seyyid Said's opinion, the sweetest water to be found on the east coast. Its third advantage was a central situation, for the island, although nearly twenty miles from the mainland, is just over a hundred miles south of Mombasa and thus in a central position for trade with the mainland. Fourthly, its climate and fertile soil have the comparatively rare qualities needed for the cultivation of spices. These are shared also by the small neighbouring island of Pemba.

Introduction of cloves. With these advantages Seyyid Said considered that he could make his new capital the chief port on the western shores of the Indian Ocean, and thus increase his own and his country's wealth. In this way he would gain power, prestige and security. Soon after his arrival in Zanzibar he took the important step of introducing the cultivation of cloves. Until the end of the eighteenth century, cloves had only been known to grow in the East Indies. Yet they were eagerly sought after both as a preservative and as a medicine. This meant that they were, and are still, a very valuable crop. The idea of planting them probably came to Seyyid Said when, on a visit to Zanzibar, he saw a few cloves growing there and realized that the island's fertile soil might prove to have the rare qualities needed for their cultivation on a large scale. Having decided that clove culture should be the primary industry of his islands, Said set an example by sowing forty-five of his own plantations with the crop. He also put strong pressure on the other landowners on the island to do the same. When a coconut palm died, or was cut down, three clove trees had to be planted in its place. Disobedience resulted in the confiscation of land. As a result, at the end of Said's reign the value of the cloves exported from Zanzibar ranked next to that of the ivory and slaves on which the island had long depended, and today Zanzibar and Pemba produce nearly 90 per cent of the world's supply of cloves.

Exports of slaves and ivory. Nor did the development of cloves lead to a neglect of Zanzibar's primary exports, slaves and ivory. These had to be obtained from the interior of Africa, and during Seyyid Said's reign more and bigger caravans were sent out further inland, so much so that Burton, an explorer who is discussed in ch. v, tells us that Ujiji was not visited by the Arabs until 1840, yet by 1858 it was already a regular trading post. Speke is another explorer who commented on the extension of the caravan routes which, by Livingstone's time, had reached the three great lakes. As these caravans all went on foot, an increase in the routes meant the establishment of outposts such as Ujiji, for it was impossible to return to a base in Zanzibar during a single dry season.

Said's commercial outlook. These small Arab settlements, however, did not mean that Said was building an empire on the mainland. His interests were commercial, not imperial. Despite the fact that all the Arab caravans that set off from Zanzibar carried the sultan's red flag, and that most of the European explorers who used Said's capital as a base carried a letter of recommendation from this powerful ruler, he did not seek to found settlements other than the outposts that were needed to feed the new trade routes. Yet by the end of his reign men were saying that: 'When they whistle in Zanzibar, the people dance on the shores of the great lakes.' Seyyid Said's part in this had not only been to introduce the profitable clove and to encourage the caravans; he also provided a background of security and peace without which trade seldom flourishes. In addition to this he had seen the need to develop new markets for the products of the African mainland.

Foreign trade. In order to do this he encouraged foreign traders. Among these were the Indian merchants or Banyans who had long been familiar with the East African coast (see chapter 1). These men were not only allowed complete liberty of worship, and freedom from taxes beyond the 5 per cent customs duty which was levied on all goods; they were also employed to deal with Zanzibar's finance. Even the important post of collector of customs was usually given to a Hindu. The result was that a large Indian colony grew up in the capital and helped to change it from a fishing village to a town which numbered 60,000 in 1859. This population was larger than that of Mombasa, and nearly ten times the size of Mozambique, the capital of Portuguese East Africa.

Consulates established. Yet Seyyid Said was too clever a man to give the Indians a monopoly of his increasing trade. He realized that the best markets for his ivory and cloves were to be found in America and Britain. He therefore anxiously sought to develop trade links with these countries. The end of the American War of Independence gave the ex-colonists the chance to share in the trade with the east from which they had previously been shut out by the mercantile system under which the British East India Company had claimed a monopoly over all British and colonial trade in the Indian Ocean. The Americans seized this chance, and the number of their ships in this region steadily increased, until finally an American mission arrived at Muscat. The delighted Seyyid Said was thus able to sign a commercial treaty with the United States in 1833. Four years later the Americans were given the right to open a consulate in Zanzibar town.

A similar treaty was signed with France in 1844, and in the same year the French also opened a consulate. Seyyid Said knew, however, that these treaties were not sufficient to safeguard Zanzibar, and it was to Britain that he looked for support. The commercial treaty that he signed with her in 1839 was to be the beginning of a close link between the two countries. Indeed, the British consulate, which opened in 1841, had a powerful influence on Zanzibar policy. This favour with which the sultan regarded Britain went back to the beginning of his reign in Oman when, as a young man, he had joined forces with the British governor of India against the Jawasmi pirates who were attacking British shipping. Seyyid Said was aware, moreover, of the dangers from other European countries, especially France, and was prepared to pay a high price for British friendship.

The Zanzibar slave trade. The price Britain asked was his support in putting down slavery in East Africa. For centuries slaves had been captured in the land behind the east coast of Africa and used to transport the valuable ivory down to the coast, where Zanzibar was the chief slave market. As the Arabs penetrated further inland the number of slaves increased, until at the beginning of the nineteenth century about fifteen thousand were obtained annually. Many of these were shipped from Zanzibar to Arabia, Persia, Egypt, etc.

Britain's attitude to the slave trade. Britain, having played the chief part in stopping the transatlantic slave trade, was now anxious to check the Arab slave trade. Seyyid Said's support in this aim was the price that Britain asked for her friendship and her permission to trade freely with the ports of British India. She realized, however, that suppression of the slave trade would mean a big drop in revenue for Seyyid Said, who would also have to face the indignation of his Arab subjects. Britain, therefore, decided to work in stages. In 1822 pressure was successfully put on the sultan to sign the Moresby Treaty. Details of this are given in ch. IV, in which it is shown that a loophole existed whereby the terms of the treaty could be evaded. In 1845, therefore, Britain forced the sultan to take further steps to suppress the slave trade; by the time Seyyid Said died in 1856, the slave trade had been very much restricted, although slavery itself was still unchecked.

Benefits of association with Britain. In the opinion of many of the leading Arabs, Seyyid had had to pay a heavy price for British friendship, but he had secured British support against the French, whose interest in East Africa was becoming dangerously active at this time; his kingdom gained so much materially from his connexion with the greatest merchant nation in the world that by 1856 Seyyid Said had transformed his backward East African lands. This was shown by the great increase in the volume of trade which passed through Zanzibar and brought the sultan a very satisfactory revenue through the only tax he imposed, the 5 per cent tax on all imports. It also meant wealth for the merchants of Zanzibar. The value of the trade between Zanzibar and India in 1859, for instance, was over £333,000, and that between the United States of America and Zanzibar was £245,000.

Extent of Seyyid Said's power. When Seyyid Said died in 1856 his business ability was acknowledged by all who were in touch with East Africa. These men would, however, have found it harder to define the lands over which he ruled. This vagueness was largely due to the fact that Seyyid Said was interested in securing the sole right to levy taxes and develop trade in as much of Africa as possible; he was much less interested in political boundaries, and the phrase 'effective occupation', which was to be discussed so often in the future of Zanzibar, was meaningless to him.

On the coast the sultan's authority was undoubtedly acknowledged from Rovuma in the south to Warsheikh in the north. Yet the governors whom he placed in the chief coastal towns were often almost independent rulers. So long as they paid a large part of the customs duties to Seyyid Said he seldom interfered with them. For the rest, his system of government was not complicated by departments or ministers or courts of justice, nor even by the actual collection of taxes. The sultan himself judged all serious criminal offences, and this was typical of the way in which he himself was the government. But he kept in touch with the people by means of *baraza*, and held such audiences two or three times a day.

The Canning award. On Seyyid Said's death his unwieldy lands were divided as he wished. His eldest son inherited Oman, while

Zanzibar went to the second son, Seyyid Majid. After a brief struggle this arrangement was confirmed by the award of Lord Canning, Governor-General of India, who intervened in 1861 to enforce the peace which England's interests needed in East Africa and India. The Canning award set out the details of the division, and the two kingdoms have had separate rulers ever since.

CHAPTER III

THE SLAVE TRADE AND AFRICA

Slavery. Slavery is the absolute possession of one person by another, and it is as old as history itself. The ancient civilizations of China, India, Persia, Mesopotamia, Egypt, Greece, and Rome all accepted it as a necessary part of their society, and there is probably no race on earth which at some time has not participated in slavery, either as one of the enslaved or as the possessor of slaves. But although slavery has been universal, no continent has been so widely and consistently ravaged by it as Africa, from whose interior slaves have been drawn for at least two thousand years, and where slavery still existed when our fathers were born.

The responsibility for the African slave trade. The responsibility for slavery and the slave trade in Africa rests mainly upon the Africans themselves, the Arabs, and the countries of Europe.

Slavery was a normal feature of African life before any slave raider set foot on the continent. Sometimes slaves were obtained as a result of tribal wars, in which case the conquering tribe would enslave the women and children of the conquered tribe, and possibly the men as well if they had not been killed. Sometimes too an offence which was regarded as serious, but which did not deserve death, was punished by enslavement. Again, a man might voluntarily offer himself as a slave to another, in order to obtain food or protection. Usually slaves would be employed in cultivation, or in watching cattle and

25

sheep. Sometimes, as with the Baganda and Ashanti, they were used as human sacrifices. It is impossible to estimate with any accuracy the number of slaves in the continent before the demand from other countries developed, but certainly there were fewer in Africa than Asia. Nevertheless it was from these beginnings that the slave trade with outside countries began. It was not usual for slave traders themselves to capture the slaves. On the western coast they often never even landed on the shore. They relied instead on the African chiefs to supply them with the slaves they wanted, either by selling slaves from their own village, or by attacking a neighbouring village and selling the people in it who were caught. Tempted by presents of guns, alcohol, clothing, and trinkets, the chiefs strove to enslave increasing numbers of people, with the result that tribal wars and raids on neighbouring villages increased also.

Motives for the Arab slave trade. By far the most important outside traders who promoted the slave trade in East Africa were the Arabs. They were Muslims, and the Koran, although it did not explicitly forbid slavery, laid down strict rules for the treatment of slaves and positively forbade any Muslim to enslave another. It was therefore necessary for the Arabs to look outside their own country for slaves, and East Africa became their source of supply. From the ninth century a stream of slaves left the East African ports for the markets of Turkey, Arabia, India, and Persia.

Slaves and ivory were the commodities on which the wealth of the Arab settlements in East Africa was based. Unfortunately for the Arabs they were also the most difficult commodities to obtain. Gum-copal, coconuts, copra, and palm oil were easily obtainable from the coastal belt, but the revenue from these was comparatively small. The main wealth came from the caravans which penetrated further and further into the interior, searching for the long elephant tusks and the men, women, and children to carry them to the coast. There, both the black and white ivory could be sold at a very handsome profit.

Area and routes of the Arab slave trade. The main hunting ground of the caravans was the very heart of the continent in the region of the lakes. The main market in the nineteenth century was Zanzibar. Although some slaves were taken from the interior north-westwards across the desert, and still more were taken northwards along the Nile to Khartoum, the main slave routes lay across what is now Tanganyika. One of these main routes started from Bagamoyo (or from Saadani or Pangani) on the mainland opposite Zanzibar island, and climbed from the coastal plain inland to Tabora. This was for the interior what Zanzibar was for the coast: the main centre of communications and trade. Tabora was probably founded about 1830 and by the time Speke and Burton arrived (1857–8) it consisted of about twenty-five Arabs and a few Indians living 'comfortably and even splendidly' in separate little groups of huts and houses.

The houses, though single-storied, are large, substantial, and capable of defence. Their gardens are extensive and well planted; they receive regular supplies of merchandise, comforts and luxuries from the coast; they are surrounded by troops of concubines and slaves whom they train to divers crafts and callings (Burton).

From Tabora one route continued westward towards Lake Tanganyika and another struck northward through Karagwe. The westward route in 1842 ended at Usenga, but when Burton and Speke made their expedition it stretched to Ujiji on the shore of the lake itself, which by then had become a regular outpost of the Arab slave trading route. In 1876 Stanley found the market prices of slaves there quoted as follows:

A girl aged 13–18 worth 80–200 cloths.
A woman aged 18–20 worth 80–130 cloths.
A boy aged 13–18 worth 16–50 cloths.
A man aged 18–50 worth 10–50 cloths.

From Ujiji the Arab caravans explored southward and westward across the lake where Livingstone found them collecting slaves and ivory on the upper reaches of the Congo.

The northward route passed through Karagwe to the northern end of Lake Victoria where it forked north to Bunyoro and north-eastwards to Buganda. As early as 1852 the wealthy Arab trader, Snay-bin-Amir, had reached Kampala fom Tabora, but it was not until the

1870's that the route came into general use. By that time the slave traders pushing southward from Khartoum had almost reached the Victoria Nile, and but for the European intervention they might well have come into sharp collision with the traders from Zanzibar as the distance between them was very small.

As well as the routes through Tabora there was to the south another route from Kilwa towards Lake Nyasa, which was extremely important. To the north there was yet another route, of rather less importance, which started from Tanga and struck inland past Kilimanjaro towards Lake Victoria. To the north of this the route from the coast to Lake Victoria was made dangerous by the warlike Masai, whose reputation kept most of what is now Kenya comparatively free from the curse of slave raiding. The route from Mombasa (probably via Kilimanjaro and along the Rift Valley) was attempted by a considerable number of caravans, but many which made the attempt disappeared, so that the prudent Arab slave dealer considered the southward diversion well worth while.

Methods and effects of the Arab slave trade. The size of the caravans varied. On the shorter trade routes a caravan might consist of only fifty men, but for long, dangerous journeys inland, parties might join together, making a total of a thousand or more. With the native guide in front carrying his tattered blood-red flag, the sign of Seyyid Said's protection, the file would set off westwards in search of its prey, through the coastal forest, the hated thorn-scrub, and the long grassland, watching for hostile tribes and wild animals by day, and camping by night beside the watch-fires which kept off the marauding hyenas, jackals and lions. Progress was slow. The journey from Tabora to Ujiji, for example, though only about one hundred miles, usually took over three weeks. When the rainy season started, movement became almost impossible, so most of the caravans started in the dry period of April or May after the long rains, and sometimes they remained away from the coast for two years or more. In the interior slaves would either be purchased from chiefs or Arab merchants, or the caravan might raid a village itself. These raids, whether carried out by hostile tribes or by the Arabs themselves, were devastating and merciless. A shot in

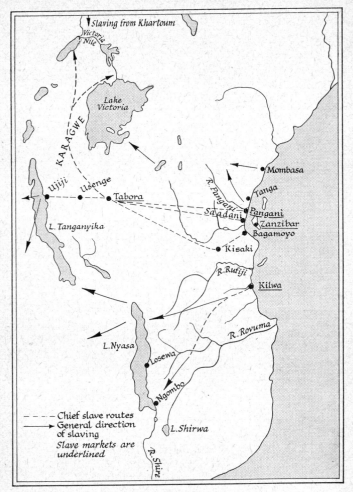

Map. 3. Slave Routes.

the night would be followed by a bonfire of blazing huts while the screaming inhabitants rushed into the bush. Those who were fit would be enslaved, and those who were useless would be massacred. Then the raiders would depart leaving the village a smouldering graveyard. Such was the picture Livingstone saw. Apart from the human misery involved, the unrest and depopulation caused by these raids were enormous. When the explorer Speke visited the east side of Lake Tanganyika in 1858 he wrote:

How the shores should be so desolate strikes one with much surprise. Unless in former times this beautiful country has been harassed by neighbouring tribes and despoiled of its men and cattle to satisfy the spoilers and be sold to distant markets, its present state appears quite incomprehensible. In hazarding this conjecture it might be thought that I am taking an extreme view of this case; but when we see everywhere in Africa what one slave-hunt or cattle-lifting party can effect, it is not unreasonable to imagine that this was most probably the cause of such utter desolation here. These war-parties lay waste the land for endless time.

On the return journey of the caravan the guide would be followed by the long, infinitely pathetic, line of slaves yoked together and carrying on their heads elephant tusks, and bundles of cloth, beads, and grain. Beside them marched the exultant Arab traders with ready whips for the weary, and ready swords for those who could march no more. At the rear of the file came the most important of the Arab merchants. When the caravan reached the coast the ivory and the slaves might be sold on the spot or else shipped to the main market at Zanzibar. For this journey they were heaped in tiers on top of one another and many never reached their destination. By the middle of the nineteenth century about 15,000 slaves a year passed through the squalid, sandy square of the Zanzibar slave market, where men and merchants in every variety of costume from mere rags to the brilliant gold and vermilion raiment of the Arab aristocracy gathered each afternoon from five until sundown to purchase the haggard wretches who were ornamented and arrayed for their inspection. Some of their purchases were kept for the merchants' own use, but most were exported under appalling conditions to Arabia and the Persian Gulf.

For every five captured in the interior only one reached his or her destination. Most died before they even reached the coast.

Upon the great expansion of the slave trade which took place during his reign Seyyid Said smiled with satisfaction, as well he might considering the increased prosperity of his dominions which it brought. But the results of the trade upon the African interior were catastrophic. Tribe attacked tribe to obtain profit from those they captured and enslaved; whole villages were destroyed and their inhabitants removed or massacred, while the slave routes themselves were strewn with the skeletons of those who perished. Constant internal war and depopulation on a vast scale were the price of the East African slave trade.

Motives for the European slave trade. The first of the European countries to import slaves from Africa was Portugal. In 1441, when Henry the Navigator's seamen searched the West African coast looking for the sea route to India, they captured twelve men, women, and children, and brought them back to Portugal as slaves. Within seven years nearly a thousand slaves had been imported and sold at the Lisbon slave market, where we are told Henry the Navigator looked upon them with great pleasure, thinking that these people would now be converted to Christianity. By the end of the fifteenth century the determination of the Portuguese explorers was rewarded, Vasco da Gama had established the route by sea to India, and the Portuguese carracks carried home the immensely profitable spices of the East. In comparison with this cargo slaves were of little value, and interest in them might have been expected to decline. But whereas the discovery of the route to India made the collection of slaves comparatively unprofitable, Columbus's discovery of the West Indies and America made them the most profitable cargo of all. By one of the ironies of history the discovery of the continent which now has the Statue of Liberty standing outside its greatest city was responsible for the greatest increase in the slave trade that the world has known.

During the fifty years after Columbus first landed on the Bahamas in 1492, the Spaniards conquered Mexico, Peru, and the main West Indian islands, while in 1531 the Portuguese began the colonization of Brazil. Not only were extremely rich deposits of gold and silver found, but also plantations of tobacco, indigo, and sugar were laid out. But to mine the silver and gold, and to work the plantations, labour was needed in large quantities. Neither the Spanish nor the Portuguese had the numbers, the inclination, or the stamina to provide this labour in the tropical heat; they turned to the Indians with no success, although a considerable part of the Indian population was wiped out in the attempt. The situation was saved by the importation of slaves from West Africa, the first batch arriving in 1510. The Spanish missionaries, led by Las Casas, the first bishop of Mexico, encouraged this importation. They realized that it would relieve the Indians, whose sufferings they, and the Spanish government, had been trying to prevent. Throughout the sixteenth century the number of slaves imported to America increased. In theory Portugal controlled the area of export in West Africa, and in 1580 the supply of slaves to Spanish colonies was entrusted exclusively to them by the Spanish government under an agreement known as the 'Asiento'. But in fact other countries took part also, and the voyages of John Hawkins to the region of Sierra Leone were among the earliest.

The slave trade and the West Indies. But so far as Britain was concerned the Atlantic slave trade did not become a matter of supreme importance until the second half of the seventeenth century. Before 1660 the British colonies used slaves, but not on a great scale, and as a result the English Guinea Companies had been small associations maintaining a few insecure African posts, and the number of interlopers was small compared with later years. But in the second half of the seventeenth century the plantation colonies developed rapidly, and as they did so the slave trade on which they depended became a matter of vital importance. The greatest cause of the development of these colonies and the slave trade which it involved was the realization that sugar could be grown in the West Indian islands, and that it brought tremendous profits. It was in 1643 that the sugar industry took root in Barbados, which had previously grown mainly tobacco and cotton, and had supported a population of 18,000 male whites, with comparatively few slaves. By the end of the seventeenth century the exports of Barbados to Britain, which were composed almost entirely of sugar, were worth more than the exports of all the rest of the British American colonies put together. Meanwhile the population had entirely changed. The small plantation had given way to the large; the many small owners had given way to a few fabulously wealthy ones; and the proportion of slaves had increased tremendously.

Where Barbados led the other West Indian islands followed, and in the eighteenth century Jamaica became the greatest British sugar island, with a slave population of 300,000. But slaves were required not only for sugar, nor in the West Indies alone. Tobacco, and later cotton, plantations also needed slave gangs, and by 1760 half Virginia's population of 400,000 were slaves. North of Maryland the proportion was far smaller, and it was domestic, not plantation, slavery.

The figures for the Spanish, Portuguese, and French colonies were also alarming. By 1800 there were 776,000 African slaves in Spanish America; in the last half of the eighteenth century 642,000 slaves were shipped into Brazil; in 1775 there were over half a million slaves in the French West Indies alone. The total number of slaves carried by the Atlantic slave trade from its beginning until its end has been variously estimated. Probably it was at least fifteen million.

The slave trade in West Africa. The vast majority of these slaves came from West Africa. The remainder came from Angola and a few from Mozambique. In the early days of the Atlantic slave trade the area between Gambia and the Gold Coast was the main source, but before the end of the seventeenth century the huge increase in the demand for slaves resulted in the spread of the trade to the whole Gulf of Guinea. As Zanzibar was the centre of the east coast slave trade during the nineteenth century, so Calabar was the chief centre of the slave trade on the west coast from 1600 until in the nineteenth century Lagos superseded it as the worst slave depot of the region. Slaving gradually developed from a mere affair of kidnapping to a highly organized trade. During the late seventeenth and eighteenth centuries, when it was at its height, the British, Dutch, French, Danes, Portuguese, Germans, and Swedes had between them nearly fifty forts along the West African coast to which slaves were brought from the interior, and particularly from the area north of the Niger delta. From these fortresses the slaves would be purchased and shipped across the Atlantic.

The extent and organization of the trade. The British took a leading part in this trade from the middle of the seventeenth century, with the development of the plantation colonies. New impetus was given when at the Peace of Utrecht in 1713 she obtained the Asiento. By 1770 half the total slave trade of the Atlantic was carried by nearly 200 British ships with cargo space for nearly 50,000 slaves. The French came next with 30,000, and the Portuguese third with 10,000. Most of the British trade was managed from Liverpool, and the remainder from Bristol and London.

Some of the slaves were carried by companies, and others by individual traders. For a man, or a group of men, with capital there could be no better investment than to hire a ship and an experienced captain, and to load at Liverpool a cargo of cloth, hardware, or spirits. From Liverpool the ship would sail to one of the forts on the West African coast where the cloth, the beads, and the spirits would be exchanged for slaves and probably some gold and ivory as well. With this new cargo the ship would turn westwards across the Atlantic to the West Indies and perhaps some of the mainland colonies also. Here the slaves would be sold, and sugar, cotton, and tobacco would be loaded in their place. Then, with a cargo many times more valuable than the original, the ship would return to England. The whole trip usually took about six months and fell clearly into three stages—the outward passage from England to West Africa, the middle passage across the Atlantic, and the homeward passage from the West Indies or American mainland to England. So great were the profits that if only one ship in three made a successful voyage the enterprise was well worth while.

A comparison of East and West African slave trade. There are interesting similarities and contrasts between the slave trade in East and West Africa. The volume of each was enormous, but while we can make some sort of a guess at the number of slaves taken from West Africa it is extremely difficult to make an estimate for East

Africa, because the volume varied and figures can only be obtained for the comparatively few final years. But we do know that the European slave trade across the Atlantic did not begin until the sixteenth century, that it did not reach its maximum until the eighteenth century, and that at the start of the nineteenth century it was abolished. But the Arab slave trade across the Indian ocean began before the Christian era and did not stop until the end of the nineteenth century, so that although its volume in any one year did not reach the highest figures of the European slave trade the total number of Africans exported during two thousand years may well have exceeded fifteen million. The treatment of slaves by those who transported them was dreadful in both cases, but whereas about half those captured as slaves in West Africa reached their destination, we have seen that only about one-fifth of those captured in East Africa survived. Yet those deported from East Africa who reached their destination in the Middle East were usually treated with comparative kindness and were used as domestic slaves, while those who were deported from West Africa to the American or West Indian colonies were used in gangs on plantations. Sugar is perhaps the most exhausting of all crops to harvest, and the overseers were interested in making the greatest profit in the shortest time so that they could return to England. Consequently their treatment of the slaves does not make happy reading. The Spanish alone, among the European countries, made a sincere and effective attempt to treat their slaves with something like kindness. The results of the slave trade upon Africa went deep, and even when internal warfare ended at the abolition of the slave trade, the population in both the east and the west remained low.

Other evils of the time. It is tempting to conclude that the people who encouraged and took part in this trade were some of the most inhuman brutes that have ever lived. Some were, but many others were not. Lord Nelson, for example, was a strong supporter of the trade, and John Newton, who later became a convert to the abolition movement and wrote some of the best-known hymns in the English language, in his early days worked on one of the Atlantic slave ships.

2-2

The fact was that most people in Europe had no idea of the details of the trade. Nor did they have a clear idea about other evils of their time. While Wilberforce and the Clapham Sect were rousing the British on account of the slave trade, in England itself English children of six and seven years old were forced to work for over twelve hours a day with the aid of 'strappers' who beat them when they fell asleep; English men and women crawled along pitch-black mine shafts pulling coal trucks and never saw the light of day except on Sundays; starving children were hanged when they stole a shilling. A West Indian planter remarked on a visit to an English factory that he never worked his slaves as hard as the factory worked its children. The slaves were not the only sufferers of the time, and the abolitionists were not the only humanitarian reformers. While Wilberforce attacked the slave trade, and then the institution of slavery itself, Lord Shaftesbury struggled to improve conditions in the factories and mines in England. Both met opposition from vested interests, from people who believed that reform would ruin the economic life of Britain, and from the majority of timorous folk who preferred to let things stay as they were rather than risk trouble by trying to put them right.

Contemporary attitude to the slave trade. In the middle of the eighteenth century the slave trade was regarded by most people as essential. Without it they believed that the plantation colonies in general, and the West Indies in particular, would be rendered useless, and from them Britain drew her most valuable commodities. The West Indies were the centre around which British Imperial policy revolved, and to ruin them by stopping the slave trade seemed unthinkable to most contemporary economists. Moreover, if Britain abolished the slave trade while other nations did not, the other nations participating in the trade would gain at Britain's expense. The view which Lord North, the kindly though somewhat idle chief minister of George III, expressed in 1783 was typical. 'It would be found impossible to abolish the slave trade,' he said, 'for it was a trade which had in some measure become necessary to almost every nation in Europe, and it would be next to an impossibility to induce them all to give it up.'

Forces against abolition. The West Indian planters themselves naturally emphasized the necessity for slaves, the vital part which sugar played in imperial profits, and how these profits would disappear if the slave trade were abolished. Moreover, the voices of these planters were extremely influential. Sugar had made them some of the richest men in the world and in England in the eighteenth and early nineteenth centuries a seat in Parliament was something that could be bought. Their influence in the eighteenth century had been strong enough to force through the Molasses and the Sugar Acts. In the late eighteenth and early nineteenth centuries they opposed abolition with all their force, which was very considerable. They were fully supported by the slave-trading ports of Liverpool and Bristol, whose wealth and prosperity were linked with those of the planters. Apart from commercial motives and vested interests, there was also a general fear that as so many merchant ships were employed in the trade its abolition would result in a serious weakening of the British mercantile marine, which supplied so large a proportion of men for the British navy in time of war. If Britain abolished the slave trade and France did not, it was feared that the relative strength of their merchant shipping would be seriously affected. It was this belief which made Nelson, and many others, oppose the abolitionists.

But despite the great weight of opinion supporting the trade, and despite the fact that many who deplored it thought it necessary, there were, from the seventeenth century onwards, people who condemned it outright. Political thinkers such as Locke condemned it; poets, including Pope condemned it; Defoe condemned it; George Fox, the founder of the Quakers, condemned it, and so did a number of individual preachers and novelists. But these were voices crying in the wilderness, and a very barren wilderness it seemed.

Forces assisting abolition. It was not until the latter half of the eighteenth century that the movement to abolish the slave trade began and was effective. This was partly due to the two great political upheavals which took place in that period. The first was in America when the thirteen colonies broke from Britain and at their Third

Congress solemnly declared, 'We hold these truths to be self-evident, that all men are created equal, that they are endowed by their Creator with certain unalienable rights, that among these are Life, Liberty, and the pursuit of Happiness....'

The French, who had helped the colonists, caught the spark from them and took it home. Thirteen years later the French Revolution, with its watchwords of 'Liberty, Equality, and Brotherhood', began. A new outlook had grown, with a tremendous emphasis on freedom. To this slavery stood in violent contrast.

While political revolutions swept through America and France, two revolutions of a less spectacular but extremely important sort swept through Britain. The first was moral and its leader was John Wesley, who travelled the length and breadth of Britain preaching in market-places, on village greens, at pit-heads and wherever men would listen, in an attempt to make Christianity a reality to the poor instead of a veneer for the rich which it had almost become. By 1774, when the evangelical movement was near its height, he published his *Thoughts upon Slavery*, appealing to all concerned with the slave trade and slavery to give it up. The effects of the evangelical movement spread far and deep and supported abolition throughout. The second revolution was in economic thought. When Adam Smith, the Scottish professor, published his *Wealth of Nations* in 1776 he upset the economic beliefs of at least two centuries by arguing, among other things, that slaves were not a profitable form of labour. 'It appears', he wrote, 'that from the experience of all ages and nations the work done by free men comes cheaper in the end than that performed by slaves.' Thus were denounced the ideas on which slavery was based.

Granville Sharp and the abolition of slavery in England. The abolition movement, to which these new ideas contributed, was started unofficially by the twelfth child of an archdeacon of Northumberland. His first step was to get slavery abolished in England itself. Granville Sharp was a man of many parts. He was an expert on the flute, the oboe, the books of Daniel and Revelation, and anything else which took his fancy. He started his career reluctantly as a linen draper's apprentice, failed lamentably in attempting to start a manufacturing business of his own, and then settled down as a junior civil servant, from which obscure position he forced the most learned lawyers of his day to declare that slavery in England was illegal. By the eighteenth century there were about 14,000 African slaves in Britain brought home by West Indian planters. In 1765 one of them, Jonathan Strong, was so severely beaten by his master, Mr David Lisle of Barbados, that he was thrown out as useless. Granville and his brother William helped Strong to recover and found him a job, and there the matter might have ended had not Strong's master claimed him again and resold him. This action turned Granville Sharp into the first effective abolitionist. Not only did he start to study law with such effect that he succeeded in establishing that Strong was legally a free man, but he then sought for another similar case which would force a decision as to whether slavery was allowed in England at all. From such a decision Lord Chief Justice Mansfield shrank because he knew that if a decision were given against slavery then the owners would lose £700,000 worth of property, while 14,000 freed slaves would be cast into society without any means of support. At last, in 1772, the case of James Somerset, which was almost identical to that of Strong, was brought before Mansfield by Sharp. Although the Lord Chief Justice was convinced that slavery was wrong, he gave a fine display of legal gymnastics to avoid giving a direct judgement; but by this time both Sharp and the planters wanted to know where they stood. On 22 June the judgement came. Slavery was not approved by English law. This judgement automatically applied to Ireland, and in Scotland it was confirmed by the case of Joseph Knight in 1778.

The importance of abolition in Britain. The Somerset case was the first decisive step in the abolition movement, and it marks a revolution in the ideas of the British concerning slavery. Before that time it had been generally accepted without question. After that time the opposition to it grew stronger and the support for it became weaker, until at length it was abolished not only in Britain but throughout the world.

CHAPTER IV

THE ABOLITION MOVEMENT IN THE EMPIRE AND IN EAST AFRICA

I. ABOLITION IN THE EMPIRE

The expansion of the empire and emigration. While the abolition movement was developing, the British Empire was growing at a speed which people were slow to realize. There were several reasons for this rapid growth.

In the first place, during the Napoleonic wars new colonies were gained and old ones were expanded, so that by 1815 when the wars came to an end, Britain was by far the greatest colonial power in the world. In Australia, New South Wales had grown from a settlement for convicts into a community which was already producing small quantities of wool. A foothold had been gained in Malaya, and soon Singapore was to be added. In the Indian Ocean, Ceylon, Mauritius, and the Seychelles had been gained, and the Dutch settlements at the Cape of Good Hope had been permanently taken over in 1806 to safeguard the route to India. In India itself Wellesley and Hastings had made Britain the supreme power. Meanwhile, across the Atlantic British North America was expanding into the region of Ontario as loyalists from the U.S.A. and emigrants from Britain arrived. In the West Indies Trinidad, Tobago, and St Lucia helped to offset the declining productivity of the older British islands, and on the mainland of South America, Demerara, Essequibo and Berbice were added and in 1831 were combined into the Crown Colony of British Guiana. In European waters Heligoland, Malta and the Ionian islands were occupied as useful naval bases. Lord Castlereagh, who was chiefly responsible for the peace of 1815, did not intend to be an empire builder, and like his predecessors regarded colonial possessions mainly as trading bases and military outposts. Neither he nor anyone else realized that they would expand into flourishing colonies of settlement. Yet that is what happened, partly owing to the great increase in the population of Britain, which rose from seven and a half to fourteen million in the single reign of George III (1760–1820), making large-scale emigration possible, and partly to the Industrial Revolution which provided an incentive for new markets to absorb the increased production. The government at first made no serious attempt to encourage or organize this growth, and in fact the two groups of people who exercised the greatest influence on the growing empire were the radical school of colonial reformers and the evangelicals.

The influence of the evangelicals. Of the radicals, led by Gibbon Wakefield and including Lord Durham, it must suffice to say that their influence in persuading the government to assist and organize colonization, and in encouraging the growth of responsible government, was of vital importance in imperial history. In connexion with the abolition movement, however, the evangelicals must be mentioned more fully. Drawing their inspiration from the Christian gospel and the revival headed by Wesley and others, the Evangelicals included such men as Wilberforce, Buxton, and Sir James Stephen. From their meeting at Wilberforce's residence at Clapham they became known as the 'Clapham Sect', and from the large annual meetings they held each May at Exeter Hall in the Strand they were known also as the 'Exeter Hall' party. Their representatives in Parliament had still another name—the 'Saints'. As the radicals concentrated upon the rights of settlers and the necessity for some clear policy concerning emigration and land, so did the evangelicals concentrate upon the rights of native peoples and the necessity for realizing the moral responsibility which the colonies involved, and from 1836 to 1847, when Sir James Stephen was Permanent Under-Secretary, their influence in the Colonial Office was supreme. But it was not only in emphasizing native rights that its influence was shown in the colonies. The evangelical revival also led to a great revival of missionary activity which had previously been weak, so far as the Protestant churches were concerned. The Baptist Missionary Society was started in 1792, the London Missionary Society in 1795, the Scottish Missionary Society in 1796, the Church Missionary Society in 1799, the British and Foreign Bible Society in 1804, and the Methodist Missionary Society in 1813. In the Pacific Islands, China, and in South, Central, and West Africa the influence of these Protestant missions was tremendous. It was paralleled by the efforts of missions from America and also of the Roman Catholic Church, whose missionary activity, stretching back through the centuries, branched out afresh in 1868. In that year the White Fathers were formed, whose influence on Africa was of great importance. Thus, morality as well as trade claimed its share of the new possessions. But the most spectacular success of the evangelical movement was the abolition of the slave trade in 1807, and of slavery itself in 1833.

The development of the abolition movement. We saw in the last chapter that the judgement in the Somerset case of 1772 was the first step in the abolition movement. The second step came in 1783 when the Quakers appointed a committee of six to agitate 'for the relief and liberation of the negro slaves in the West Indies, and for the discouragement of the slave trade on the coast of Africa'. In 1787 this committee was increased to twelve. Sharp was its chairman and its members included Thomas Clarkson, who supplied the abolition movement with the majority of its facts, which he gained by constant travelling and visits to the slave ports in England. This committee soon realized that the essential need was not only to convince public opinion that abolition was necessary, but more particularly to convince Parliament that the slave trade should be made illegal. This was by no means easy, for representatives of the slaving interests were strong in Parliament, as we have seen, and no responsible Whig or Tory leader was willing to commit his party to an abolitionist policy that seemed certain to fail. But individuals in Parliament were not all indifferent or hostile to the abolitionists. What was needed was a man who was not a party leader and yet had influence enough to draw votes from both parties.

Wilberforce. By one of the great coincidences of history this need was met exactly by William Wilberforce. In his early days Wilberforce was a gay young man, with a gift for talking wittily and continuously, and among the fashionable upper class in which he moved he was extremely popular. He came from a wealthy Yorkshire business family, and finished his education at Cambridge. Well supplied with money, he then lived a leisurely life in London, where he made friends with Pitt, his contemporary at Cambridge. In 1780 both Pitt and Wilberforce were elected to Parliament, and when Pitt became Prime Minister in 1783 Wilberforce was his most loyal supporter. It was at this time that the gay young man of leisure suddenly had his career turned into an unexpected channel. Between 1784 and 1785 Wilberforce was touched by the influence of the evangelical revival, and partly through the influence of John Newton—the fierce old slaver turned clergyman—he was converted. For the rest of his life he was guided by a sense of the nearness and goodness of God. His old interests faded, and clubs, parties, and theatres saw him no more. He even thought of resigning his seat in Parliament. In this new spirit he became interested in the slave trade. He read Clarkson's book and interviewed him; he heard John Newton's tales of his bad old days, and he became convinced that the trade should be stopped. The final push came from Pitt, who, during a country walk one summer's day, persuaded Wilberforce to take up the abolition of the slave trade in Parliament.

There are many great names connected with the abolition movement, but that of Wilberforce is easily the most important. In some ways this may seem strange, for it is doubtful whether he was, for example, more zealous than Clarkson, or had more intellectual ability than Zachary Macaulay who edited the *Anti-Slavery Monthly Reporter*; among the abolitionists zeal and intellectual ability were common. But the great contribution which Wilberforce made, and which no one else could make, was that Parliament, and only Parliament, had authority to enforce abolition, and that Wilberforce alone had sufficient influence to persuade it to do so. This influence depended on three things. First, he had Pitt as Prime Minister and his best friend; secondly, he possessed a quite extraordinary power of speech, and his exceptionally pleasant voice gained him the title of the 'nightingale of the House'; and finally he belonged to no political party and thus could gain support from both Whigs and Tories. These assets, in addition to his high ability and character, gave him the influence in Parliament without which the abolitionist cause might have failed, and would certainly have been delayed. Yet such was his power that not only were the slave trade and slavery abolished but also their abolition took a suprisingly high priority. Factories and mines in Britain still depended on the extreme exploitation of child labour, when slavery no longer existed in the British Empire. Wilberforce made the victory of the abolitionists certain; he also hastened its arrival.

Abolition of the slave trade in the British Empire. The campaign to abolish the slave trade began in Parliament in 1788, but its early hopes of success were soon crushed. In 1792 the French Revolution reached its most bloodthirsty stage, and was followed by the Napoleonic Wars, in which Britain fought for her life against the French. During this struggle all suggestions for reform were regarded as unpatriotic, and even Pitt felt that the abolition of the slave trade should be temporarily neglected so that all energies could be concentrated on the war. Consequently the abolitionists lost almost all their supporters, although Wilberforce in every session reminded Parliament of the cause they had abandoned.

It was in 1807 that success was at last achieved. This was partly because the war then seemed less formidable than it had at first. It was much more particularly due to the death of Pitt in 1806 and the formation of a coalition government led by Grenville, with Fox as Foreign Secretary. This meant that now a majority of government ministers favoured abolition, and Fox himself was so strong a supporter that he considered abolition even more important than the war with France. Fox died in the autumn of 1806, but already the triumph of abolition was clear, and in 1807 the Bill prohibiting 'all manner of dealing and trading' in slaves in Africa or in their transport from Africa to any other place was passed. It became operative from 1 January 1808, and was enforced by British warships. At first some British slave ships took the risk of being captured and continued to trade, but there were only a few which did so; and in 1811, when slave trading was made punishable by transportation, it virtually came to an end so far as Britain was concerned.

The anti-slavery campaign. This was the greatest victory of the abolitionists and the most hardly fought, but it did not finish there. The abolition of the slave trade was regarded, not as an end, but as a step towards the abolition of slavery itself. It was hoped that now fresh supplies of slaves were stopped the planters would cherish with greater care those they already possessed, and would therefore decrease punishments and encourage marriage. As conditions of life improved, the abolitionists hoped that the slaves would become more civilized, until their freedom would come naturally and easily, without social disturbance. It was a happy thought and not unreasonable, but the planters made it impossible by their obstinacy. They hated criticism, they hated the abolitionists, they absolutely refused to change. But it was hard for them to kick against the pricks, and their defiance merely hastened the end which might otherwise have been slow.

In the years after 1807 the abolitionist cause greatly increased in strength. In 1822 Wilberforce, on account of ill-health, handed over the Parliamentary leadership of the campaign to Thomas Buxton, and in 1823 the earlier committees were replaced by the large Anti-Slavery Society, which contained many important members of the Commons and Lords, besides veterans like Wilberforce and Clarkson. Moreover, the great majority of British opinion was also on their side. Meanwhile, the opposition had grown weaker. The planters still controlled many seats in Parliament, but the wealth which purchased those seats was declining rapidly. At the same time East Indian sugar was being produced in increasing quantities by a free community. The economic interests of the East Indies were thus opposed to those of the West Indies and further weakened the position of the planters.

The abolition of slavery in the British Empire. The increasing strength of the abolitionists made their triumph certain. The question was simply how long it would take to achieve. From 1824 to 1833 it was encouraged by the failure of the West Indian planters to make any substantial improvements, by their defiant attitude to the British government, by slave revolts, and by the Reform Bill of 1832 which resulted in a reduction in the number of members of Parliament whose financial interests lay in the West Indies, and an increase in the number of abolitionists. In 1833, when the excitement over the Reform Bill had subsided and the abolitionist cause had again become the focus of attention, the bill to abolish slavery in the British Empire was introduced and passed. By it the legal status of slavery was to cease within a year, although the slaves were to continue to work as unpaid apprentices for from four to six years. In addition £20 million was to be paid as compensation to the slave-owners. It was fitting that Wilberforce should have lived until the passing of this bill was certain. He died a month before it was actually passed. 'Thank God', he said, 'that I should witness a day in which England is willing to give £20 million for the abolition of slavery.'

Results of abolition. What were the results? So far as the West Indies were concerned the abolition of slavery did not result in chaos, bloodshed, and ruin as the planters had prophesied, and the freed slaves behaved in an orderly way. But it was difficult to fit them into the new society, and as they were reluctant to work, production fell sharply. Yet the abolition of the slave trade and then of slavery itself was only one of the factors contributing to the decline of the West Indies. The diminishing fertility of the soil, the increase of competition, and the ending of the preferential tariff for West Indian sugar in 1836 also played their part.

The only other colonies which were affected were Mauritius and the Cape. In Mauritius slave labour was replaced by Indian coolies and production rose. In the Cape the ending of slavery did not seriously upset the country's economy, for the farmers were not dependent on slave labour; but there was considerable bitterness, partly due to the great increase in vagrancy which resulted, and partly due to the dissatisfaction with the compensation which was paid. These grievances were important factors in causing the Great Trek, during which about 10,000 Boers left the Cape settlement in order to escape from British authority.

So far as East Africa was concerned the abolition movement was the greatest factor in shaping its modern history, and we must now turn to a consideration of its application and effects there.

II. ABOLITION IN EAST AFRICA

One of the most extraordinary results of the abolition movement was that it made so deep an impression upon the British people that they were not content with abolishing their own part in the slave trade; they were determined also to abolish it throughout the world. This was to be a vast undertaking.

Foreign abolition agreements. The campaign began with an attempt to persuade other European countries to end, or at least restrict, their own part in the slave trade. Thus, agreements were made with Portugal in 1815, and Spain in 1817; and in 1818 France also agreed to abolish the trade. These agreements cost the British Exchequer nearly a million pounds in bribes, but they produced such poor results that in the first half of the nineteenth century the Atlantic slave trade grew rather than declined. The reason was clear, for rarely have ethics and profits come into such sharp collision. The abolitionists had made it clear that Christianity and slavery were incompatible and therefore the Christian countries of Europe felt morally bound to agree, in theory at least, to abolish the slave trade in their dominions. But on the other hand the slave trade was such a profitable business that in most cases agreements about abolition were in fact ignored. It took nearly the whole century, the use of a large part of the British navy, and volumes of diplomatic correspondence, to stamp it out in fact as well as in theory among the European participators.

Meanwhile the East African slave trade had grown rapidly under Seyyid Said, during the early part of the century, and had attracted the attention of the abolitionists.

India and the East African slave trade. Their influence reached East Africa via India and Mauritius. For centuries India had been supplied with slaves from East Africa by the Arabs, but when the slave trade was abolished in the British Empire in 1807 abolition applied to the import of slaves to India also. However, the British-Indian governments needed no spurring in this direction, for the Bombay government had abolished the trade so far as its presidency was concerned two years previously. But it was one thing to make the trade illegal and quite another to be able to stop it effectively. Despite every effort of the Indian government the importation of slaves continued, until it became clear that it could only be stopped by a direct appeal to Seyyid Said to prevent his Omani traders from exporting slaves from East Africa.

Such an appeal had two serious difficulties. In the first place Said depended on the slave trade for the greater part of his revenue, and even were he willing to make an attempt to stop it he would quite likely have lost his throne as a result. Secondly, the British had no wish to antagonize Said who, they feared, might easily ally himself with the French against them. Therefore, it was only after the destruction of the French power in the Indian Ocean that the first approaches were made to the sultan, in 1812 and 1815. These merely consisted of polite requests by the governor of Bombay that Said should abolish, or reduce, the east coast slave trade. The Seyyid had no wish to antagonize either the British or his Arab subjects, and the requests were ignored.

Mauritius and the East African slave trade. The next attempt to attack the East African slave trade originated from Mauritius. This island of French sugar planters had been taken over by the British during the Napoleonic Wars, and its population considered the slave trade to be absolutely essential to its economy. The British governor, Sir Robert Farquhar, therefore found himself in an extremely difficult position. On one side was the French planter population of Mauritius demanding the continuance of the slave trade; on the other side was the British government in the full swing of the abolition movement. After some hesitation Farquhar realized that he must comply with the British instructions to prevent the importation of slaves to the island, but soon found that with the population dead against him this was impossible. He therefore turned his attention to cutting off the slave supply at its source. As most of the slaves came from Madagascar and Zanzibar it was the rulers of these areas that he approached. In Madagascar there was no great difficulty, and in 1817 a treaty was made with Radama, the most powerful chief of the island, agreeing to the 'entire cessation and extinction' of the trade throughout Radama's dominions, which included all but the southern part of Madagascar. This treaty had a considerable effect, but it still left the Mauritius smugglers with Zanzibar from which to draw their slaves. It was to Zanzibar therefore that Farquhar now turned his attention, and as Seyyid Said was a far more important ruler than Radama, Farquhar decided to get support of the British governments in India and Bombay. This was willingly given, for these governments too had realized that the slave trade must be ended at its source and not at its final market if abolition were to be really effective.

The Moresby treaty, 1822. In the summer of 1822, therefore, Captain Moresby was asked to visit the sultan on behalf of the Indian and Mauritius governments. His instructions were to persuade Said to limit the trade rather than to attempt complete abolition, which was considered too drastic a request at this stage, and the object was to prevent the importation of slaves to India and Mauritius. In theory Moresby was completely successful, for the sultan agreed to forbid the sale of slaves to any Christians, nor would he allow his slave ships to sail south of Cape Delgado (thus preventing importation to Mauritius), and east of a line from Diu Head to near Socotra (thus preventing importation to India). In 1839 the prohibited area was still further enlarged. This was the first of the slave-trading treaties between Said and the British. It did not in any way interfere with, or restrict, the trade between Zanzibar and the sultan's dominions in Oman, to which most of the slaves were sent; it was concerned only with the sale and export of slaves to Christians and British colonies, and it depended for its enforcement upon the British naval patrols. But the Indian Ocean was too large an area to be patrolled effectively, and the Arabs were so determined to continue their smuggling that at least three-quarters of the smugglers continued uncaught; in fact the Moresby Treaty had very little effect. But it would be quite unjust to suggest that Seyyid Said himself ignored the treaty. The evidence shows clearly that, although he regarded the British demand as a nuisance, although it meant a big drop in his revenue, and although he only agreed because he respected British naval power, having made the agreement he did honestly do all in his power to support it.

The Owen protectorate, 1823–6. On the other hand Said had good cause to accuse the British of unfair dealing, for in 1823 another attempt was made against the east coast slave trade which involved a British protectorate over Mombasa. As it happened, this was completely unofficial, for Owen's aim in establishing his protectorate was primarily to abolish the slave trade at Mombasa, and not to annex territory for the aggrandisement of Britain. He was successful in temporarily ending the slave trade through the town, but he was not successful in persuading the British government to support him, and in 1826 he was forced to withdraw, to his own disappointment and to the great relief of Seyyid Said.

The Hamerton treaty, 1845. Twenty years after the Moresby Treaty the British made another attempt to persuade Said to restrict the slave trade in his dominions. This time it was the far more radical demand that he should prohibit the trade between Zanzibar and his realm of Oman, which was the chief purchaser. In fact all exportation, except between the east coast towns and Zanzibar, was to be prohibited. It was Captain Hamerton, who had been appointed in 1841 as political agent for the government of India and as British consul under the Foreign Office, whose task it was to press this treaty upon the sultan. Naturally Said was not pleased. It was a far bigger demand than that of Moresby; it would mean a far bigger drop in revenue, and it would meet with great opposition from Said's Arab subjects. But the sultan knew that Britain would not tolerate a refusal and that her friendship was indispensable; by the Hamerton Treaty, therefore, which was signed in 1845, and became officially effective from 1847, he agreed to the demands. Again, having made the treaty he sincerely tried to carry it out, but again his subjects were determined to evade it, so that the effectiveness of the treaty depended, like that of 1822, simply upon the British naval patrols. The Indian Ocean is very large. The slave dhows were very numerous. The Hamerton Treaty was merely another check while the main trade still went on.

Difficulties of the policy of restriction. It took nearly another thirty years to convince the British government that attempts to restrict the East African slave trade instead of abolishing it completely could never be more than partially successful. Nevertheless, during that time the restrictions imposed by the Hamerton Treaty were made as strict as possible, and Seyyid Majid, who succeeded Seyyid Said, forbade any dhows to sail from Zanzibar during the time of the south-

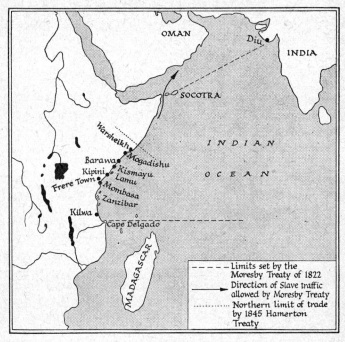

Map. 4. Slave Trade Treaties.

west monsoon, and imposed heavy punishment upon anyone selling slaves to the northern Arabs. In theory it was impossible to smuggle slaves from Zanzibar to the north. But in fact the whole system met with such universal opposition from the sultan's subjects that the laws depended for their enforcement upon the sultan's untrustworthy Baluchi garrison at Zanzibar, whom the slavers openly defied, and on the British naval patrol in the Indian Ocean. This patrol normally consisted of seven or eight small cruisers stationed along the African coast to watch the area of export, and between the mouths of the Red Sea and the Persian Gulf to watch the area of import. From these cruisers smaller boats, carrying about twenty men, were launched, and these made explorations of several days, or even weeks, up the inlets along the coast. It was an extremely unhealthy, dangerous, and heartbreaking business. Malaria took a heavy toll of life, and the Arab slavers fought desperately when caught and often outnumbered and killed their attackers. But perhaps the main difficulty was in distinguishing between a dhow carrying slaves, and a dhow carrying legal goods, for the Arabs usually claimed that their slaves were crew. Out of 400 dhows examined, for example, in the early part of 1870, only eleven were condemned as slavers, and it was reckoned that while over 2500 slaves were caught by the patrol between 1867 and 1869, 37,000 were successfully smuggled overseas. In brief, the British naval patrol, despite all its heroic efforts, was a failure.

Decision for complete prohibition. During this period Livingstone had brought home to the British people for the first time an eye-witness account of the slave trade in the interior, and his descriptions gave a new impetus to the abolitionists' efforts for East Africa. As a result, in 1871 Parliament appointed a select committee to inquire into the question. The conclusion they reached was that so long as the slave trade was still permitted between Zanzibar and the coast towns, the work of the naval patrols was made unnecessarily difficult, and smuggling was sure to continue on a large scale. Unanimously they agreed that the only answer was to prohibit the East African slave trade completely. A special mission led by Sir Bartle Frere, the ex-governor of Bombay, was sent to Zanzibar to gain the sultan's agreement to this proposal.

The Frere mission and treaty of 1873. In January 1873 the mission arrived at Zanzibar and was met with great ceremony and friendliness by the sultan Barghash. Three months later it left with less ceremony, less friendliness, and an absolute refusal by the sultan to accept complete abolition. The reason was obvious, for the abolition of the slave trade would certainly mean, within a fairly short time, the abolition of slavery itself, because the birth-rate among slaves was far below the death-rate. As the economy of Zanzibar was based upon slave labour Barghash's refusal is easily understandable. However, the British government was not to be put off, and when Frere had made his report methods of peaceful persuasion were replaced by methods of force. Sir John Kirk, the British consul at Zanzibar, was ordered to inform Barghash that unless he agreed to complete abolition Zanzibar itself would be blockaded by the British navy. Barghash had no longer any choice. On 5 June 1873 he duly signed the treaty making the slave trade illegal between all his ports, and at once messengers were sent to close the gates of the Zanzibar slave market for ever. Upon its site the Universities Mission built its Cathedral Church with the altar standing where the whipping-post once stood.

Attempts at evasion. The 1873 treaty was the death-blow to the Arab slave trade in East Africa, but the trade took some time to die. The Arabs could no longer transport slaves by sea, but they could— and they did—march them from Kilwa northwards along the coast, secretly selling them as they went. Once more Kirk, who was the greatest influence in the suppression of the east coast slave trade, pressed Barghash to take action. As a result, in 1876 the sultan prohibited the fitting out of slave caravans at the coast, and also prohibited them from entering the interior or transporting slaves from port to port. He even abolished the legal status of slavery itself in the northern part of his dominions. These proclamations had an immediate effect. Kilwa, the greatest of the slave collecting ports, had a population entirely dependent on the slave trade and prepared an army of 3000 men to resist their enforcement; fortunately Kirk arrived in a British cruiser in time to prevent the revolt. Almost at the same time a crowd of low-class Swahili slavers in Mombasa rioted and threatened to attack the Church Missionary Society's station of Frere Town, where freed slaves were kept and trained for employment. But here the Arabs supported the governor and the riot was quickly dispersed. In 1877 one more attempt by Kilwa to open the trade with Lake Nyasa resulted in one of the leading high-class Arabs of the town, Said-bin-Abdulla, being sent back to

Zanzibar, where he was arrested, put in irons, and thrown into the common prison. That example ended any more open attempts to defy authority, and from then onwards the slave trade was a trickle compared to the former flood, and legitimate trade gradually took its place. But Livingstone's lesson was nevertheless true; it was only by opening up and occupying the interior that the slave trade was finally and completely extinguished, for it was only at the very end of the century that the last slave caravan was caught on the shores of Lake Nyasa.

The effects of abolition. The end of the slave trade was the beginning of a new age for East Africa. It changed the country within a generation from a land of wars, suspicion, and savagery, where no man's home was secure, into a land of comparative peace where development was possible. For this the British abolition movement, stretching through the century from Granville Sharp to Sir John Kirk, was fundamentally responsible. Perhaps no country has ever received from another so great a gift as East Africa received from Britain. One testimony among many, is that of Joseph Thomson: 'If the Anti-Slavery Society', he wrote, 'require an argument for continuing their good work they have it here [the present Tanganyika], for undoubtedly the stoppage of the slave traffic formed the turning point in the great moral and social revolution which has taken place.'

The abolition of slavery in East Africa. With the end of the slave trade slavery itself was doomed for, as we have seen, the death-rate of slaves far exceeded their birth-rate. However, slavery was not merely allowed to die a natural death. It was hustled on its way by a series of decrees. The first was an agreement made between the British government and the sultan in 1889, by which it was agreed that all persons entering the sultan's dominions after 1 November of that year should be free, and added that children born after 1 January 1890 should be free also. This decree was followed by further instructions giving slaves the right to complain against their masters. The most important step came in 1897 when a decree abolishing the legal status of slavery on Zanzibar and Pemba was signed by the sultan on 5 April. By this decree slaves were able to obtain their freedom by application to the

District Courts, and compensation was to be paid to the owners. Many slaves were slow in claiming this freedom, and the 1897 decree was heavily criticized by the missions as inadequate. Its moderation was due to the fear that too strict and rapid a declaration might lead to the ruin of the clove plantations, and it came as a surprise to everyone when, in fact, the production of cloves rose after 1897 instead of declining. The final decree concerning Zanzibar and Pemba was signed in 1909, when the final points were settled and it was agreed that 31 December 1911 should be the last possible date for claiming compensation.

So far as the mainland was concerned abolition was less rapid. The legal status of slavery was not abolished in the British area until 1907. In 1910 Compensation Courts were set up in Mombasa, Lamu, and other coastal towns, and, in Zanzibar and Pemba, compensation could not be claimed after 1 December 1911. In the German area the pace was slower still. The Germans had indeed taken steps to improve the conditions of slavery and had proclaimed the freedom of all children born in, or after, 1905, but it was not until Tanganyika became a British protectorate that the legal status of slavery was finally abolished.

CHAPTER V

EXPLORATION

Geographical obstacles. Until modern times, deserts have been as serious an obstacle in the way of men's movements as the oceans over which they learnt to sail, the mountains they climbed, and the forests through which they pushed their way. That is why the Sahara divided Africa into two: a northern Moslem portion linked with Mediterranean Europe, consisting of Egypt, Libya, Tripoli, Tunis and Morocco; the grasslands and forests of tropical Africa, which in their turn are linked with the sub-tropical countries of South Africa and the Rhodesias.

The inaccessible interior. The second of these areas was further isolated because travel from the sea was hindered by the scarp edge of the plateau which forms the interior of Africa and causes the rivers flowing down to the coast to be broken by waterfalls and rapids. Men were unable, therefore, to reach the interior of Africa in the way they were able to reach the interior of North America; for not only was the way guarded by these obstacles, it was further blocked by forests and mangrove swamps

Limits of early exploration. Of the four main obstacles to men's movements in the southern part of Africa which have been listed in the first paragraph, only one had been overcome by the end of the eighteenth century; and Swift's well-known verse

> So Geographers, in Afric maps,
> With savage pictures fill their gaps,
> And o'er uninhabitable downs,
> Place elephants for want of towns.

still rang true, despite the great discoveries of the sixteenth and seventeenth centuries. These had merely revealed the coast of Africa to the people of Europe. The eastern side of this had, of course, long been known to the peoples of Asia. These, however, had been halted by the lack of navigable rivers which is shown in the map on p. 57. Nor had men found easy the long march up from the coast through the waterless land which stretched inland for many miles behind most of the coast. The early traders, therefore, stayed on the coastal plain, where men died from fever.

First contacts with Africans. Some knowledge of the interior was possessed by the Arab slavers, and the Portuguese had had considerable knowledge of parts of it; but there was no real contact between the Africans and the peoples of either the East or the West until the nineteenth century. It was then that the first vague outline of the features of the interior became known to the peoples of Europe. They had been known, of course, for centuries to the Africans who lived there, but travel for these was still a slow matter, and very few had knowledge of any large area. The coming of European explorers was to bring Africa into touch with the peoples of the West; and this was important for the peoples of Africa, who had hitherto lacked the stimulus that is given by the meeting of men with new ideas. These first Europeans seemed very strange to them. Bishop Hannington, whose

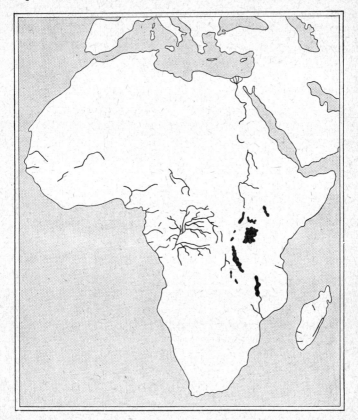

Map 5. The Navigable Stretches of Waterways in Africa.

journey to Uganda ended in his murder by the order of the Kabaka, has left a description of how he was interviewed:

'Did you ever see such a creature?' 'No, we never did!!!' 'What are those things on his eyes? Are they horns growing?'... 'Are those your feet, White man?' 'No, gentlemen, they are not. They are my sandals.' 'But, do they grow to your feet?' 'No, gentlemen, they do not. I will show you.' So I would unlace a boot. A roar of astonishment followed when they saw my blue socks, as they thought my feet must be blue and toeless.... My watch too, was an unfailing attraction. 'There is a man in it. It is *hubari*, it is witchcraft', they would cry. 'He talks, he says Teek, teek, teek!'

But years before Hannington crossed Masailand, Europeans had been fascinated by two mysteries in Africa: the source of the Nile and the course of the Niger. Old charts show that Africa was one of the three continents which were known in ancient days. Yet, on closer examination it will be seen that the Nile is drawn as rising in very queer places, and it flows in impossible directions. It even sometimes joins the Niger.

Exploration of the Niger. The course of the Niger was the first of the two mysteries to be solved. In 1788 the African Association was founded to provide the money for expeditions to find out where the Niger went. The Association was to choose the leaders, and eight years later they had their first real success when they employed a young man called Mungo Park. At the time there were considered to be two possible approaches, from the north and from the Gambia.

On his first journey (1795–8) Mungo Park tried the second way, and wrote that he was successful in seeing at Segu 'the great object of my mission, the long-sought-for, majestic Niger, glittering to the evening sun, as broad as the Thames at Westminster, and flowing slowly to the eastward'. Park went back to Scotland and married, but his thoughts kept turning to the mystery of where the Niger flowed to the sea. In 1805 he returned to Africa at the head of an expedition of forty-four Europeans, thirty of whom died. This did not check Park, who was determined to push on, even if the others died too. He wrote: 'I would at least die on the Niger.' And such was his end, reported a later explorer, Clapperton, when in 1825 he reached the spot where Park was drowned.

Five years later the mystery of the Niger was solved by Clapperton's companion, Richard Lander, who sailed down the Niger to its wide delta, and found out that it had long been familiar to men under the name of the Oil Rivers.

The problem of the Nile. In the second century A.D. there was a great Greek geographer called Ptolemy. In his time men knew that there were both a Blue and a White Nile, and it was Ptolemy's opinion that both the Niles had their source in lakes. The Blue Nile, he considered, rose in a lake in the east. The White Nile, on the other hand, he thought, rose in large lakes which were fed by the Mountains of the Moon. This was the sort of information that sometimes trickled through from traders with the east coast of Africa; but for over sixteen hundred years the peoples of Europe knew no more about the source of the White Nile. It was a fascinating problem; and the first step to its solution was taken when, in 1770, the British explorer Bruce reached the source of the Blue Nile at Gheesh in Abyssinia, south of Lake Tana.

Krapf and Rebmann. In the middle of the nineteenth century, European interest was greatly increased by the discoveries of two German missionaries, Krapf and Rebmann. They were both members of the Church Missionary Society, and when Krapf arrived in Mombasa in 1843 he had already worked for some time as a missionary in Abyssinia. In 1846 he was joined by Rebmann and together they established a mission station at Rabai. Malaria had already killed Krapf's wife and child; and throughout their work in East Africa both had to struggle with unknown diseases, master new languages, and explore the land sufficiently to establish the chain of mission posts of which Krapf dreamt as the bases from which Christianity could be spread throughout the interior.

In 1847, therefore, Rebmann became the first European of whom we have record to go into the interior of East Africa. In that year he went into the Taita hills, about a hundred miles from Mombasa. It was in these hills that a pygmy people had probably lived, some 500 years earlier, before they were poisoned by later invaders, in whose history Rebmann was interested.

Discovery of Mounts Kilimanjaro and Kenya. As, by 1847, many of the Taita tribe had spread to Taveta and to the slopes of Kilimanjaro, where they mingled with the WaChagga, Rebmann decided in the following year to follow up what he had heard about the Chagga people and the mountainous country in which they lived, and on 11 May had his first glimpse of Kilimanjaro. This was the first of four journeys which he made to and from the Chagga country. At the end of this he was convinced of the existence of a great snow-covered mountain, a fact which Krapf later confirmed. Their reports were not however believed at first; one man even wrote a book to prove that Kilimanjaro could not exist. He had not realized the passionate interest which Krapf and Rebmann had in scientific accuracy. In the former's book, *Travels, Researches and Missionary Labours*, the care with which all reports about the mountain had been checked is clearly shown. On 3 December 1849 Krapf had a glimpse of East Africa's other great mountain, Kenya, which he was shown by Chief Kivoi when staying with the Akamba at Kitui. This chief was an important trader, as well as being a typical Kamba in that he was a great traveller, and had been therefore to both mountains. On hearing that Krapf wanted to go beyond the river Tana to the country in which the mountain was to be found, he offered to accompany him there; and the trip was finally arranged in 1850. On the way the party was attacked by robbers, Kivoi was killed and his followers scattered: Krapf struggled on in the direction of the Tana, longing only for water. As soon as his thirst was satisfied, he began to explore the river, which he estimated as 150 feet wide and from six to seven feet deep.

Burton and Speke. These discoveries interested the Royal Geographical Society so much that they commissioned Richard Burton to investigate reports that there existed a lake of sweet water, 800 miles long by 300 miles broad. It seemed very unlikely; but the idea interested Burton, an Indian Army officer who was a fine Arabic scholar and had already made a daring journey to Mecca in disguise. In 1856 he set out with Lieut. John H. Speke, also of the Indian Army. As they drew nearer to Lake Tanganyika, they found, by conversation with the Arabs, that the great lake they were seeking was really three lakes, great distances apart, and that the tales Krapf and Rebmann had heard referred to Lakes Tanganyika, Nyasa, and the largest of all, later named Victoria. Despite the help they had received from the Arabs in the way of transport, supplies and information, the journey had proved a great strain and both men were ill. Speke had a form of temporary blindness and could not even see Lake Tanganyika clearly when it lay in the distance; while Burton was so broken down in health that, on their return to headquarters, the Arab centre of Tabora, he let Speke go on alone in the direction of Victoria Nyanza. On this journey he was lucky and, on 3 August 1858, he was able to write:

The pale blue waters of the Nyanza burst suddenly upon my gaze. It was early morning. The distant sea-line of the north horizon was defined in the calm atmosphere, between the north and west points of the compass, but even this did not afford me any idea of the breadth of the lake.... I no longer felt any doubt that the lake at my feet gave birth to that interesting river [Nile] the source of which has been the source of so much speculation and the object of so many explorers.

When Speke told this news to Burton he admitted that there was a lake there, but denied the possibility that it was the source of the Nile. Speke's guess later proved right.

Speke and Grant. On coming back to England, Speke was commissioned by the Royal Geographical Society to return to Africa to check the details of his discovery and to trace the link between the lake and the Nile. This time he took as his companion an old friend called Grant; they left Zanzibar in 1860.

Speke and the Nile. On the earlier expedition Burton and Speke had been forced to return to Tabora, partly because of illness, and partly because they ran out of calico, which they needed to purchase supplies on their journey. Burton said bitterly that on this kind of journey baggage was life. The truth of this statement was to be shown in the journeys of many other explorers, among them Livingstone and Stanley. Speke, too, continued to have endless trouble with porters and baggage. At one time he complained that more than half his property had been stolen; and it was not until he reached Karagwe, which is to the west of the Victoria, that he and Grant were able to rest and enjoy the generous hospitality of the local chief, King Rumanika. When they went north from here Grant became so ill that he had to be left behind, leaving Speke, in 1862, to become the first European to enter Buganda. Here, on the north shore of Lake Victoria, he reached what proved to be the Nile and told his men to bathe in the holy river for, as he wrote, he saw that 'Old Father Nile without any doubt rises in the Victoria Nyanza, and, as I had foretold, that lake is the great source of the river'. A tablet was later placed where Speke declared that the Nile had its origin. Today a growing industrial centre, Jinja, is developing there.

Return journey. Presently Grant recovered sufficiently to join Speke and they went to the kingdom of Bunyoro. The journey had to be carried out in boats made of planks and tied together with rags; and at the end of it they found a kingdom which was less developed than Buganda. Here they were detained for a time by the king, who was on bad terms with the Kabaka of Buganda, so they were pleased when they were free to continue their journey northwards to Cairo. This took longer than they had expected and, when they finally reached Gondokoro, 'Speke was excessively lean; he had walked the whole way from Zanzibar, never having ridden once during that wearying march. Grant was in rags, his bare knees projecting through the remnants of trousers.'

The Bakers. This description of them was given by Samuel Baker. He was at Gondokoro with his determined wife, who had insisted on sharing her husband's dangers. The Bakers were personal friends of Speke and had set out from the mouth of the Nile to follow it down to its source. In doing this they hoped to meet Speke and Grant and bring them stores which they would be certain to need. The latter had meanwhile been coming up from Victoria Nyanza by the course which the Bakers had proposed to follow south, and the two parties met at Gondokoro. Baker's idea of following the Nile from its mouth, and so finding its source, seems an obvious one. But the country along the Sudd portion of the Nile was a formidable obstacle which he was fortunate to have passed, and there were further difficulties ahead.

The meeting in Gondokoro was, therefore, sensational. Baker wrote: 'All my men perfectly mad with excitement; firing salutes as usual with ball cartridges, they shot one of my donkeys, a melancholy sacrifice as an offering at the completion of this geographical discovery.'

Discovery of Lake Albert. At first Baker was convinced that his friends had really solved the mystery of the sources of the Nile. But when Speke told him of a rumoured lake to the south-west of the Victoria, and when the four explorers had discussed the lie of the land, it became clear that in Baker's own words 'one leaf of the laurel remained' for him to pick. Armed with Speke's own map, the Bakers set off across country in the direction of the kingdom of Bunyoro, and reached the southern tip of the lake in March 1867. They named it Lake Albert.

Samuel Baker had meant to celebrate this by all the men giving three cheers in English style; but the knowledge that he had found a great inland sea, one of the twin sources of the Nile which men had sought for centuries, overwhelmed him. Instead he thanked God for having guided and supported the party through all dangers, with this magnificent result.

Murchison Falls. Sailing in canoes up the eastern shore of Lake Albert, the Bakers reached the point where it was entered by the Victoria Nile; and they completed their exploration by going up this river for some eighteen miles. Suddenly there was a roar of water and they came to a great waterfall of the Nile, which they named the Murchison Falls in honour of the President of the Royal Geographical Society. The christening ceremony was an exciting one. Baker shot at the crocodiles, a boatman was so frightened that he collapsed on the bottom of the canoe, a paddle was lost, a hippo rammed the boat and the African women with the party screamed. Finally it all became calm again and the boat was held steady while Baker sketched the Murchison Falls.

The Nile system. The exploration was now almost complete. It was clear that the Nile was fed by at least two lakes, Victoria and Albert (see map on p. 117). Another map (on p. 69) will also show one reason why men were so long confused by the Nile, the Congo and the Zambezi. This reason is that the watersheds of these great rivers all lie near together. The whole Nile system, indeed, was not

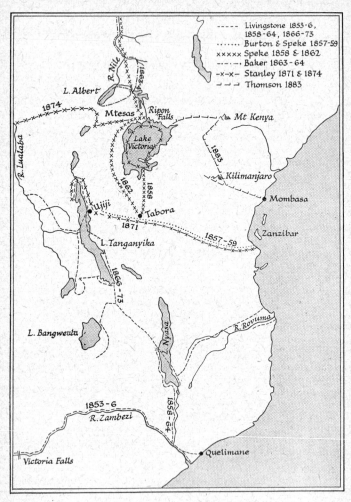

Map 6. Explorers of East Africa.

accurately mapped until another explorer, Stanley, paid a visit to this area years later. Before this a very great explorer, Livingstone, had puzzled over the problem for years.

Livingstone. Mungo Park, Speke, Burton, Grant and Baker were all geographers and naturalists whose interests were in scientific exploration; but Krapf and Rebmann had shown the close link that could exist between the spreading of Christianity and the discovering of more about the unknown continent; and the greatest explorer of all was a medical missionary, David Livingstone.

Youth. By the time he was ten David Livingstone had shown great determination. As there was no money to educate him, he went to work for fourteen hours a day in a cotton mill, but that did not mean that he gave up hopes of learning. When he was ten he bought a Latin Grammar with his first week's wages and studied after working hours. In this way he qualified himself to be accepted by the London Missionary Society; and while waiting to be posted abroad he studied medicine and became a doctor.

First post. He went to his first post in Bechuanaland in 1841, and from there he crossed the Kalahari Desert and got into touch with the Africans living round Lake Ngami. Pushing further north still in search of sites for missions he met the Makololo, who were to give him his most faithful followers; and it was through his good relations with this tribe that in 1851 he found the mighty river Zambezi. He also learnt that the Makololo had recently combined with another tribe to raid for slaves with which to buy guns from the Arabs. This helped to convince him that it was essential to adopt a positive policy in regard to this evil, if it was to be stopped. To do this he thought it was necessary to establish a mission station which should also be a centre for farmers and traders; for in his opinion the greatest obstacle to the spread of Christianity among the Africans was the poverty and ignorance which surrounded them with fear. If they were to be freed from this, they would have to be introduced to a higher standard of living and shown that it was possible for the different tribes to work together, thus increasing their power to resist violence.

First expedition. In those days a settlement of the nature Livingstone had in mind depended on climate and communications. He considered that he had already found a healthy area in the Bakota uplands: the problem was to link it with the civilization of the coast. In searching for this, Livingstone set out on the first of his three great journeys. This lasted from 1853 to 1856 and took him right across Africa, from Makololand to the Atlantic Ocean at Loanda, and then back to reach the sea on the east coast at Quelimane. For a large part of this journey he had followed the course of the Zambezi, and in doing so he had in 1855 discovered the Victoria Falls. Now he wondered whether this river would not be a better means of communication than any land route.

Appeal to Cambridge. On his return to England he found himself famous through the publication of his book *Missionary Travels and Researches*; and he used his fame to appeal to Cambridge University for help in carrying on the work he had begun in opening the way for commerce and Christianity in Africa. The result was the foundation of the Universities Mission to Central Africa whose work is described in ch. VI. He also secured government support for his second important expedition, the object of which was to explore the Zambezi valley up from the mouth of the river in the hope that it might prove a good means of communication.

Second expedition. This second expedition lasted from 1858 to 1864; and was different from the first in that Livingstone travelled on a steam launch, the *Ma Robert*, and took with him European companions, with whom, however, he did not get on so well as with Africans. The first difficulty was the discovery that the Zambezi was not as easily navigable as Livingstone had hoped, and, when he had surveyed its mouth, therefore, he turned to the Shiré River. This flows into the Zambezi not far from its mouth and led Livingstone to the Murchison Falls. At this point he left the steamer and set out on foot for a great lake which he was told was nearby. It took a month to reach and proved to be Lake Shirwa. The highlands around seemed to be a possible site for the kind of missionary colony Livingstone had in mind, and after he had returned to Tete, he marched off again to find out more about the land. Information, however, was not easily obtained. This was country where the slave trade had turned fertile land into a wilderness, and the results were to be seen in starving people and corpses. In these circumstances the Africans were afraid of the explorers; however, Livingstone persisted, and in 1859 he reached the southern end of Lake Nyasa. The size of this lake convinced him that it could prove a valuable waterway and strike a blow at the slave trade, which he was more determined than ever to uproot. He reasoned that if a steamer were placed on the lake, ivory could be bought for European goods and transported by water all the way to England, except for one stretch above the Murchison Falls. If ivory were carried in this way, the slave trade would be cut out, for it would never pay to drive slaves all the way to the coast by land, unless they could pay for their keep by carrying ivory. His letters home telling of his ideas persuaded several missionaries to come out, but the area proved too unhealthy, and the mission was abandoned. It was later that Livingstone's discovery of Lake Nyasa led to mission stations, followed by traders, and eventually to the establishment of the Protectorate of Nyasaland. At the time the importance of his new discoveries was not realized; and he had also to face great personal distress through the death of his wife, who had come out to join him.

Object of third expedition. Undaunted by the disappointments at the end of his second expedition, Livingstone set out on his third important journey in 1866. This was to be his last. Its object was geographical: Speke and Baker had reported their discoveries, but Burton and some others maintained that their theories of the source of the Nile were incorrect, or at least incomplete. Besides, no one yet knew where the central watershed lay. The President of the Royal Geographical Society suggested that Livingstone might be able to settle the question by going from the Upper Rovuma to Lake Tanganyika and then exploring westwards. This would give him a chance to see if the Nile not only flowed out of Lakes Victoria and Albert in the north, as Speke and Baker had shown, but first flowed into the southern end of these lakes. If this idea should prove correct, the true source might be Lake Tanganyika. Livingstone was far from convinced that Speke and Baker were right and was delighted at the opportunity of exploring these possibilities. He at once agreed, provided he was allowed also to use every opportunity to fight against the slave trade and to spread Christianity.

Results. In view of these plans, Livingstone decided to operate from two bases. In the first, Zanzibar, he planned to recruit porters, obtain supplies and arrange for reinforcements. The second was to be Ujiji on Lake Tanganyika. From here Livingstone meant to explore the land around, looking for the Nile and endeavouring to identify the central watershed. Although far to the south of his goal, the true Nile sources, Livingstone's last journey was not unproductive of results. He discovered Lake Bangweulu in 1868 and was exploring the Lualaba, or upper reaches of the Congo, when he died.

Difficulties. Throughout this last expedition Livingstone had great difficulties to overcome. He hated the atmosphere which he thought slavery created in Zanzibar, and could not recruit sufficient reliable porters. Nor was he popular with the Arabs, or the Banyans of the coast, who knew his ceaseless efforts to get slavery stopped. This made it difficult for his friend Kirk to send further supplies to his second base at Ujiji, near Lake Tanganyika, especially as few were willing to carry the explorer's letters back to Kirk for fear of what they might reveal about the slavery in the district.

Lack of supplies. Yet Livingstone was in great need of further supplies, for a porter had deserted with his medicine chest, and without drugs he was soon dangerously weakened by fever. Despite this he carried on to Lake Tanganyika, undaunted by the desertion of most of his porters. From here he discovered Lake Bangweulu in 1868, then returned to Lake Tanganyika, where he found that the supplies which he had arranged to have sent on from Zanzibar had nearly all been stolen. After resting awhile, he set out again looking for the Nile and found the Congo, or Lualaba River as he called it, in 1871. He then returned to Ujiji, where in 1871 he was met by Stanley, whose commission to find out what was happening to Livingstone will be described later.

Death. Stanley failed to persuade him to return. He was determined to solve the problem of the Nile while he still had the strength

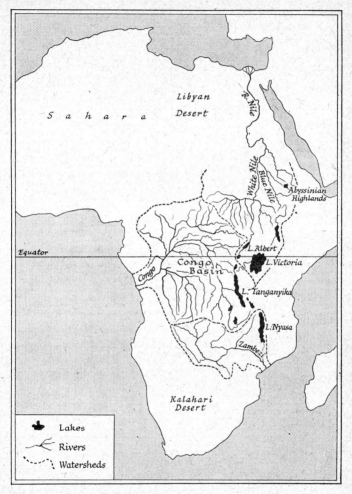

Map 7. The Watersheds of Central Africa.

to do so; but his once magnificent body was fast failing, and on 30 April 1873 he died near Lake Bangweulu.

Achievements. It is not easy to sum up Livingstone's achievements: he carried on Wilberforce's work for the abolition of slavery, enlisting the sympathy of the British for the Africans by making Africa real to them through his letters and books. As an explorer he changed the map of Africa. Lastly, it was through his work that Nyasaland eventually became a part of the British Commonwealth. Today his reputation still stands high as an utterly fearless man, serving the highest ideals, and marked by a real understanding of the Africans, which may have come from his great affection for them. This was returned in full measure by the faithful Susi and Chummah who had followed him in all his travels, and on his death carried his journals and his body for hundreds of miles to the coast.

Stanley. Among those bearing Livingstone's coffin at the state funeral in Westminster Abbey was Henry Morton Stanley (1841–1904), who in his turn was to rank as a great African explorer. All his life he was to be a great admirer of the man to whom he had brought supplies and news when he was cut off from the world at Ujiji. It is more doubtful whether Livingstone would have continued to feel a similar admiration for Stanley if he could have known how bitterly the latter was to attack Kirk, Livingstone's faithful ally and friend in the fight against slavery. Stanley even made a speech in Edinburgh, where Kirk had been a student, in which he spoke of the indfference of the 'gentleman [Kirk] who had got his fame and position as the friend of Dr Livingstone', and 'left him in Africa, silent, alone, deserted and almost at death's door'. In saying this he referred to the fact that Kirk had not been able to get supplies to Livingstone when he had been stranded in Tanganyika and that Livingstone was eventually relieved by Stanley himself. This failure, however, was not due to indifference on Kirk's part, but to the fact that the caravans had not been able to get through.

Character. This readiness to attack others, regardless of the damage he could do to their careers, was typical of Stanley, who troubled very little about other people's feelings. It is for this reason that before condemning Stanley's character, and praising his achievements, his early life must be described. Its hardships exceeded by far the difficulties that faced Livingstone, so that by the time Stanley had won success in life, he had become a self-confident man who was convinced that those who could not overcome difficulties were weaklings. He thought he knew by then the rough ways of the world and was prepared to give as good as he received, with the result that people found it difficult to accept his successes.

Youth. John Rowlands, later to be called Henry Morton Stanley, lost his father soon after his birth at Denbigh in 1841, and his mother left him to be brought up by his grandfather and two uncles. When he was four his grandfather also died and the two uncles sent him to live with a couple to whom they paid half a crown a week. Later, on being asked to increase this sum, they refused and John was sent to the workhouse. This shock was made even worse because he was told that he was going to live with his aunt Mary who lived in a big house. When he got inside it proved to be the workhouse. Here food was scarce and beatings frequent; but through it all John grew in strength and intelligence until at ten years old he was head boy in the workhouse school. At fifteen, being no longer prepared to be beaten by the cruel head of the workhouse for something he had not done, he turned on his master and gave him the thrashing instead. He then ran away to his other grandfather, who refused to do anything for him and told him to get out of the house. Fortunately John had worked successfully at his lessons, and in the end was accepted as a pupil teacher by a schoolmaster cousin. He was not really welcome, however, and eventually he ran away to sea. Here he lived again in a world of blows and kicks. On landing in America fortune was kind to him and he was adopted by a Mr Stanley, who gave him his own name. Mr Stanley, however, did not live long enough to make provision for his adopted son. So Henry Stanley, as he must now be called, was caught up in the American Civil War out of which he was finally invalided. He then worked his way back to England and in his journal wrote later:

Like a bride arraying herself in her best for her lover, I had arranged my story to please one who would, at last, I hoped prove an affectionate mother! But I found no affection, and I never again sought for, or expected, what I discovered had never existed.

I was told that 'I was a disgrace to them in the eyes of their neighbours, and they desired me to leave as speedily as possible'.

'*How I found Livingstone.*' Eventually a gift of vivid description and aptitude for a life of adventure gave Stanley the chance to become a press correspondent; and a brilliant piece of reporting won for him the commission to go wherever dramatic events were taking place. In this way Stanley became the first explorer to be financed by a newspaper when he was commissioned, in 1871, by the *New York Herald* to find David Livingstone. This mission was not likely to be popular with the more conservative Englishmen, who rightly said that although Livingstone might be cut off his whereabouts were perfectly well known to the well-informed, and who did not care for the idea of the British national hero being rescued by an American newspaperman. Nor was Stanley's account conciliatory. His book, however, *How I found Livingstone*, was a best-seller. In 1874 the British *Daily Telegraph* and the American *New York Herald* fitted out an expedition under Stanley's leadership which was to complete the work of Speke, Grant, Baker and Livingstone.

'*Through the Dark Continent.*' This was geographically a most successful expedition and was later described by Stanley in *Through the Dark Continent*. It began with a long march towards Lake Victoria. As soon as the column entered Ituru it was clear that they were not welcome. Stanley, however, fought his way through, pursuing the defeated Africans from village to village and setting fire to each as soon as captured. From Ituru he entered friendly and hospitable land and travelled safely to Lake Victoria, which he circumnavigated, and so finally settled the question of its size and nature. This stage of the journey revealed the two sides of Stanley's character. On the one hand it brought him into touch with Mutesa, the Kabaka of Buganda. Their relations were friendly, and he wrote afterwards of the Kabaka's desire to imitate the ways of the Europeans which gave an opportunity to talk to him of Christianity. Later Stanley followed this up by appealing to the C.M.S. to send missionaries to Buganda. The other side of his nature was shown, however, to those who lived on Bumbireh Island in the Nyanza. The inhabitants had made it very clear that they violently resented Stanley's landing on the island to buy food on his journey to Uganda. He and his followers had indeed with difficulty escaped with their lives from the place. After further considerable trouble, Stanley maintained that the hostility of Bumbireh was blocking his route to Uganda. In his opinion, the only action he could take to clear the route was to attack the islanders with guns, having tempted them to show themselves in the open. The uselessness of spears against guns in these circumstances was shown. Forty-two Africans were killed and over a hundred were seen to retire wounded. Against this only two of Stanley's followers were injured, and those were by stones which had been thrown. This incident resulted in very strong protests from England condemning Stanley's savage behaviour. It should be noted that his judges had not themselves lived through the terrifying moments when Stanley's first landing on Bumbireh was met with treacherous violence.

The source of the Nile. Next came the exploration of the land between Lakes Edward and Victoria. So began the final stage in solving the mystery of the Nile; for it was now clear that it had its principal source in Victoria Nyanza, which is higher than the secondary source in the Lakes Albert and Edward which are linked by the Semliki River. Some people, however, consider that the real source of the Nile is to be found in the Ruchuru, which the map on page 117 shows as the largest river flowing into Lake Edward.

The Congo. After this, Stanley carried out an equally thorough survey of Lake Tanganyika and then turned his attention to the river which Livingstone had called the Lualaba, but which is known today as the Congo. He reached this at Nyangwe, the place where Livingstone died. From here he had to force his way through land from which Livingstone had been forced to turn back by the unfriendly attitude of its people. Stanley partly solved the problem by coming to an arrangement to travel in the same party with Tippoo Tib, a well-known Arab slave dealer, and for a fortnight he marched through a forest so dense that it shut out the daylight and left the men to stumble in the half-light through streams and over fallen trees. At the end of this he was able to launch on the waters of the Congo the boat which his party had carried. Nor was the passage an easy one. The Stanley Falls, for one thing, blocked the way further down; and the boats had to be dragged past these in the face of ceaseless attacks from cannibals, shouting for human meat. But at last Stanley reached the great pool named after him, and in 1877, after losing his last European companion, struggled to a point which had already been surveyed on the lower Congo. For the rest of his career in Africa he was closely connected with the Congo. This was an area rich in commercial possibilities. Stanley, who had seen the pioneers in their wagons developing the west of the United States, was quick to appreciate these possibilities and to urge that England should take control of the Congo, a task which she refused. Leopold of the Belgians, however, was eager to undertake it and he eventually persuaded Stanley to return to Africa to open up the Congo for trade under Leopold's control.

Communications and trade. From 1879 Stanley spent five years developing communications and trading stations on the Congo, and signing treaties with over 450 independent African chiefs who gave their rights of sovereignty and ownership to Leopold's Association. These were the years when Stanley was nicknamed Bula Mutari, or the Breaker of Rocks, by the Africans, who watched him working 2352 miles backwards and forwards to carve out only fifty-two miles of road.

Emin Pasha. Stanley returned to Africa a fourth time in 1887, on an expedition to rescue Emin Pasha, the governor of the equatorial province of the Sudan. Many felt that he was in danger of being overwhelmed by the forces of the Muslim prophet (the 'Mahdi') who had defeated the English General Gordon; for when Emin Pasha sent out an appeal for help a number of people not only wished to rescue him but also hoped that the rescue might result in his province of equatorial Africa being added either to the Congo State or to the Imperial British East Africa Company. Stanley was now so famous that he could make his own terms. He refused to lead the expedition unless it followed the short, but hazardous, route up the Congo. From his point of view this had two advantages. First of all, it gave him the chance of dealing with Tippoo Tib, who was threatening to get control of the new state of the Congo which was largely Stanley's creation. Tippoo Tib was now appointed governor of the Stanley Falls station, in which position he was to put down slavery below the Falls. Secondly, it offered the chance of further exploration.

The impenetrable forest. Stanley seized this opportunity when he set off from the Congo through the unknown forest to meet Emin Pasha. The horrors of this jungle were so great that only one-third of those who went into it with Stanley came out alive. Giant trees of one hundred and fifty feet high were so interlaced with thick creeper that there was no space between them, and all the time the men were attacked ceaselessly by painful insects and snakes, while in the undergrowth the pygmies lurked with their poisoned arrows and skewers. Over all there often hung a thick white mist, and food was so scarce that the expedition was threatened by starvation.

An unwelcome rescue. Five months later the survivors came out on a plateau leading to Lake Albert. Emin Pasha came to greet them, and to rescue his rescuers with gifts of supplies.

They did not receive the welcome they expected. Emin did not even wish to be rescued, if it meant leaving Equatoria, and it was with difficulty that Stanley persuaded him and his followers to come back with him to Bagamoyo. (Before that was achieved Stanley had crossed the Great Congo Forest three times.) On this return journey Stanley saw the Mountains of the Moon for the first time. Later he was able to tell Europe of this important discovery in the book *In Darkest Africa* which he published on his return.

The last part of Stanley's life. This last journey was really the end of Stanley's work as an explorer. The rest of his life can be summarized very shortly; he married, was elected to parliament in England, was knighted, and in 1904 died.

Joseph Thomson. One major task remained for those who sought to establish links between Europe and East and Central Africa. This was to find a quicker route from the coast to Uganda than the old track from Zanzibar via Bagamoyo, Tabora and Ujiji. It was known that a better way probably existed, for in 1882 Dr Fischer had reached Lake Naivasha from Kilimanjaro; but this route meant passing through Masailand, and travellers did not dare face the powerful tribe who lived there. However, the Royal Geographical Society was aware that a shorter path was badly needed if the slave trade was to be suppressed and trade encouraged. In 1883, then, Joseph Thomson was chosen to lead an expedition, 'To find whether a useful direct route for European travellers exists through the Masai country from any one of the East African ports to the Victoria Nyanza, and to examine Mount Kenya; to make a preliminary survey and to make observations regarding the peoples, rocks, animals and plants of the regions traversed.' Thomson's qualifications for this post were, first the success with which he had taken over the lead of an earlier Tanganyika expedition when he was only twenty, and secondly his qualifications as a scientist. His first attempt was, however, a failure and he was forced to retreat, because the numbers of his caravan proved too small to face the Masai who were threatening to fight.

Across Masailand. His second attempt was luckier. The El Moran 'Masai Warriors' were away on a raid, so that he was able to reach Kikuyuland. Here the dense forests sheltered the Akikuyu, who attacked the expedition with poisoned arrows and stole all they could. From there he pushed on, past Lake Naivasha to El Menteita. He then took the great risk of leading a small party to Mount Kenya, through the Masai of Lykipia. That he got through, and was the first European to see the Aberdares and Thomson's Falls, was largely due to the skill with which he acted the part of a great Laibon (medicine man), who was able to cure a disease which was killing the cattle. After rejoining the main party, Thomson travelled on to Victoria Nyanza, being thus the first European to cross Masailand and find a quick route from Victoria Nyanza to the coast. He was also able to return with information about Mount Elgon, which he had included in his return journey.

Views on Kenya's prospects. Thomson's remarks about the prospects of the country that was soon to be crossed by the Uganda railway show that he had grasped its relative poverty:

Many people have proved with most convincing logical power that a railway is the proper means to open up the country. They have sketched with a daring hand a few thousand miles of the iron road, connecting the coast with the various great lakes: bringing untold wealth to Britain, and taking unlimited quantities of its Brummagem [industrial] wares and flimsy adulterated cottons instead. To make the picture complete, they have told us to expect, as an important result, the stoppage of wars and of the slave trade—industrious and contented tribes taking to civilized ways, and shouting unanimously for missionaries to come over and help them. The utter absurdity of such brilliant schemes will require no further proof than the remarks I have made upon the hopeless prospect of developing any trade in the interior for several generations to come.

CHAPTER VI

MISSIONARY SOCIETIES AND THE EARLY DEVELOPMENT OF EAST AFRICA

African beliefs. Akamba. When the Christian missionaries came to East Africa they found that the inhabitants were used to the idea of one God (Mungu), but, unlike the Christians, they did not think of him as bothering about what happened among men. The practical Akamba, for instance, thought it was wasteful to give sacrifices to the creator of all things, or Mumbi as they called him, because he lived in the skies and was too far away to be influenced by men. They made their sacrifices to a man's aiimu (spirits) who go and live in a wild fig tree when he dies. That is why small huts were often built close to fig trees.

Akikuyu. The Akikuyu also worshipped a god 'Ngai' who lived on Mount Kenya and was a god of love. He concerned himself with men in so far as he punished those who disobeyed him by sending famine, disease and death; but the Akikuyu considered that more ordinary troubles were due to the spirits of the dead.

Baganda. The Baganda had rather different ideas. They believed in Lubare who lived in certain places. These Lubare had special power over some objects. The most important Lubare, for instance, was called Mukasa, and lived in the Victoria Nyanza. He not only controlled the waters of the lake but also had a fair amount of power over the whole of Buganda.

Masai. In Mr Richard's manuscript, *History of the C.M.S. in the Highlands*, he quotes an early missionary who wrote about the Masai beliefs that: 'Beyond their word for God, "Engai", I cannot find that they have any word for soul or spirit, not even for the spirits of the departed; in fact they seem to have no idea of a future existence. To them a man is like the beasts that perish.' He was worried also about their morals because they had no word for good that did not also have a bad sense.

These few examples serve as an indication of the kind of religions existing in East Africa before the coming of the Muslims and Christian Missionaries.

Spread of Islam. Most of the Muslims on the coast today are Shafite Sunnis, and it is reasonable to assume that the conversion of the coast people began some time after A.D. 813 when Muhammad bin Idris es Shafi, the founder of the Shafite school, started his teaching. After Seyyid Said's transfer of his capital to Zanzibar, the Arab traders carried their religion inland as far as the great lakes and later Uganda. At this stage Islam took root in several places and secured some African followers. However, converting people was solely the work of isolated Arabs, Swahili and Somali traders, and their African converts. It was not directed by any missionary organization and lacked plan, money or literature. Despite this, the period of European occupation from 1885 onwards was one in which the Muslim faith spread to parts of central and western Tanganyika, southern Uganda and a number of townships in Kenya; for European penetration of the interior meant that the Swahili population, who were Muslim, found openings as troops, traders, skilled craftsmen, interpreters, domestic servants etc., and could thus help to spread Islam.

Today, in British East Africa, there are thought to be over two million Muslims, that is, one-tenth of the total population, and among the African converts there are several hundred former Christians.

The first Muslim Mission to East Africa was opened in 1935 in Tabora, Tanganyika, by the Ahmadiyya Mission, and is now active in all three territories. The first task of its present head, Sheikh Mubarah Ahmed, was to prepare a Swahili translation of the holy Koran with a commentary. Other Islamic literature is being produced; but, apart from this, the Muslims have mostly conducted village Koranic schools, where the standard of religious and secular learning is low. As many Muslims are afraid of religous pressure if they send their children to Christian schools, the African and Arab communities are apt to be backward and economically handicapped. Nor has the Ahmadiyya mission yet undertaken hospital work of the type undertaken by the Christian missionaries. The Muslims who follow H.H. the Aga Khan, on the other hand, established schools, hospitals, dispensaries and libraries after the end of the First World War. They do not, however, support missionaries, for they believe that conversion should result from the activity of the individual.

Hinduism. From very early days, the Hindu religion has been practised along the coast by traders who visited East Africa from India and settled there. Hindus do not, however, regard it as part of their religion to make converts, for they recognize that their vegetarian and teetotal habits make it difficult to absorb those who were not born Hindu. This lack of missionary work accounts for no further allusion being made to Hindus in this chapter.

Christian missionaries: Krapf. The first Christian missionaries belonged to the Church Missionary Society which had been founded for work in Africa and the East. The pioneer in this society was Dr Krapf, whose large part in exploring his new country has been described in the previous chapter. In 1844 he set out from Zanzibar, armed with a letter of introduction from Seyyid Said which told the Arab governors of the coast that 'This letter is written on behalf of Dr Krapf, a good man who wishes to convert the world to God. Behave well to him, and be everywhere serviceable to him.' Two years later he was joined by the Rev. John Rebmann, and together they opened a mission station at Rabai, some fifteen miles inland from the present Mombasa. From here Rebmann moved to Kilimanjaro, home of the Chagga people, whence he startled Europe in 1848 by announcing that a snow-capped mountain was to be found near the Equator. But it was at Rabai that East Africa's first school was started a little later by Krapf, who realized that his converts must be taught to read the Bible, which in future was to be their guide.

The study of Swahili. These early missionaries were quick, too, to realize the importance of studying the languages of the people among whom they worked; and Krapf gave much time to this, with the result that he was able to publish the first Swahili dictionary, together with a translation of part of the Bible. He was followed in this work by Dr Steere of the Universities Mission to Central Africa, who gave a great deal of his time to studying Swahili. He was determined that this knowledge should be spread, and trained some of the young men at his first mission as printers; in 1865 the first copies of his book *A Handbook of the Swahili Language as spoken in Zanzibar* were produced in Zanzibar. Today his *Swahili Exercises* are regarded as the standard grammar of the language and studied by all those who have to pass examinations in the subject. Steere, however, like Krapf, regarded his studies as a means to an end, which was to make the Bible available to those who knew the widely spoken language of Swahili; and to this end he translated the Bible and a good deal of the Church service into Swahili. While he was doing this work, Dr Steere became interested in some of the tales he heard, and made an interesting collection of them in Swahili.

Livingstone. As an early missionary, explorer, linguist and teacher, Krapf laid the foundations for a line of missionary stations which he thought of as a chain of Christian 'forts' linking up eastern and western Africa, but few would have noticed the foundations when he left. It was Livingstone who was to introduce East Africa to a wider public. His travels caught men's imaginations; and his attacks on the slave trade filled them with sympathy for the African, whom they now saw as suffering from a poverty which limited his ambitions to satisfying his immediate material needs, and haunted by fears: fears of the slavers, and the fears that arise from ignorance.

The Universities Mission to Central Africa. In 1857 Livingstone appealed to Cambridge for help to destroy these handicaps from which the Africans suffered. The result was the foundation of the Universities Mission to Central Africa. This aimed at raising the African's standard of life and at the same time bringing him into the Christian fold. Unfortunately the first expedition started in the Shiré River district where so many of the party died that Bishop Tozer, who came out to take over its leadership in 1863, decided that the difficulties of carrying on in Nyasaland were too great and moved the mission's headquarters to Zanzibar. Here he began to train young African boys for the Christian ministry: and here his assistant Dr Steere began the study of Swahili. After the slave market was closed in 1873, Dr Steere, then Bishop Steere, also took over the building of a stone church on the site. It took four years to complete; and the bishop himself supervised the mixing of the mortar and showed his trainees how to place the stones, as well as doing all the really skilled work himself.

The freed slaves. The work of the Universities Mission to Central Africa soon began to spread out from Zanzibar town; and a new responsibility was taken on when Mbweni was started a few miles south. This village was to be a centre for freed slaves, for the missionaries who were coming to work in Africa were drawing increasing attention to the evils of the slave trade. This meant that the government was having more and more pressure put on it to check the East African slave trade. At the same time it was not much good to free a slave and then leave him hundreds of miles away from his tribal lands. It was necessary, therefore, to cater for the freed slaves before more could be rescued. The Universities Mission played their part in this work; and in 1867 they started their first station on the mainland at Magila, in the hilly country behind Tanga. From this centre they opened up a number of mission posts with schools and hospitals; and in 1875 they went further afield and explored the area round the Rovuma River. Here Dr Steere selected a place called Masasi and led there a number of Africans from Mbweni.

The Society of the Holy Ghost. The third mission society to rank among the pioneers in East Africa was that of the Fathers of the Society of the Holy Ghost, together with the Sisters of the Sacred Heart. They also landed at Zanzibar, where Catholics had already opened two hospitals, one for European sailors, and the other for Africans, together with an elementary and an industrial school. The Holy Ghost Mission, however, intended to use Zanzibar only as a depot, the headquarters of the Society being established in 1868 on the mainland, at Bagamoyo. This village concentrated on the care of freed slaves, the majority of whom were bought from slave traders and helped to pay for their keep and training by their work. Père Horner, who was in charge, reckoned that £5 would pay for the training that would make a man self-supporting. After this he would be married off before going to settle in one of the Christian villages that had been planted inland to act as Christian oases. In this way hundreds of people were rescued from slavery, taught Christianity and given a chance to live a successful agricultural life. Bagamoyo was like a torch on a dark night. The Africans who lived there learnt to use the plough instead of the digging stick, saw the first coffee bushes, and cast away many of their superstitious fears as they entered the fold of the Church.

Freretown. This concern of the Universities Mission, and that of the Holy Ghost, for the freed slaves was shared also by the C.M.S., who deliberately placed their settlement of Freretown near to Mombasa. It was such a disturbing influence among the domestic slaves and their owners that the Mombasa Arabs took a vow to make soup of the missionaries' livers. Concern for the slaves also caused the Society of Friends to start their mission on Pemba, just before slavery was finally abolished in Zanzibar.

Two other pioneer missionary societies. Two other mission societies belong to the pioneer group who settled on or near the coast. They are the United Methodists, who came out to Ribe in 1876, and the society which Livingstone had joined as a young man, the London Missionary Society. A year later this society accepted the offer of £5000 made towards the purchase of a steamer for work on Lake

Tanganyika. This mission was very unlucky in the number of deaths it suffered, and eventually it moved down to Northern Rhodesia. Its decision to undertake work on Lake Tanganyika is interesting for three reasons. First it was typical of a change which was coming over mission work in East Africa, which was moving inland; secondly, it led to a link being made between Lake Nyasa and Lake Tanganyika, and this helped in influencing Rhodes to occupy Northern Rhodesia. This connexion between missionary work and politics was also typical of East African history in the last part of the nineteenth century. Thirdly, there is an odd coincidence between the offer of £5000 made to the London Missionary Society and another offer of the same sum which was made to the C.M.S. on condition that they undertook missionary work in Uganda. This was made three days after the explorer Stanley had written a letter describing the opportunities in the country for Christian missionaries. On the strength of this offer, a small party of C.M.S. missionaries set out on the long tramp to Uganda, where they were at once followed by Catholic missionaries, members of a new order, the White Fathers, which had been founded by Cardinal Lavigerie. The Catholic Church owed the rapid development of their work in East Africa to the Cardinal, for he was deeply moved by the needs of this continent. His ambitions for the Church were also limitless, and acute friction soon developed in Uganda between the Catholic and the Protestant missions, both of whom were faced with the rivalry of the Mohammedans who were also keenly seeking converts. Finally a 'religious war' developed between their converts, further details of which will be found in ch. VIII.

The position of the missions at the end of the pioneer period. The close of the pioneer period saw the C.M.S. established at the coast and with their work beginning in Uganda; the Universities Mission with their bases in Zanzibar, the hilly country behind Tanga and the area round the Rovuma River; the United Methodists at Ribe, and the London Missionary Society at their temporary base on Lake Tanganyika. All these were Protestant missions with their headquarters in Britain. The Catholic Missions were drawn from France and consisted of the Holy Ghost Fathers and the White Fathers.

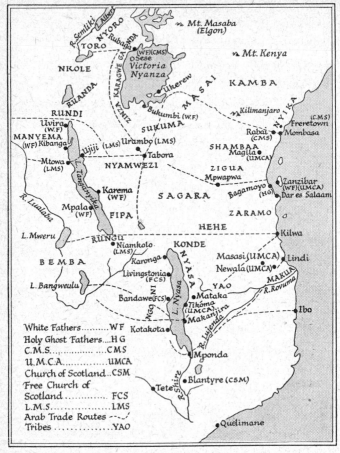

Map 8. Missionary Occupation of East Africa to 1885.

These had established centres at Zanzibar, Bagamoyo, Tabora, Lake Tanganyika and Uganda.

The social achievements of the missions. The missions were now playing an important part in East Africa, of which Dr Oliver has summed up one aspect in his book *The Missionary Factor in East Africa*. He wrote of the Africans' new mission settlements:

All acquired some new tool which made life easier. Digging sticks were replaced by iron hoes, sometimes even by the plough. Saws came to the aid of axes, metal cooking pots to the aid of earthenware. With settled agriculture houses became more permanent and more comfortable. Doors and windows made their first appearance, together with the simplest kind of furniture. Clothing became more plentiful and more hygienic, if not more becoming, and soap made its debut in East African life.

The influence of the missions. Judged by the European standards the missionaries were poor men living simple lives, but they were all employers of workers whom they paid in trade goods, and the wages they paid made it possible for the chiefs to enjoy the calico and other goods for which they had once exchanged slaves. It is no wonder that in one slave-centre the price of cloth fell by more than 50 per cent in the first ten years that the missionaries were there. Nor were they without political influence, for well-informed chiefs were interested in securing the friendship of those who were in touch with the influential British consul at Zanzibar. Indeed, much of England's information about the interior of East Africa came from missionaries at this time, and reference has already been made to their work as explorers. Apart from the sensational discoveries made by men like Krapf and Rebmann, there was the work done by such men as the members of the U.M.C.A. who were the first Europeans to find their way about the Rovuma district; and this was supported by the work of many who travelled on new routes and methodically recorded their findings. Finally the missionaries of this period were the first students of the African languages, of which they drew up dictionaries and grammars.

Bishop Hannington. The work did not proceed without opposition. In Uganda, for instance, when Mutesa died and was succeeded as Kabaka by Mwanga, the persecution of the Christians was begun which is described on p. 128 in ch. VIII. It was to aid the Christian missionaries that Bishop Hannington hurried to Uganda in 1885.

Dawson's biography of Bishop Hannington shows the courage that was possessed by the best of Christians. On one occasion, for instance, Hannington killed a lion cub, which was quickly scented out by the enraged parents. When he heard them approaching, Hannington turned round and faced them. They suddenly checked and stood glaring a few paces away. He then fixed his eyes on them, slowly increasing his distance until he could walk away. Later Hannington went back to get the skin of the cub. When he got near he heard low growls and saw the lion and lioness licking its body. Hannington, however, was more interested in a rare flower growing nearby. He picked it carefully and inspected it, and only then did he fling up his arms and shout at the lions. They looked up, turned tail and ran away.

Such a man naturally took the shortest route to the place where he was needed; but it was unfortunate in 1885 that this was Thomson's route across Masailand, by way of Kavirondo to the north-eastern shores of Victoria Nyanza, for this was the path by which ancient prophecies declared that the conquerors of Buganda would one day come. The Kabaka feared that the Bishop might be coming to take his country away by the same means which the Germans had used further south. He therefore ordered his death.

I.B.E.A's decision to retire from Uganda. Events like this had political results. In 1888, twelve years after the arrival of the first C.M.S. missionary in Uganda, the Imperial British East Africa Company had been founded to spread British influence in East Africa. In doing this it had been led to dispatch caravans to Uganda. During the reign of the weak Kabaka, Mwanga, the Company found that England looked to it also to keep order in Uganda, a task which was complicated by the bad terms on which the different religious bodies in Kampala were living. Details of this are given in ch. VIII. Here it is sufficient to say that the French Catholics, who had arrived in the country soon after the C.M.S., feared that if the Kabaka supported the Company it would result in the Protestant C.M.S., with its headquarters in Protestant England, having a monopoly in Christian converts. The Catholics, therefore, favoured the German efforts to secure control of the country, hoping that Germany would be more friendly to Catholic missionaries than England. The third, or Arab party, was that of the Muslim missionaries. In 1891 the Imperial British East Africa Company, feeling that they could no longer afford to stay on in Uganda, announced their intention of retiring. This greatly dismayed the C.M.S., who feared for the safety of their followers. The outcome of this is described in ch. IX, pp. 147–9.

Trouble round Lake Tanganyika. Nor was Uganda the only area in which the position of the missions was challenged. There was trouble round Lake Tanganyika, where the Arabs had come to realize that their power was being undermined by the European missionaries, whom they suspected of being in league with the Europeans at Zanzibar, with the object of undermining their influence in Africa. This suspicion was increased by the activities of the Germans who, led by the German East Africa Company, were actively seeking influence and power for their country. In these circumstances some of the missionaries believed that the Arabs had been 'commissioned by the sultan of Zanzibar to take possession of all countries round the Lakes'. The years 1884–8 were troubled ones in this area for the missions, which were threatened with violence.

The arrival of new missionary societies. At the same time the European occupation of East and Central Africa, which will be described in ch. VII, resulted in the coming of new missionary societies: in 1891 the Church of Scotland Mission, in 1895 the Africa Inland Mission and the Mill Hill Fathers; those societies also which were already established received considerable reinforcements.

This spread of missionary activity was followed by another increase after British East Africa had been linked by the railway to the coast: the Society of Friends settled on the Uganda border in 1902 and the African Institute of God began its work, while in 1907 the Consolata Fathers opened a mission at Nyeri.

Proposed federation of the missions. This was the period when the influence of the European missionary was at its greatest; it was soon followed by a development of African Christianity, marked by steady recruiting of African clergy. These developments led to the calling of a conference at Nairobi to discuss proposals for a federation of missions as the first step towards the establishment of a United African Church. These proposals were not accepted in the end, although the Kenya Missionary Alliance, the parent of the Christian Council of Kenya, was an important result of the movement.

The missions and education. As time went on there was an increasing demand on the missions for educational and medical work. Reading and writing had begun to be looked on as a means of obtaining well-paid work. It was felt, too, that the Africans were faced with new problems: they needed medical care and education, and the European missionaries were therefore called on to devote a larger proportion of their time to supplying these services. Indeed, up till 1911 all education for Africans in East Africa was in the hands of missionaries, who often met with a good deal of opposition. The Akamba, for instance, considered that they ought to be paid for attending school; and at Kabare, according to Richards' (unpublished) *History of the C.M.S. in the Highlands*, rumours were spread that 'schoolboys, if they continued to read, would never be allowed to eat cold food or to marry, would be given the nickname of Mwalimu (teacher) and eventually would suffer much harm'. Despite this, education spread like a fire; and in 1911 the government of British East Africa laid down rules whereby they gave grants-in-aid to mission schools. At first a few isolated grants only were given. But by 1926 sufficient Africans had secured a primary education for it to be possible to start secondary education, and in this year the Alliance High School was opened in Kenya.

Buganda had already led the way by the founding of secondary schools some twenty years earlier. Before that, primary education had begun with the start of a school in 1895–8; and in 1898 when the first educational missionary arrived there were ninety-eight boys and twenty-eight girls at school. Later schools were supported by the chiefs, but they received no financial help from the government. Despite the increasing interest taken by the government in education, in 1952 it could still be said of Uganda that its system of African education was based almost entirely upon schools supplied, staffed and managed by Christian missions. In 1925 a Department of Education had been set up and the first grants-in-aid were made to Indian schools. Two years later the active Muslim community in Uganda founded a training college called the Uganda Muslim Association.

Education in Tanganyika. When German East Africa was taken over by England as a mandated territory under the League of Nations, many of her administrators were impressed by the relatively high educational standard prevailing, and declared that it was the best in East Africa. The change in administration involved, however, a change in policy. In the period 1920–37 the foundation was laid of the present government school and aided Indian school system. In 1925 a special conference was held in Dar es Salaam which drafted a Bill to give effect to a state scheme of African education. Regulations governing a system of grants-in-aid for mission schools were included. This system was severely hit, first by the depression of the 1930's, and then by the Second World War. Through all these difficult years the Christian missions continued to take an active part in education, and in 1952 it was still true that the majority of African children who received primary education went to a mission school.

Medical missions. The Christian missions realized, too, that European medicine had a big part to play if the witch doctor's hold was to be weakened. The medicine men also were quick to see the threat to their position in this and Mr G. C. Richards, in his (unpublished) history of the C.M.S. in the Highlands, writes that they were disturbed when the services of Dr Crawford, a medical missionary, were sought by such numbers of men that half of them had to sleep on the earthen floors of the reception huts, while another 250 called at his dispensary: all within a few months. This, the witch doctors thought, must stop, and they tried to poison some of the patients so that Dr Crawford should not seem so successful. It was not long before the position changed, so that by 1936 it was generally agreed that European medicine had considerable value. The efforts of the missionaries were now greatly increased by those of the government, which maintained a number of hospitals.

The government and mission hospitals. In Kenya, for instance, the government in 1936 had three principal hospitals for Europeans, together with six for Asians and Africans in the towns, supplemented by twenty-three in the Native Reserves and six small hospitals in the northern part of the Colony. An active government policy, however, did not mean that the missions could now disassociate themselves from medical work—they realized the great need that still remained. This can be illustrated by Tanganyika, where in 1936 the government maintained a number of hospitals, and at the same time the missions had a staff of about eighteen qualified doctors, with whom they ran a number of hospitals, while also undertaking maternity work of high quality and the training of African orderlies and nurses. In Uganda the C.M.S. mission hospital of Mengo stood to remind men of the pioneer work of Sir Albert and Lady Cook who had built it.

The missions and Christianity. In stressing the part played by the missions in supplying vital social services to East Africa the growth of the Church itself must not be ignored; for the primary purpose of all Christian missions is to spread Christianity. In doing this it is doubtful if they were really helped by the vague belief in one God which lay in the background of most tribal religions in East Africa. In fact Dr Oliver suggests, in *The Missionary Factor in East Africa*, that this belief was so overlaid by the cult of tribal ancestors that the African who came into contact with a religion stretching beyond the bounds of any one tribe had his own tribal faith shaken.

African clergy. In spreading the knowledge of Christianity, the missionaries relied a great deal on the services of the African lay catechists whom they taught. These were the men who started the Bush school and through whom many consider that virtually every convert to Christianity is still being made. The catechists, who were 'pupils of a few years' standing able perhaps to read the gospel or recite the catechism', could not build up the Church by teaching the Bible and administering the sacraments. The number of ordained European missionaries therefore imposed limits on the growth of the Church. Once Africans were ordained those limits could be extended, but time was needed before this could happen.

In 1893 seven Africans of mature age who had shown their sincerity by long years as lay-readers and catechists were ordained deacons, and three years later three of them became priests. By 1938 in all six of the Anglican dioceses African clergy outnumbered the ordained European missionaries, and by 1950 they were about four to one. A similar position existed in other branches of the Protestant Church. As the Roman Catholics aspired from the first to a celibate African clergy having roughly eighteen years' education, their numbers grew more slowly, and by 1948 they had 208 African Catholic priests. Considering the Christian Church as a whole, by the middle of the twentieth century the growth of the African clergy has reached the point where the European missionary is required chiefly for specialized aid.

Church government. Church government is closely linked with the position of African clergy. To the Catholic this was an international concern: Africans who were ordained priests would not only gradually replace the missionaries, they would be eligible for service anywhere in the world, in any office of the Catholic Church. The Protestant organization was more local in outlook, and they developed Church government and council, with Europeans and Africans working together. This has been the pattern for much that has followed in the field of secular government.

That the foundation of the Christian Church in Kenya was well laid has recently been demonstrated by the gallant resistance offered to the Mau Mau by so many African Christians.

CHAPTER VII

THE SCRAMBLE FOR AFRICA AND THE FIRST PARTITION OF EAST AFRICA

I. THE SCRAMBLE FOR AFRICA

The change of attitude towards the empire in the later nineteenth century. The first half of the nineteenth century was a time of social unrest in Britain, during which the poor suffered from very squalid living conditions, very low wages, very long hours of work, and very harsh laws. In fact there were so many social evils to be put right at home that it is not surprising that the interest of many was mainly absorbed in home affairs, and the rapid growth of the colonies aroused comparatively little concern. But in the latter part of the nineteenth century this attitude changed. A period of great prosperity started for Britain, and at the same time there developed a widespread interest in imperial affairs. At its worst this interest was mere boastful pride in British might, and became known as 'Jingoism' from a song of 1878:

'We don't want to fight, but by jingo if we do,
We've got the ships, we've got the men, we've got the money too.'

This was the worst side of imperial interest. In happy contrast to it was a developing sense of duty towards the areas within the empire which was reflected by the thoughtful words of Lord Lugard's *The Dual Mandate*:

The civilized nations have at last recognized that while on the one hand the abounding wealth of the tropical regions of the earth must be developed and used for the benefit of mankind, on the other hand an obligation rests on the controlling power, not only to safeguard the material rights of the natives, but to promote their moral and educational progress.

This popular interest in empire spread from the people of Britain to the government. The two leading statesmen of this time were the Conservative leader, Disraeli, and the Liberal leader, Gladstone. Of these Disraeli was the first to realize that the British public had a lively interest in overseas possessions, and the purchase of the Suez Canal shares in 1875 has rightly earned for him particular praise. But to both Disraeli and Gladstone the additional responsibility of new areas was something to be avoided if possible. It was only in 1895, when Joseph Chamberlain took over the Colonial Office, that the government began a positive policy towards the empire. Before then it had been pushed by circumstances and by the pressure of public opinion into acquiring new areas. This was particularly noticeable in East Africa where later developments were to show clearly how reluctant the government was to accept any new colonial responsibilities.

British Africa was acquired, as Lugard put it, 'not by the efforts of her statesmen, but in spite of them'.

Imperial expansion in the later nineteenth century. While interest in the colonies was developing, the empire was expanding rapidly in Asia, the Pacific, and in Africa. Not only Britain, but also Germany, France, Italy, Japan, the United States of America, and Portugal attempted to gain an empire or to increase their existing possessions in one, or all, of these areas. The 'scramble for Africa' was only one of the scrambles for empire which took place in the latter part of the nineteenth century, although it was also the most important.

Motives for imperial expansion. Why was it that this scrambling took place at all, and why should so many countries have pursued the same purpose at the same time? We may trace the growth of competition through several stages. First came the explorers. They brought news of conditions and resources in the regions they explored. Their reports further aroused the interest of missionaries, geographers, and manufacturers. To the missionary there was a new kingdom to be won for Christ; to the geographer there was a new field of information, and to the manufacturer came the realization that the new areas might be extremely useful as a new source of raw materials and as a new market for his products. But however the newly discovered areas were regarded, missionaries, geographers, and traders all desired the same thing—that the new regions should be opened to peaceful trade and administration without delay. Fortunately the development of the steamboat and railway engine during the nineteenth century made this possible for the first time.

Nationalism and Germany. The other major factor leading to competition was the new sense of nationalism which developed in many parts of the world. It was particularly noticeable in Europe, where the various German states had united under the leadership of Prussia in 1862, had defeated Austria and then France, and in 1871 proclaimed the formation of the German empire with the King of Prussia as emperor, or Kaiser, and Bismarck as his chancellor. The confidence and excitement of the Germans was tremendous, and many of them urged that Germany should gain further prestige and wealth by acquiring colonies. But the man who had been responsible for Germany's development, and who still guided her policy, was Chancellor Bismarck, and at first he firmly opposed overseas possessions. When his mind changed, in 1884, the pace of colonial competition was greatly increased.

Leopold and the partition of Africa. Such were the motives leading to partition, which, so far as Africa was concerned, took about twenty years (1879–99) and was most intense in the 1880's. The main rivalry was over the tropical regions of West Africa, East Africa, and the Congo, and the chief powers concerned were France, Germany, Britain, Portugal, and King Leopold of the Belgians. Leopold was the man who started the scrambling in earnest, when he looked from his little neutral kingdom in Europe to the vast unclaimed stretches of tropical Africa, and decided that he would be the leader of the movement to open up the interior. In 1876 he called a meeting of all who were interested and this developed into the International African Association, presided over by Leopold himself, and having as its aims the abolition of the slave trade and the civilization of Africa. At first Leopold hoped to reach the interior of Africa from the east coast, but finding this approach unsatisfactory he sent Stanley to explore the approach from the west, by way of the Congo, in 1879. The French had also sent an expedition there under De Brazza, and both explorers laid claim to the area. Portugal also revived her ancient claims to the Congo mouth, and in order to gain Portuguese support in abolishing the slave trade in that area Britain recognized her claims in 1884. Both Leopold and the French objected.

The Berlin conference, 1884–5. It was at this point that Germany, in the person of Bismarck, intervened by inviting all the European countries concerned to a conference in Berlin to discuss the future of the Congo in particular, and the partition of African territories in general. This Berlin conference (November 1884–February 1885) was willingly attended, and its decisions were stated in the Berlin Act of 1885. The particular importance of this was to state that the 'conventional Congo basin' was to be an area under international protection, whose trade was open to all. At the same time all the powers recognized Leopold as sovereign of the new Congo Independent State. The general importance of the conference was to assert that protectorates should not be claimed and would not be recognized, unless evidence could be shown that they were, or could be, effectively managed. At the same time all the powers agreed that the slave trade should be destroyed wherever it still existed.

Rivalry in West Africa. In the Niger area, as well as in the Congo, rivalry was keen. The French and British had both been interested in the West African coast since the seventeenth century, and both had started to extend their influence inland in the nineteenth. But Sir George Taubman Goldie had bought out his French rivals in 1884, so that the British claim to Niger was recognized at the Berlin Conference, and the delta region became the Oil Rivers Protectorate. At this stage the Germans also competed for the region. They had traded along the west coast since about 1850, but it came as a surprise to the other European countries when Dr Nachtigal visited the region in June and July of 1884 to 'report on German commerce', and in fact made treaties with the chiefs of Togoland and the Cameroons and claimed them as German protectorates. Rather than quarrel with Germany the British recognized these claims.

Rivalry in South-west Africa. Further rivalry took place in the south. German missionaries and settlers had established themselves in Damaraland and Namaqualand in South-west Africa from the mid-nineteenth century. They complained that the British gave them no protection against native attacks, which the British countered by asserting that, apart from Walfish Bay, the Cape government had no responsibilities north-west of the Orange River. Therefore, when Herr Luderitz took a German expedition to Angra Pequena Bay, 150 miles north of the Orange, in 1883, and purchased part of the hinterland from the Hottentots, the British government should not have been surprised. But in fact they were surprised and attempted to claim the whole region from the Orange to the Portuguese Congo, although in June 1884 these belated claims were withdrawn and the German Protectorate over South-west Africa was officially recognized. Yet the Germans did not have things all their own way, for at this same time Cecil Rhodes was dreaming of an Africa which he hoped would be British from the Cape to Cairo. With his millions from the diamond mines of Kimberley and the goldfields of Johannesburg he made at least part of his dreams come true. In 1885 he was instrumental in annexing Bechuanaland in order to secure the 'missionaries' road' into the interior and prevent the Boers from the Transvaal joining up with the Germans in South-west Africa. This was the essential preliminary to the much greater expansion which took place into what became Southern and Northern Rhodesia, after he had formed his British South Africa Company in 1889.

Rivalry in North and East Africa. Meanwhile in North Africa the French pushed south from Algiers and westwards from Senegal, thus encircling the British west coast possessions, and established a huge area of influence across the Sudan which joined with their area north of the Congo. From there an attempt was made in 1898 to extend the area right across to the east coast, but this was halted at Fashoda on the Upper Nile, and in 1889 the French withdrew and recognized the British status in the eastern Sudan. In East Africa France occupied Madagascar in 1886, and the Portuguese claim to the whole interior of Africa between Mozambique and Angola—which cut across the region of Nyasaland and the ambitions of Rhodes—was happily settled by the Anglo-Portuguese Treaty of 1890, which fixed the boundaries which still exist. The areas of what are now Kenya, Uganda, and Tanganyika, were divided between Britain and Germany by the treaties of 1886 and 1890; they are considered more fully later at pp. 109 and 114. Meanwhile the Italians, despite their defeat at Adua, had maintained their hold on Eritrea, and by the end of 1889 had established a protectorate over all the Somali coast.

The effects of partition on the European powers. Thus was Africa partitioned. France had gained in prestige from her African colonies what she had lost by her defeat in Europe in 1870. Leopold of the Belgians soon gained a virtual monopoly of the Congo trade, but his reputation as a philanthropist was ruined when his unprincipled exploitation of the native population was revealed. Bismarck had failed to achieve the friendship with France which he had desired at the Berlin Conference, and was left with colonies whose political value he strongly doubted. Britain had acquired new protectorates to prevent them falling into the hands of her European rivals, but was

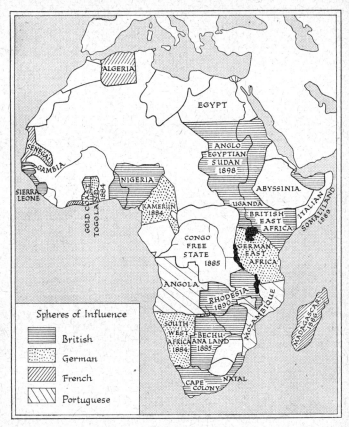

Map 9. The Partition of Africa, 1879–99.

unwilling to develop them. Their development was therefore left at first to chartered companies. In the west coast region Goldie's Royal Niger Company was chartered in 1886; on the east coast Sir William

Mackinnon's Imperial British East Africa Company was chartered in 1888; and in South Africa Rhodes obtained a charter for his British South Africa Company in 1889.

The effects of partition on Africa. It would be quite wrong to think of the partition of Africa as a struggle for profit alone. Some people did see it as this, but that was only part of a very large picture. There were also the missionaries and abolitionists who in many cases gave their lives and received no tangible reward. In East Africa they dominated the early picture. A comparison of conditions in East Africa before and after the scramble is also revealing. When Burton passed through the Usambara district on his way back from the expedition to Lake Tanganyika with Speke, he wrote of stockaded villages, hostile people, violence, extortion by chiefs, and the deep underlying curse of slave trading. Twenty-three years later Joseph Thomson was astounded to find that these same villages no longer had stockades, that the people were friendly, and that the whole countryside had an atmosphere of peace in which trade and agriculture were the only interests of importance. Thomson emphasized the fact that this rapid change was due to the establishment of law and order, trade, and particularly to the abolition of the slave trade, all of which were the direct result of European interest. On the other hand, while Thomson applauded the beneficial results of this interest another great traveller, Elton, wrote a warning against the dangers colonization might involve in connexion with the land: 'Probably the land', he wrote, 'is wastefully occupied, and plenty of spare elbow-room might be found. But native ideas of land-holding are very enlarged, and it is probable that European cultivation might lead to grave misunderstandings.' But although in some areas this prophecy has proved true, the fact remains that since the partition Africa has enjoyed a far greater measure of peace, health, and wealth, than ever before. Partition brought more gain than loss to the African.

The Brussels Conference, 1889–90. Of the meetings which were held between the countries concerned in the colonization of Africa, one at least shows that the interests of the African peoples were not ignored. The Brussels Conference (1889–90) had three aims, all of which were humanitarian: first, to destroy the African slave trade completely and finally; second, to protect the African population; and third, to ensure for Africa 'the benefits of peace and civilization'. The conclusions of the conference are dealt with in ch. XI, but it is mentioned in connexion with partition as evidence of the genuine good will of the countries concerned.

II. THE PARTITION OF EAST AFRICA

The extent of the Sultan's dominions in 1875. In 1875 the coast and the interior of East Africa between Warsheikh in the north and the Rovuma River in the south were, in theory, the dominion of the Sultan of Zanzibar. In fact his lack of resources and the difficulties of communication over so large an area prevented him from keeping a tight hold over the whole of the region, so that his main interest was confined to the area nearest to Zanzibar and the main trade routes to Lake Tanganyika from which he drew so large a proportion of his profits. Over this central region his rule was effective though not always secure against revolts. To the south and to the north it was less effective, but garrisons with governors or sub-governors were stationed in most of the coastal towns.

The Sultan warned by Egyptian invasion, 1875. Before the Germans staked their claim to East Africa in 1884 the Sultan had been well aware that he was in no position to defend his dominions from any invasion from without. In 1875 he had watched with some apprehension the Egyptian occupation of Barawa and Kismayu in the north. In fact this occupation, which had aimed at establishing a route from the Indian Ocean to the Great Lakes to help General Gordon exterminate the Nile slave trade, only lasted two months, but it showed the Sultan that East Africa had a strategic importance. The journeys of the explorers had shown what might be the value of East Africa as an entrance to the heart of Africa. The Sultan, therefore, rightly feared that the Egyptian invasion would be the prelude to others which might lead to permanent occupation, and not being strong enough himself to prevent an attack he decided that his safest

4-2

course would be to invite Britain to safeguard and develop his dominions for him.

The Mackinnon concession, 1877–8. In 1876 Sultan Barghash first requested that British 'capitalists' should help him in 'the development and civilization of Africa, and the opening up of trade on the coast and in the interior'. The request was taken up by Sir William Mackinnon. This energetic little Scottish business man had already done much for East Africa. It was he who had started the first steamship and mail service, and he had also helped in providing a telegraph cable to Zanzibar. In the same year that Barghash made his request Mackinnon was busy on plans for opening up the interior by means of a road from Dar es Salaam to the northern end of Lake Nyasa. By 1881 this road was over seventy miles long and carrying considerable traffic. But the request which the Sultan had made was for much more than a road. It was virtually a request for a British company to colonize his East African dominions. At first Mackinnon took up the idea with enthusiasm and in 1877 negotiations between his representatives and the Sultan began. Both parties were assisted by Sir John Kirk, who gave whole-hearted encouragement to the scheme, and for a year negotiations continued on excellent terms. But by May 1878 the atmosphere had changed; the next month negotiations finished and the proposed 'Mackinnon concession' was dead. The reason for the failure, Kirk said, was not the attitude of the British government but the delay of the company in taking over the area, and the tactlessness of one of Mackinnon's negotiators, Badger, who 'made an ass of himself' by trying to bully the Sultan. But whatever the causes of failure, there can be no doubt that when the proposed concession failed both Britain and the Sultan lost the golden opportunity for the peaceful development of East Africa. The time of the scramble was approaching and competitors were coming into the area in increasing numbers.

The work of the explorers has been described already in ch. v. They included missionaries, geographers, naturalists and patriots. In this chapter we shall only be able to mention briefly those on an official national basis.

The Belgian expeditions to East Africa, 1877–84. Well to the fore among the competitors for East Africa was Leopold of the Belgians. The Africa International Association which he had started in 1876 to promote the exploration and civilization of Central Africa decided that the easiest approach to the centre of the continent would be from Zanzibar. At the end of 1877 the first expedition arrived, but as three of its four leaders were Belgians, and as it was organized by the Belgian national committee of the International Association, it was virtually King Leopold's expedition rather than an international one. Within six weeks of their arrival two of the four leaders of this expedition were dead and one had deserted, but Lieut. Cambier, who survived, started with a caravan to the interior, and despite many difficulties succeeded in establishing posts at Tabora and at Karema on Lake Tanganyika which he reached in August 1879. In the same month another expedition started inland from Bagamoyo, led by the Belgian Captain Popelin and the Englishman Carter. The most important members of this expedition were four elephants which Carter had brought to see if they could survive the climate, in which case they would have provided a useful means of transport. By the time Tabora was reached in October two of the elephants had died, but a triumphal entry was made into the settlement on the two that remained, to the huge delight of the inhabitants. By the end of the year when the caravan entered Karema only one elephant remained and in a few months that too was dead. But Leopold was not content with the footholds which his expeditions had gained at Tabora and the small marshy settlement at Karema. A foothold on the coast was also needed, and in the June of 1880 he sent M. Emile de Ville as consul to Zanzibar to request a part of the coast near Malindi as a training ground for elephants, with the intention that it should in fact become a Belgian colony. This request was refused by the Sultan and Leopold did not press his claims. Nevertheless, Belgian interest in East Africa continued, and between 1880 and 1884 three more expeditions were sent and another post was established on the western shore of Lake Tanganyika at Mpala. The last expedition, however, never went beyond the East African coast, for in 1884

Leopold had realized, as a result of Stanley's efforts, that the Congo was his most profitable approach to Africa, and from that time his interest in East Africa ceased.

The French expeditions to East Africa, 1878–81. Meanwhile the French had also made a series of attempts to open up the East African coast. Their connexion with Muscat was about as old as that of Britain, although their influence in Zanzibar during the time of Barghash was nothing like so great. In 1878 they equipped one of the most interesting and pathetic expeditions that ever penetrated into the Sultan's dominions. Its leader was the Abbé Michel-Alexandre Debaize, a young French priest, who felt that both God and his country were calling him to help in the exploration of Africa. The French government gave him permission to blaze a trail for the French National Committee of the International Association, which was still being formed. In 1878 Debaize landed at Zanzibar. By October he had reached Tabora with his 800 porters and his amazing collection of supplies, which included two suits of armour, two dozen umbrellas, and a barrel organ. In May of 1879 he was in Ujiji with a caravan much decreased by desertion, but still full of enthusiasm. 'The thought', he said, 'that I am working for the glory of God and the glory of France will sustain me in all my trials.' Not content with having reached the lakes, he planned to press on to the Congo, but in November fever caught him and on 12 December he died. In the next year the French were ready to make another and more serious attempt to open up East Africa; a French business firm asked Barghash for a concession to build a quay and docks at Bagamoyo and a railway along the main route from Bagamoyo to Ujiji. For a while the Sultan looked favourably upon this proposal, but in 1881, as a result of Kirk's influence, he finally decided to reject it. With the collapse of this scheme the French government virtually abandoned official interest in the Sultan's dominions and turned their eyes southwards. By 1886 they had succeeded in establishing protectorates over part of the Comoro Islands and had gained a foothold on Madagascar.

So far as Britain was concerned these were wasted years.

Britain's wasted opportunity. While European interests in Africa increased, and as one expedition after another plunged into the interior from East Africa, the British government deliberately rejected opportunity after opportunity for helping the Sultan to develop his territory. So far from trying to 'grab' colonies, the Gladstone government did its best to avoid having colonies forced upon them. Yet, for several reasons, the British had by far the best claim of all the nations to govern and develop the East African dominions. In the first place the opening up of the interior was the work of British explorers, and of the few Europeans who had already settled there by 1880 the great majority were British missionaries. In addition to this there were, at Zanzibar and all along the coast, Indian traders who had been in East Africa as long as the Arabs, but whose numbers had much increased since the British consul had been established at Zanzibar. These people managed almost all the business and provided nearly all the revenue, and they felt that they were entitled to British protection. But the chief claim of Britain lay in the abolition of the slave trade in 1873, for without British aid the slave trade would have turned the interior of East Africa into a despoiled and depopulated waste. Yet, despite these reasons, and despite the forceful suggestions of Sir John Kirk, the British government refused to accept any sort of commitment in East Africa. The last chance came in 1882 when the Sultan asked the British government to be responsible for seeing that his son succeeded him, and to act as regent in case of a minority. This request might well have involved the government in establishing the equivalent of a protectorate over Zanzibar, a responsibility which Sir John Kirk would have welcomed, for he believed that the ideal way of developing East Africa was through the rule of the Sultan supported by British commercial and military power. But the Gladstone government would have none of it, and the request was politely refused.

This was Britain's last chance, for at the end of 1884 a party of four Germans led by Carl Peters landed at Zanzibar and staked out a claim to East Africa which they maintained for over thirty years.

Early German expeditions to East Africa. They were not the first Germans to take an interest in East Africa, for the German National

Committee of the International Association had, like those of Belgium and France, sent expeditions into the interior in 1880 and 1881 with the purpose of starting trading bases. Moreover, the Denhardt brothers, who were Germans, had been interesting themselves in

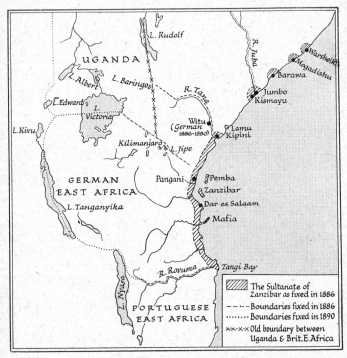

Map 10. Anglo-German Agreements of 1886 and 1890.

scientific expeditions along the Tana river since the 1870's, and were about to appear on the scene again. At the same time the Germans had decided to obtain a more official position at Zanzibar by sending Rohlfs there as consul. He arrived in the January of 1885 and looked forward to obtaining a substantial area of the interior for Germany.

Carl Peters's expedition, 1884. Such was the position when Carl Peters and his expedition made their claim upon East Africa. Peters himself was then a young man of twenty-eight who had started the Society for German Colonization early in 1884 with the purpose of acquiring part of the East African coast and interior. Supported by funds from the society he and his companions sailed in disguise to Aden and then re-embarked for Zanzibar where they arrived on 4 November 1884. Within a week they had crossed to the mainland and were journeying up the Wami river to Usagara, where they made twelve treaties with different chiefs by which the chiefs signed agreements giving up their territories to the German company. The treaty made with the Sultan of Msovero is a typical example:

Treaty of eternal friendship: Mangungo, Sultan of Msovero in Usagara, offers all his territory with all its civil and public appurtenances to Dr Carl Peters as the representative of the Society for German Colonisation, for exclusive and universal utilization for German colonization.

By December the expedition was over and Peters was back at Zanzibar, and by February 1885 he was in Berlin.

The importance of Peters's treaties. For two reasons the treaties he had collected did not deserve to be treated seriously. In the first place it was extremely unlikely that the chiefs who signed them understood what they were about, and in the second place the areas concerned were part of the dominions of the Sultan of Zanzibar. But for an equally clear reason the treaties were very important indeed—they were recognized and supported by Bismarck. This support, and this support alone, gave the expedition and the treaties of Peters their importance. The previous expeditions had penetrated deeper and taken much longer, but Bismarck had then maintained that Germany was not interested in colonies; the expeditions, therefore, had come and gone without leaving any appreciable mark on East African history. But Peters's expedition came at the right moment when Bismarck had changed his mind and was seeking colonies wherever they could be found.

The official annexation of Usagara, March 1885. When Peters arrived back in Berlin the conference on Africa was still sitting. Bismarck had already laid claims to regions in West and South Africa, besides annexing the north coast of New Guinea, and he therefore decided not to bring up another claim before the conference. He waited, therefore, until the day after the General Act of the conference was passed before getting the German emperor to sign a bill officially taking the areas gained by Peters under the protection of the German government, and he then waited until the day after all the delegates had left before he published it, on 3 March 1885.

The Sultan's protest. It was not until 25 April that Sultan Barghash heard that the government of part of his dominions had been handed over to Peters's company by the German government. He was very indignant. Not only had the Germans made their expedition to the interior with the utmost secrecy, but the claim which they now made was for the most valuable area of all his mainland possessions; it included the mainland opposite Zanzibar and the first part of the main trade route to the interior leading to Tabora and Ujiji. Barghash sent a vigorous protest to the German emperor: 'These territories are ours', he wrote, 'and we hold military stations there, and those chiefs who profess to cede sovereign rights to the agents of the Society have no authority to do so.'

So indignant was the Sultan that he considered following the telegram by a personal visit to the emperor, but Sir John Kirk dissuaded him.

The annexation and significance of Witu, April 1885. Usagara was not the only part of the Sultan's dominions in which Germany was interested. In January of 1885 the younger Denhardt left Zanzibar for the port of Lamu in the north, and started negotiations with Simba, who was sometimes referred to as the Sultan of Witu, but who was, in fact, an old ruffian with a following of over 3000 bandits who were the scourge of the northern coastal area. When Denhardt started negotiations with him Barghash was apprehensive, and with good cause, for in April 1885 Denhardt calmly announced that a 'covenant of friendship' between Simba and Germany had been made giving Germany a protectorate over 'Witu and the neighbouring Swahili lands'. Of course Simba had no right to make such an agreement, and the Sultan Barghash protested. Nevertheless the German emperor confirmed the agreement. The possession of Witu was of considerable strategic significance, for it meant that now Germany controlled an area to the north as well as to the south of the British region. If only these northern and southern regions could be joined by the acquisition of the area to the west of the British sphere then the British possessions would be encircled by those of Germany. As we shall see, this was precisely the plan which the Germans pursued, first by trying to expand their northern possessions, and secondly by the expedition which Peters made to Uganda.

The attitude of the Sultan, Kirk, and the British government. The Sultan Barghash had good cause for indignation, but it was quite useless. Without British support he could do nothing but protest, and British help was not forthcoming. To both Kirk and the Sultan this was a bitter disappointment, and both felt that they had been let down. Yet the British government had reason enough to hesitate about picking a quarrel with Germany at this time, for when 1885 opened East Africa was a comparatively small worry among British overseas possessions. In the Sudan General Gordon was murdered on 26 January by the Mahdists; in Egypt there was serious tension with France which might have led to war; on the Indian frontier a Russian army was threatening Afghanistan. Considering these threats to her position in North Africa and India it is not surprising that the British government thought it unwise to risk a war with Germany over the ownership of the Usagara area. But however difficult the circumstances were the Sultan had been let down, for he had conformed to British desires even to the extent of abolishing, in 1873, the most profitable trade of his subjects, and he therefore had a right to expect some effective support when his dominions were annexed. Moreover, the Anglo-French declaration of 1862, recognizing the independence of his dominions, implied some willingness to uphold that independence against aggressors. In view of this, one can only suppose that Gladstone did not fully understand the position, or was not referring to Usagara, when in March of 1885 he remarked, 'If Germany becomes a colonizing power, all I can say is "God speed her".' Thus Germany had nothing to fear from Britain, and alone the Sultan could offer no effective opposition.

Germany forces the Sultan to accept the annexations, August 1885.
Thus Bismarck settled the question as he chose, and his methods
were by no means so gentle as those of the British. Instead of sending
a friendly diplomat to negotiate he sent a squadron of battleships and
an ultimatum that the Sultan Barghash must withdraw all protests
against treaties made by Germany with the Sultans of Usagara,
Nguru, Useguha, Ukami, and Witu, or else Zanzibar would be blown
to bits. The Sultan, as might be expected, agreed, but he did so under
protest.

The Zanzibar Commission, 1885–6. The claims of Germany to the
Usagara area raised the question of what exactly were the limits of the
Sultan's territories. On this point the British government did take
an active interest and in June 1885 persuaded Bismarck to agree to
a commission with representatives of Germany, Britain and France
'to investigate what are the just limits of the Sultan's dominions'.
The Zanzibar Commission met at the end of the year and inspected
the coast from south to north in three separate voyages. No one
disputed the Sultan's claim to the islands of Zanzibar and Pemba, but
the distance inland to which the Sultan's authority extended on the
mainland was hotly disputed. The German representative, Schmidt,
who was anxious to make it appear as small as possible, estimated it at
a maximum of ten miles inland, and in parts denied that the Sultan
had any authority over the coast at all. The British and French commissioners estimated that the Sultan's rule was effective to a depth of
about forty miles inland. In the middle of 1886 the Commission
broke up without coming to any clear decisions except that Zanzibar,
Pemba, and the chief mainland ports were definitely in the Sultan's
dominions.

Kirk advises partition. So far as Britain was concerned the problem
of East Africa had resolved itself into the question of whether Germany
was to be allowed to take over the whole region, or whether Britain
should claim a part of it. Sir John Kirk made this very clear in his
dispatches.

The question to be decided, [he wrote], is practically this: whether
we are prepared to see Germany paramount over all the Zanzibar

coast, using the trading capacities of our Indian subjects to advance and develop her commerce, or whether some compromise cannot be come to whereby our influence is upheld and admitted as legitimately paramount over a certain district, without necessarily affecting the independence of the Sultan of Zanzibar.

Kirk not only posed the question. He also answered it—Britain's duty was to demand partition. It remained to be seen whether the British government would act on his advice.

Other factors favouring partition. Besides the fear of German domination of the whole coast, other minor considerations also made partition desirable. Ever since Johnston's expedition to the slopes of Kilimanjaro in 1884, when rights had been acquired over Taveta, there had been serious consideration as to whether the area should be taken over. Now, in 1886, the Taveta concession was made good by a British expedition which established a post there. Moreover, in 1886, H. H. Kitchener, while serving on the Zanzibar Commission, had written a dispatch on the defence of British communications with India and the East. In this he emphasized the need for a British key-point in the northern part of the East African coast to offset the German harbour of Dar es Salaam. The key-point he recommended was Mombasa. Besides its use for protecting communications in the Indian Ocean Kitchener also pointed out that 'Mombasa is the most probable port from which any railway system for the opening up of the interior would start, and its possession would give to England a commercial base, without which it would be impossible to develop the trade of Central Africa'.

The partition treaty of 1886. While the British government were considering the possibility of partition, Bismarck once more took action, this time because he wished to settle affairs in East Africa before the dispute between Britain and France concerning Egypt was settled. He sent Dr Krauel, a high Foreign Office official, to London to bring the affairs of Zanzibar to a satisfactory conclusion with the suggestion that if Britain would help Germany at Zanzibar Germany would support Britain against France over Egypt. Both Bismarck and Krauel realized that it would be worth making some concessions in order to reach an agreement; the talks in London, therefore, were far more profitable than the Zanzibar Commission had been. By the end of October 1886 the settlement was made. The main points were: (i) Britain and Germany recognized the Sultan's authority over the islands of Zanzibar, Pemba, Mafia, and Lamu, and also over the coast to a depth of ten miles from the River Rovuma in the south to Kipini in the north. North of that the towns of Kismayu, Barawa, Merka, Mogadishu and Warsheikh were also recognized as the Sultan's. (ii) The territory between the rivers Rovuma and Tana was to be divided into German and British 'spheres of influence' by the line which now marks the boundary between Kenya and Tanganyika. (iii) Britain agreed to support Germany's claim to establishing a customs house at Dar es Salaam. Dar es Salaam thus became virtually a German possession leased from the Sultan. (iv) Britain agreed to recognize the German possession of Witu and its corridor to the sea at Manda Bay.

The effects of the partition treaty. The only things which were left undefined were the western boundaries of the protectorates. Britain, on the other hand, had succeeded in maintaining her influence over a large part of East Africa, so that the possibility of Germany taking over the whole region was removed.

There were several regrettable results of the intrusion of Germany into East Africa. One was that as Barghash's authority in the interior decreased slave trading revived, and reports that slave dhows were reappearing on the coast, and that parents were selling their children, reached Zanzibar during these two years. Worst of all was the belief which developed among the Africans that what the white man really wanted was land—the Africans' most treasured possession. They did not realize that the British and Germans were interested in the land as a political possession for strategic reasons and had no intention of dispossessing individual landholders, and there developed a hatred of all white men which had not been felt before. In 1885 missionaries in Uganda reported that this hatred and fear that Europeans wanted 'to eat the country' was felt by Mwanga. In the same year Bishop Hannington was murdered. Had he come two years before he would have been safe.

The Imperial British East Africa Company. The development of the German and British spheres was not undertaken by the governments of those countries but by companies. The British East Africa Association with Sir William Mackinnon as chairman was therefore started in 1887, and in the following year the Sultan gladly conceded all his mainland possessions opposite the British area to the Association. Later in 1888 a royal charter was granted and the Association was re-formed as the Imperial British East Africa Company. The German East Africa Company also started in 1888, and like the British company it received from the Sultan a concession to administer the mainland opposite its sphere of influence.

Difficulties of the Company. The years which followed the partition were not easy either for the Company's administrator, Mackenzie, or for the British consul, Colonel Euan Smith. One of the troubles was the new Sultan Khalifa who succeeded Barghash in 1888. He was mentally unbalanced as a result of long imprisonment, and he was not respected by his subjects. Moreover he disliked Colonel Euan Smith and put his faith in two worthless favourites. His death in 1890 was regretted by none. Another trouble was the attempt of the Italian consul at Zanzibar to claim the province of Kismayu on the pretext that the Sultan had insulted the King of Italy. This annoyed not only the Sultan but also the British and German consuls, who paid a visit of protest to the Italian consulate. Thus ended Italian claims to the Zanzibar dominions. A third difficulty arose over the question of runaway slaves who had taken refuge in the mission stations near Mombasa. Many slaves from the Arab coastal plantations had escaped and taken refuge in the mission stations of Rabai (C.M.S.) and Ribe (Methodist), and while the missions were naturally reluctant to give them back to their masters, the Arabs were equally reluctant to accept this refusal to return what they considered to be their rightful property. A state of great tension developed and war between the Arabs and missions seemed imminent until the tact of Mackenzie, the Company administrator, solved the problem by a promise to pay the Arabs £3500 as compensation if they would agree to give up their claims to the runaway slaves. The offer was accepted and on 1 January 1889 nearly 1500 slaves were freed amid great rejoicing and with good feeling on all sides. Apart from this episode the relations between the British Company and the inhabitants of the area which it administered were good, largely because very few changes were made. Mombasa became the Company's headquarters and an advance post was set up at Machakos. At the same time treaties were made with the Nyika, Kamba and Taita tribes and preparations were made for the occupation of the interior.

The British and German Companies. By far the greatest trouble came from the German Company. Almost at once a rebellion broke out in the German-administered area as a direct result of their harsh and arrogant methods of colonization. The leader of the rebellion was a fiery bearded Arab, Bushiri bin Salim. Bismarck reproved the Company for its inefficiency and appointed a new Imperial commissioner, Captain Wissman, who arrived with a force of 600 Sudanese troops early in 1889 to restore order. Throughout the year the rebels were steadily harassed until the end came in December, when Bagamoyo was stormed and Bushiri was hanged. Meanwhile Bismarck had suggested that Britain and Germany should carry out a combined naval blockade of the coast to prevent the export of slaves and the importation of arms and ammunition. To this Lord Salisbury agreed, chiefly because he feared the results of allowing a purely German naval force to patrol the area. The suppression of the rebellion in the German sphere and the blockade caused great anti-European feeling, and for a while a general attack was expected on all Europeans in Zanzibar; but it did not materialize.

Another serious problem in these early years came from German claims in the north. We have seen already that by the 1886 agreement the British recognized the possession of Witu by the Germans. As Witu itself had little value it was regarded by the Germans simply as the first step towards gaining control of the northern part of the coast, and in 1887 the Witu Company was formed to promote this expansion. This company promptly claimed the island of Lamu, which was a useful port, but in August 1889 the claim was rejected by a special international committee set up to investigate it. Two months later the

Witu Company made a still more extravagant claim. This time it was for all the territory between Juba and Witu, and later the islands of Manda and Patta (north of Lamu) also, which were already occupied by the British. Once more an international committee was appointed to investigate the claims and once more it rejected them (1890). The third German attempt to gain profit from their region was more subtle. No official claims were made this time. Instead, a force of men from Witu simply established a customs house on the Belesoni Canal and demanded that all who used it should pay. The purpose of this canal was to provide an outlet for the considerable trade of the Tana River. As the Tana is unnavigable at its mouth, the coastal tribes had built the Belesoni Canal to join it with the Ozi eight miles from the sea, at a point where the rivers were only two miles apart. Thus goods from the interior could reach the sea by sailing down the Tana, through the Belesoni Canal, and finally down the Ozi to the coast. It was this trade which the Witu detachment started to tax. The British immediately protested that the region was not in the German sphere, and this time the trespass was so plain that the German government itself ordered the detachment to withdraw.

The expedition of Peters to Buganda, 1889–90. It was from Witu also that Peters made his bid to extend German East Africa by gaining the area to the west of the British sphere. This had not been defined by the 1886 treaty, and Peters hoped that he might be able to form a continuous belt of German territory from Witu to Tanganyika via Uganda, thus encircling the British area and cutting the British off from the headwaters of the Nile. He landed at Witu in June 1889, and led an expedition up the Tana, over the Kenya highlands into Uganda. His excuse was that he was going to relieve Emin Pasha, but this was merely an excuse, because two other expeditions had already set out for that purpose, one from the Congo led by Stanley, and one from Zanzibar led by Sir Frederick Jackson on behalf of the I.B.E.A. Company. Sir Frederick Jackson, as it happened, reached the border of Uganda before Peters, but despite the kabaka's request for help, Jackson, who had strict orders from the Company not to enter Uganda, refused to commit himself. Instead, hearing that Emin Pasha had already been found by Stanley, Jackson set off to the Mount Elgon district to shoot elephants, hoping that the ivory might pay for the expenses of his expedition. While he was away Peters arrived and without scruple made a treaty with the Kabaka by which the kingdom of Buganda was placed under German protection. He then moved off southwards before Jackson returned, and reached Bagamoyo in July. There, this unscrupulous treaty-maker had a salutary lesson, for he learned that the territory which he thought he had just obtained for Germany had already been recognized as a British sphere of influence. In his book *New Light on Darkest Africa*, Peters wrote that his feelings on hearing this news were so strong that he had to withdraw to a private room for two hours to regain his composure.

The Heligoland treaty, 1890. The chief reason for the 1890 agreement between Britain and Germany, which settled the western boundaries of their East African possessions over the head of Peters, was Bismarck's desire to secure Germany's position in Europe. His great fear of French or Russian attack caused him to become increasingly anxious for the friendship of Britain. To gain this he was quite prepared to make concessions in East Africa.

From the British point of view three things were desirable: (i) That a British protectorate should be recognized over Zanzibar, where German influence had grown at such an alarming rate since Wissman had made it the headquarters of the German Company that the German residents there outnumbered other European residents by six to one. This protectorate the Sultan was very ready to accept, for he feared that the Germans would soon overshadow his own authority there. (ii) That the western frontiers of the German and British spheres should be continued westwards to Lake Victoria and across it to the boundary of the Congo Free State so that Uganda should be included in the British area. (iii) That the Germans should abandon all claims to regions north of the British sphere, which would mean the end of the Witu protectorate.

The Germans on their side were willing to agree to this in return for two main concessions: (i) That the British would help to persuade the Sultan to cede absolutely to Germany the ten-mile coastal strip of the mainland which had been held on lease since the 1886 agreement. The Sultan, with some reluctance, agreed to this in return for a compensation equivalent to £200,000. (ii) That the island of Heligoland in the North Sea should be given to Germany by Britain. The Germans believed that this would be a valuable naval base, although the future was to show that it was not.

Such was the 1890 agreement which ended the scramble so far as East Africa was concerned. There were some who criticized it, especially the French who maintained that the 1862 declaration had been ignored. By way of compensation Britain therefore agreed to recognize French claims to a protectorate over Madagascar. The indignant Peters criticized it and remarked bitterly that two kingdoms in Africa (Witu and Uganda) had been sacrificed for 'a bath-tub in the North Sea (Heligoland)'. But on the whole the agreement was a good one, for it achieved its main purpose, which was to end the dangerous rivalry in East Africa between Britain and Germany. It also confirmed Sir John Kirk's belief that British economic and strategic interests could not be maintained without some fairly clear political control. Nor was it a mere land-grabbing bargain, for if Britain had not taken over the area Germany certainly would have done so. In view of the German Company's methods in Tanganyika this might not have been entirely beneficial to the inhabitants.

CHAPTER VIII

THE HISTORY OF UGANDA UP TO 1890

The history of Uganda before the nineteenth century is a shadowy affair depending partly upon fact and partly upon speculation. The difficulty is not so much that the African people of Uganda took no interest in their past. They did, and the story passed on by word of mouth from one generation to the next included the names and clans of hundreds of royal wives and children which were carefully memorized. But unfortunately the stories told in different parts of Uganda have only a few points in common, and each clan and tribe usually magnified its own part in the story to such an extent that the story of Uganda's early development varies from place to place.

The peoples and kingdoms of Uganda. Despite these differences there are still some facts about which we may be reasonably certain. In the first place it is generally accepted that the population of the areas which now comprise Uganda is composed of Bantu, Nilotes, and Half-Hamites. These races are mixtures in varying proportions of the original negroes who may have come from Asia five or ten thousand years ago, and groups of Hamites of Caucasian stock who probably entered Africa at a very much later date from the north-east. The purpose of the Hamitic emigrations was to find new grazing grounds for their long-horned cattle. The last group of them to arrive in Central Africa probably travelled via Abyssinia and reached the highlands between Lakes Edward and Tanganyika in the late sixteenth century. From this centre these later Hamites, or Bahima as they are often called, spread out still searching for new pastures. As they spread, their organization and knowledge gave them superiority over the existing agricultural groups, and the kingdoms of Ruanda, Urundi, Karagwe, and Ankole came into existence. Further to the north the traditional kingdom of Kitara was started, of which Bunyoro claims to be the successor, and it was probably from Bunyoro–Kitara that outposts were pushed eastwards into what became Buganda, although tradition also suggests that Hamites had arrived in the Buganda area earlier from the region around Mount Elgon. It is at this time, in the latter part of the sixteenth century, that we also get the first names in the Buganda list of kings, which included Kintu, who is said to have entered with his people from the Mount Elgon area and eventually to have disappeared with his companion Nambi, the mother of the race, because he was so distressed at the behaviour of his people. Another of the kings was Kimera, who is said to have conquered Buganda from Bunyoro.

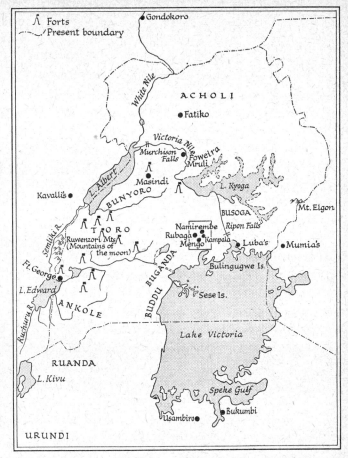

Map 11. Uganda.

The growth of Buganda. During the seventeenth century these
various kingdoms which now comprise Uganda began to develop each
its own way of life and to achieve some sort of unity. At first Bunyoro
seems to have been the most powerful and her warriors raided southwards into Ankole and Ruanda, and eastwards into Buganda and

Busoga. During the eighteenth century Buganda became pre-eminent and in the reign of Mawanda raids began into Busoga. In the reign of Kyabagu, who died about 1780, Busoga was completely overrun. It was also during Kyabagu's reign that the first contact with the outside world was made, when cups and plates were brought in by way of Karagwe. Before the end of the century further articles, including cotton cloth, copper wire, and cowrie shells also arrived by the same route. In the last quarter of the eighteenth century the attack by Buganda upon Bunyoro began, and Kyabagu's son Junju drove the Banyoro from Buddu, which has since been part of Buganda. He was also accepted as overlord of Koki and Kiziba. At about the end of the eighteenth century Junju was killed by his brother, Semakokiro, whose son, Kamanya, continued the attack on Bunyoro by conquering Buwekula. Kamanya was succeeded by his son, Suna, who ruled from about 1831–56. He was a bloodthirsty old tyrant whose corpse the funeral bearers threw upon the ground in contempt, but nevertheless by the end of his reign Buganda had built up the most advanced society in Central Africa and was the strongest power north and west of Lake Victoria. However, new powers, of whom the Arabs were the forerunners, were about to enter upon the Central African scene. But let us first look at the condition of Buganda before they appeared.

The political and social organization of Buganda. The political organization of Buganda before any Arab or European arrived was very similar to the feudal system on which European society was based during the Middle Ages. At the head was the king (Kabaka) who was elected by an assembly of the great chiefs and court officials. Usually the candidates from whom the new Kabaka was elected were the sons of the previous king, who would have had at least one wife from each clan (or kika), and it was the usual practice for each chief to vote for the son of the wife from his own clan. When the election to the throne had been decided the unsuccessful candidates were either imprisoned or executed. Apart from the Kabaka, the queen-mother (namasole), and the queen-sister (lubuga), who was chosen from the princesses, also occupied positions of great influence. In addition to the queen-mother and queen-sister the king would also have several hundred wives. They were of less importance, however, although the chief wife (kadulubare) often exercised considerable influence.

The great chiefs (bakungu). To assist the king there was a council (lukiko) composed of the great chiefs (bakungu) who were non-hereditary officials appointed by the king. The most important of these great chiefs were those who ruled the four main districts other than Buganda proper. These districts were Kyagwe to the east ruled by Sekibobo, chief of Kyagwe; Bulemezi to the north-west ruled by Kangao, chief of Bulemezi; Buddu to the west ruled by Pokino, chief of Buddu; and Singo to the north ruled by Mukwenda, chief of Singo. In addition to these and other less important great chiefs, there were also officials in the royal household who were considered to rank as chiefs. Among these were the chief butler (musenero) and the chief baker (mufumbiro). All great chiefs had to spend several months each year at the king's capital (Kibuga), where each would have some honorary office. The rest of their time would be spent in their own province, where they acted as petty kings, each having his own body of officials, including a second in command, a head of slaves, a head of the upholsterers, and a chief of the gate-keepers. In addition each had a large number of wives, pages and slaves. From their subjects the chiefs were entitled to collect taxes, and in time of war it was the chief's duty to lead the army. When a chief died he would be wound in strips of bark-cloth and buried in one of his houses.

The sub-chiefs (bataka). Besides the great chiefs there were also the heads of clans (bataka). As clan elders they were guardians of clan lands, and formed an important class in Buganda, their position being an hereditary one and not depending on royal appointment like that of the great chiefs. Like the great chiefs, however, they kept large households of wives and slaves.

The peasants (bakopi). Far below them came the great peasant class (bakopi). They attached themselves to chiefs and in theory were allowed to change their service from one master to another if they wished; in fact such a change would usually be followed by severe punishment from the deserted chief. The main duty of the peasant was to follow his chief to war, which was for him an affair of tremendous suffering: small-pox took a very large toll of soldiers, and almost as many lives were lost in obtaining slaves as there were slaves obtained. At home the peasants' work consisted of cultivation and building houses. In return for his services the peasant would be given one, or possibly two wives, by the chief, but these were loaned rather than given permanently, and might be taken away by the chief at any time.

The slaves (badu). The lowest class were the slaves (badu). These were mostly drawn from the raids on the neighbouring countries of Bunyoro to the north-west, and Busoga to the east. Each would be worth an average of 15,000 cowrie shells (about £5). They had no rights, and Mackay mentions an instance when a chief with whom he was dining killed his slave for upsetting a gourd of cider. In general the slaves were used for cultivation and for service in the houses of the king and the chiefs.

Occupations, clothing, and housing. The Baganda were essentially a fighting people, but nevertheless a considerable standard had been reached in peaceful occupations. One of their chief staples of wealth was bark-cloth made from the bark of a type of fig tree; and bead work, which was exclusively a woman's occupation, had reached a remarkable standard of skilfulness. The two most usual articles of clothing were the bead necklet worn by both men and women, and a girdle made of grass and worked over with very small beads into beautiful patterns, worn by women only. Other clothing consisted of cow, goat, and antelope skins. The leopard was considered to be the royal animal, and for any one other than royalty to wear a leopard skin was high treason. The houses in which the Baganda lived were simply beehive-shaped structures of grass supported by wooden poles, and the importance of the person to whom the house belonged could be estimated from its size.

Religion. The religion of Buganda was chiefly a mixture of witch-craft and ancestor worship known as Lubareism. Underlying this was the vague idea of a sublime creator, 'Katonda', of whom nothing was known and from whom nothing was expected. Next came Lubare, the upper air and waters, including the gods who inhabited them.

The chief of these gods who inhabited the upper air and waters was Mukasa, the god of Lake Victoria, who was responsible for the lives of sailors, all of whom tried to win his favour by throwing offerings of bananas into the lake before starting a voyage. Lubare was also the giver of wealth and the giver of children. Among the many demi-gods Kintu, the traditional hero king, was outstanding. Others were Budo and Kibuka, and of these Budo may be taken as a typical example of how these demi-gods were worshipped. Budo was the mummified corpse of a very large man who was kept in a sitting position behind the curtains of his temple; he was guarded by a virgin who was honoured as his wife, and whose sacred person no one dared approach. On certain days drums were beaten and Budo was brought from behind his curtains to hold a reception attended by the neighbouring chiefs and important people, who knelt in his presence. Unfortunately, however, Lubareism did not stop at such harmless practices, for on important occasions such as the accession of a king, a vast human sacrifice known as a 'kiwendo' were necessary. On the accession of Mutesa in 1856, for example, many hundreds of slaves had their throats cut as a sacrifice.

An estimate of Buganda in the mid-nineteenth century. Because early explorers were surprised to find a society such as we have described in Africa they sometimes tended to represent Buganda as better than it really was. Indeed, there was little resemblance to Paradise in the kingdom over which Kings Mutesa and Mwanga ruled. Each was a despot with no regard for human life. When Speke first showed Mutesa his gun the king immediately ordered a page to go outside and test its efficiency by shooting at the first man he saw, and he was delighted to hear that the man had been killed. On a picnic to the lake one of Mutesa's wives playfully offered him a fruit, and he immediately ordered that she should be executed because, he said, it was the first time a woman had ever had the impudence to offer him anything. For more serious offenders a permanent set of executioners were ready who mutilated and killed their victims in the most horrible ways they could devise, the standard method of finally killing a man being slow fire. Nor were the activities of the king confined to his court and to those who offended him. His chief interests were war and slave raiding, which necessitated a permanent army and kept the route through which the army passed and the areas which it raided in desolation, while peasants perished, slaves were captured, and children were killed by the thousand. In West Africa at the same time the same despotic rule by chiefs with absolutely no regard for human life was found. Perhaps it reached its most hideous depths at Benin, where the King and Juju priests, and most of the population, practised wholesale human sacrifice, torture, and mutilation on such a scale that the smell of blood was overpowering and the roads were lined with crucified corpses, skulls, and skeletons. Few now living in West Africa or on the sunny lands of the central African plateau would choose to step back a century in time.

The arrival of the first Arabs, 1848–52. Such was Buganda when it was first visited by Arabs and Europeans. The first outside influence of modern times to penetrate into Buganda was Arabic. Somewhere about 1848, in the reign of Suna, an Arab half-breed named Saim entered the country and was followed a few years later by Isa bin Hussein, a Baluchi deserter from the Sultan of Zanzibar's forces, who became one of Suna's advisers and was found at the capital when the great Tabora trader, Snay bin Amir, visited it in 1852. From these beginnings grew the substantial Arab population which the first missionaries found in Buganda when they arrived in 1877. The chief interests of the Arabs were—as usual—slaves and ivory, and this, together with the guns they brought, gave a disastrous impetus to slave raiding. The result was that the kings of Buganda rapidly became the greatest slave-hunters in the world. Mutesa kept a permanent army of 6000 men continually devastating the neighbouring tribes merely for the sake of slaves who were sold to the Arabs at the rate of one musket for two slaves, or one red cloth for one slave, or one hundred bullets for a female slave. The effect of the Arabs on the court was to increase luxury and immorality; although they preached the Koran and gained a considerable number of converts, they were mainly interested in trade, and Mohammedanism never established a hold comparable to that of Christianity. In one way it actually helped the Christian missions by its effects in undermining the old beliefs in Lubareism, which was already in decline when the C.M.S. arrived. By the 1870's the Arab traders in Buganda were some of the most influential people in Mutesa's court. They brought him guns and ammunition for his raids; they brought him cottons, silks, and bracelets for his clothing; and they brought him news of an outside world which he could not understand, but whose power he grew to fear.

The arrival of Speke, 1862. Before the Arabs had become influential in Buganda the first European had appeared on the scene. This was Speke, who arrived in 1862 and provided Mutesa and his court with a great deal to laugh at and a great deal to think about. His hat and his umbrella were regarded with tremendous admiration, and his rifle and pistol created a great impression. Speke was also impressed by Mutesa:

> The king was a good-looking, well-figured, tall young man of twenty-five. He sat on a red blanket spread upon a square platform of royal grass and was scrupulously well dressed in a new raiment of bark-cloth. The hair of his head was cut short, except on top, where it was combed into a high ridge. On his neck was a large ring of beautifully worked small beads. On one arm was another bead ornament, prettily devised, and on the other a wooden charm, tied by a string covered with snake skin. On every finger and every toe he had alternate brass and copper rings, and above the ankles a stocking of pretty beads. Everything was light, neat, and elegant.

From February until July Speke was detained at Mutesa's court, where Grant joined him in May; thence he marched first eastwards, looking for the Nile, and then northwards to Gondokoro, where he met Sir Samuel Baker and his wife and encouraged them in their southward exploration of the Nile, which resulted in the discovery of Lake Albert. After Speke's departure from Mutesa, twelve years passed before the next white man, Colonel Long, entered Buganda.

The Egyptian invasion. During these twelve years two things of great importance occurred. First, in the southerly part of what is now Uganda, and especially in Mutesa's court in Buganda, the Arabs greatly increased their influence. Secondly, in the north an invasion came from the Sudan. The root cause of this invasion lay again in the

zeal of the British anti-slavery movement. As the British had requested the Sultan of Zanzibar to abolish the east coast slave trade,
so they had also requested the Egyptian rulers to end the trade in
slaves and ivory which came down the Nile to Khartoum from areas
including what is now the Acholi area of Uganda; but despite British
protests Egyptian rulers had in fact encouraged and profited from the
Nile slave trade, until in 1863 Ismail became the ruler, or khedive, of
Egypt. Ismail was by no means the perfect ruler—he was reckless with
finance and brought Egypt to bankruptcy—but at least he did make a
sincere effort to stop the Nile slave trade which his predecessors had encouraged. His method was to occupy the southern Sudan, from which
most of the slaves were drawn, and which became known as Equatoria.
Since Mehemet Ali's invasion of the Sudan in 1819 the Egyptians had
maintained a loose occupation of the country as far south as Gondokoro.
Now, in 1869, Ismail extended this southwards to include the whole
of the equatorial Nile region, and as governor-general of this province
of Equatoria he appointed Sir Samuel Baker. No doubt Ismail was
interested in exploiting the resources of Equatoria, but had he not
sincerely desired the abolition of the slave trade also, he would not
have appointed men like Baker and Gordon as its governors.

Baker's work for Equatoria, 1872–3. Equatoria included the northern part of what is now Uganda, and the first act of Baker after his
arrival at Gondokoro to assume his office as governor-general was to
advance southwards into Acholi and Bunyoro. He arrived in Bunyoro
in 1872 and formally announced its annexation to Egypt. Naturally
enough King Kabarega of Bunyoro resented this, and attacked Baker
at the battle of Masindi, forcing him to withdraw northwards again.
On his northward march Baker fortified Foweira and Fatiko and then
proceeded down the Nile to Gondokoro. When he resigned in 1873
he had gained a great reputation amongst Africans and Europeans
alike, but the Nile slave trade had not been seriously checked and the
posts of Foweira and Fatiko, which had been intended to stop the
trade, became themselves centres of oppression to the local population.

Gordon's work for Equatoria, 1874–6. Mutesa of Buganda had observed this activity with considerable alarm, and when General Gordon

took over from Baker as governor-general of Equatoria in 1874, Mutesa hastened to send him presents and messages for the khedive. In return Gordon sent his American lieutenant, Colonel Chaille-Long, to Mutesa and obtained from him an acknowledgement of Egyptian sovereignty. In the following year, 1875, Gordon sent his second envoy to Mutesa. This time it was a Frenchman, Ernest Linant de Bellefonds, and his purpose was to obtain Mutesa's promise to forbid the buying and selling of slaves in his country. Again Mutesa was alarmed, but gave immediate consent, for, although he had no intention of keeping the promise, he had no desire to gain the enmity of the governor-general of Equatoria. Meanwhile Gordon was struggling with his tremendous task of bringing Equatoria into some sort of order and ending the slave trade by establishing a network of forts to safeguard the route from the Sudan up the Nile into Lake Albert, and then via Lake Kyoga to Lake Victoria. In January 1876 he was constructing a fort at Mruli on the western end of Lake Kyoga and from there he sent to Mutesa his third mission, this time under an Egyptian, Nuehr Aga, and supported with troops, to ask permission to establish a fort at the place where Speke had first encountered the Nile. In July yet a fourth mission was sent to Mutesa, this time led by the German Emin Pasha, with presents for the king and to support Nuehr Aga. Fortunately, however, for Mutesa in the next month Gordon finally decided to abandon any attempt to occupy Buganda; he had become convinced it was impossible to control the area with soldiers of such poor quality and with a line of communications 2500 miles long constantly interrupted by the jealous governors of the Sudan. Much to Mutesa's relief, Emin and Nuehr Aga were accordingly withdrawn from Buganda and rejoined Gordon at Mruli in September. But although Gordon had abandoned his scheme for occupying Buganda he had no intention of abandoning interest in Bunyoro, and from Mruli he had marched across Kabarega's kingdom and arranged for a greater degree of control over it which resulted in the establishment of forts at Masindi, Kisuga, and Londu. Then he turned northwards to return to England, and resigned his post. The resignation was only temporary, however, for in the next year, 1877,

Gordon returned to Egyptian service, this time as governor not only of Equatoria but also of the northern Sudan; in this capacity he appointed Emin Pasha as governor of Equatoria under his supervision. Emin was an efficient governor, and although the Bunyoro forts were withdrawn in 1879 the presence of Emin's troops so near his frontier kept Mutesa uneasy.

The arrival of the C.M.S., 1876–7. By this time another invasion had taken place which was primarily neither political nor concerned with the abolition of the slave trade. It was simply concerned with bringing Christianity to Buganda, and it was the direct result of Stanley's visit to Mutesa's kingdom in 1875. During that visit Stanley—the rough, tough journalist of African exploration who had looked upon the face of Dr Livingstone at Ujiji and never forgotten it—had taken the opportunity of introducing the precepts of Christianity to Mutesa, who listened so attentively that Stanley sent a letter to the *Daily Telegraph* appealing for missionaries. De Bellefonds, who was at Mutesa's court at the same time, took this letter back to Gordon, who forwarded it to England. In fact Mutesa saw in Christianity not a new spiritual inspiration but the possibility of a new political power which might prove a useful weapon against the Egyptian advance from the north and the Arab influx from the east. At the time this was not realized and when Stanley's letter appeared in the *Daily Telegraph* in November 1875 an anonymous offer of £5000 was received by the C.M.S. within three days, and others followed rapidly. From the missions' point of view it was a wild idea: for the route to Buganda along the old Arab route from Zanzibar through Tabora and then north to Lake Victoria, which was the only route yet explored, took at least six months; moreover, even when the mission had been established it would be completely isolated from any others. Despite these disadvantages eight missionaries volunteered to go to Buganda, and the expedition, under the leadership of Lieut. Shergold Smith, landed at Bagamoyo in July 1876. Within a year only half of them were still alive, two having died of fever, and two, including Shergold Smith, having been killed in a skirmish on Ukerewe Island. By the end of 1877 only Wilson was in Buganda. Next year he was joined by the greatest of all the early Buganda missionaries, Alexander Mackay, who had been struggling through from the coast for over two years. Mackay was a professional engineer, and from the outset Mutesa had a very genuine respect both for his personal character and for his technical ability. In 1879 three more Anglican missionaries, Litchfield, Pearson and Felkin, arrived, having travelled up the Nile; like Mackay and Wilson they were warmly welcomed by Mutesa.

The arrival of the White Fathers, 1876. The Anglican missionaries were not the only invaders of Buganda on behalf of the Christian faith. The Roman Catholic White Fathers, governed by Cardinal Lavigerie, were also interested, and a week after the arrival of the three Anglican missionaries Father Lourdel and Brother Amans reached Mutesa's capital, soon to be followed by three more White Fathers.

Mutesa and the missions. Buganda was not the only region of Africa where both Roman Catholic and Protestant missionaries worked, but it was the only place where they were brought into close contact with one another, both sets of missionaries being obliged to stay at Mutesa's court. The results were unfortunate. Mackay and Lourdel, the Protestant and Roman Catholic leaders, were not men who were fond of compromise, and from the outset both misunderstood and opposed the teaching of the other, so that fierce rivalry grew up between the two missions. To increase the difficulties the Mohammedan Arabs were a still greater enemy to both Protestants and Roman Catholics, and they took every opportunity to discredit the Christians before Mutesa, who became increasingly confused and hostile. To him religions represented political powers. Behind Mackay he saw Queen Victoria; behind Lourdel he saw the power of France; and because he believed England and France to be more powerful than the Sultan of Zanzibar, he at first favoured the Christian missions in preference to the Mohammedanism of the Arabs. Before long he realized that the rival missions could not provide him with armies, and his favours to them ceased. By the end of 1879 both Mohammedanism and Christianity were out of favour and Lubareism, accompanied by its human sacrifices, temporarily revived.

The work of the missions, 1879–82. Meanwhile the missions proceeded with their work. In 1880 Lourdel baptized the first of his converts into the Roman Catholic Church, and in 1881 Mackay received a request for baptism from one of his most trusted pupils, Sembera, who was received into the Church with four others in 1882. At the same time Mackay's little printing press produced the first translations of parts of the New Testament in Luganda. The next step was to teach the people to read, and soon both missions had more 'readers' than they could easily manage. Protestant and Catholic rivalry did not prevent Christianity from gaining in Buganda one of its most rapid conquests.

The years of persecution, 1882–5. But the path was far from easy. By November 1882 the king had become so unfriendly that the Roman Catholic Fathers withdrew their mission altogether from Buganda to the south of Lake Victoria, although Mackay and O'Flaherty remained. The worst years, however, were 1884 and 1885. Several circumstances made these the worst from the missions' point of view. Mutesa died in October 1884. He died a pagan and at first the missions had high hopes that his son Mwanga, who was elected Kabaka and had been one of Mackay's 'readers', would be a great improvement. He was, indeed, the first Buganda king whose accession was not accompanied by vast human sacrifices to Lubare. But hopes were soon disappointed, for Mwanga was cowardly, cruel, and stupid. Almost at once he supported the Arab party and became a Mohammedan. At the same time he started persecuting the Christian mission, partly because the Christian pages opposed the immorality of his court, and in January 1885 he seized, mutilated, and then burnt to death three young boys who were helpers of Mackay and Ashe. Behind this persecution there lay also the political fear that the Europeans would take his kingdom. Several incidents had suggested this to him. In December 1883 Joseph Thomson had reached the northern end of Lake Victoria by the direct route from Mombasa through Masailand. No one had taken this route to the lake previously, and as the Baganda tradition was that Buganda would be conquered by people approaching from that direction Mwanga was particularly alarmed. His alarm was greatly increased when, early in 1885, news reached him of Carl Peters's annexations on the mainland opposite Zanzibar, and the Arabs did all in their power to persuade him that Thomson's journey and Peters's treaties were all part of a determined plan by the Europeans to conquer Buganda. The missionaries, they said, were secretly assisting this plan. Mwanga believed them.

The murder of Bishop Hannington, 1885. It was therefore a particularly unfortunate moment for the newly appointed Bishop of Eastern Equatorial Africa, James Hannington, to attempt to take up his work in Uganda, at the earliest possible moment, by taking Thomson's route. He took the direct route because he was enthusiastic and brave, and because General Mathews and Kirk had both sanctioned it, but he took it in direct opposition to the advice of his missionaries in Buganda and of the only man who had taken it before—Joseph Thomson. He left Rabai on 3 July 1885. On 1 January 1886 the following telegram was sent from Zanzibar:

Bishop Hannington, who left Mombasa in June last, in order to find if possible a new road to the Victoria, which will obviate the long detour by Unyanyembe, has been seized by order of the king within two days march of Buganda. The latest report is that the king has given secret orders to have the Bishop executed.

And such was the unfortunate truth. In October, as Hannington entered Luba's in Busoga he was imprisoned, and eight days afterwards, on Mwanga's orders, he was killed.

The martyrs of 1886. Having taken such a decisive step, Mwanga now considered murdering the European missionaries at his capital, and for a while their lives were in extreme danger. Then, in May 1886, he decided to get rid of the pages in his court who opposed his immorality, and he demanded which of them were 'readers'. Of those who stepped forward twelve Protestants were done to death and thirteen Roman Catholics, while in a general persecution of Christian converts in and around the capital 200 victims were martyred. As a proof of the sincerity of the Baganda Christians the persecution was a lasting inspiration, but as an attempt to wipe out Christianity it was an utter failure. In fact it left the Church in Buganda and the neighbouring areas stronger than ever, for even when persecution was at its height converts came to the missions by night asking for baptism, while converts who fled spread their faith to the friends who sheltered them. By August 1886 persecution had died out, but in the next year Mackay was exiled to Usambiro on the southern shore of the lake for his persistent criticism of Mwanga's behaviour. In 1887 his place was taken by another missionary, Cyril Gordon.

The revolution of September 1888. In September of 1888 a revolution took place in Buganda. The occasion was a childish plot of Mwanga's to get rid of all the Mohammedan and Christian supporters, whose growth he found alarmingly rapid, by marooning them on an island in the lake. Then he planned to revert to Lubareism and rule in absolute power unhindered by the rival parties whom he found so difficult. His plot was discovered; the Protestants, Catholics and Mohammedans refused to embark for the island, and the Baganda of all three parties combined to depose Mwanga, who fled to the south of the lake. His elder brother, Kiwewa, was made Kabaka in his place; freedom of worship was declared, and the most important official positions were shared among the three parties.

The importance of the revolution and the growth of parties. This revolution was a turning point in Buganda history, for Mwanga, by his exceptional incompetence and cruelty, destroyed his own prestige and some of the enormous traditional respect of the Baganda for their Kabaka. The loyalty of the chiefs, which had once been wholly his, was now divided into factions. Under a strong Kabaka this division would have been most unlikely, but Mwanga was not strong, and the chiefs who crowded his capital were in many cases 'readers' and had developed a certain loyalty to one or other of the missions. As Mwanga's conduct made loyalty to him increasingly difficult, so were the chiefs thrown more towards the missions in their loyalty, and began to divide into parties centred on the new religions. But it would not be accurate to describe these parties as only religious in their origin. Many of the chiefs simply saw in Mwanga's weakness and the development of rival parties a chance to increase their own power, and joined what they considered to be the strongest party in the hope that when war came they would share in the spoils. Politics was also a major factor, for the Mohammedans corresponded to the Arab party, the Roman Catholics to the French party, and the Protestants to the English party. How deeply politics entered into the question varied, but with the scramble for Africa in full swing suspicion was rife. The Protestant missionaries hoped that Buganda would become a British protectorate and not come under the power of the Arabs, French, or Germans. The Catholic mission also had some slight hopes that Buganda might become French, but they were especially anxious to prevent its becoming a British sphere of influence; fearful of losing their own influential position, they did everything possible to discourage Mwanga from accepting a British protectorate. Above all, the Arabs, no longer content with no more than their trading profits, were quite clearly aiming at the domination of Buganda instead.

The Arab conquest of Buganda, October 1888. It is not surprising, therefore, to find that the month after Mwanga had been deposed and Kiwewa had been installed as Kabaka it was the Arabs who attempted to dominate him and drive out the Christian missions. For a time their method was most effective. They simply persuaded Kiwewa that the Christians intended to depose him, and then secretly filled the royal enclosure with armed men and forced the Christian chiefs to leave the capital. The European missionaries also, both Roman Catholic and Protestant, were obliged to escape to the south of the lake, the Protestants to Usambiro and the Roman Catholics to Bukumbi. Thus the Arab, or Mohammedan party, was left in complete control with Kiwewa as their figurehead. When he refused to submit to the Mohammedan rite of circumcision he was deposed by the Arabs, and his younger brother Kalema was proclaimed Kabaka. Buganda became in fact an Arab state.

The Arabs expelled, October 1889. It did not remain Arab for long. The Christian chiefs and their supporters who had fled from the capital in October 1888 had taken refuge in Ankole to the west, where their numbers steadily increased, for the Mohammedan rule was intolerant and unpopular. At the same time an unexpected event had suggested a plan to the exiled missions on the south of the lake. In December 1888 Mwanga had paddled up in a canoe to the White Fathers' base at Bukumbi; he had appeared to be penitent and had been given refuge. The idea was now put forward by the White Fathers that the Christians at Ankole, assisted by the Protestant and Roman Catholic missions, should combine to drive out the Arab party from Buganda and restore Mwanga to his throne. Mackay refused to help, having had quite enough experience of Mwanga already, but the Christians of Ankole readily agreed and Charles Stokes, who had come to Buganda in 1879 as a C.M.S. missionary, but was now a trader, offered to lend his boat to help in the restoration. In April 1889 Stokes took Mwanga across the lake to Buddu. From there he advanced towards the Buganda capital, but his forces were poorly organized and were at first defeated by Kalema's troops. The defeat was not decisive, however, and Mwanga and his supporters were able to withdraw from the mainland and establish a new base first on the Sese Islands opposite the Buddu shore, and then, in June, on Bulingugwe Island in Murchison Gulf, only eight miles from the capital. Here he was joined by Lourdel and Denoit of the White Fathers, and Walker and Gordon of the C.M.S. Meanwhile the Christian refugees in Ankole, led by the Protestant chief Apolo Kagwa, started their advance towards Buganda in September; aided by Mwanga's troops from Bulingugwe they defeated Kalema and the Arab party, and re-took the capital. On 11 October Mwanga entered in triumph. Apolo Kagwa was appointed Prime Minister in recognition of his leadership of the victorious Christian army; the chief offices of state were divided equally between the Catholic and Protestant chiefs; and Mwanga built for himself a new capital at Mengo.

The Christian victory was a brief one, however, for after their defeat the Arab party had withdrawn north-westwards into Bunyoro and made an alliance with King Kabarega. Thus reinforced, they returned to Buganda in November 1889, and reoccupied the capital, Mwanga and the Christians being forced to withdraw again to the islands. For three months Kalema and the Arab party remained in power; then once more the Christians rallied, and in February 1890 they decisively defeated the Arab-Muslim troops at Bulwanyi. Once more Kalema and the remains of his army withdrew to Bunyoro, and Mwanga re-entered his capital.

Roman Catholic predominance. It was, perhaps, natural that after this triumph Mwanga should rely most for advice upon the Roman Catholic party who had sheltered him and helped to organize the movement which resulted in his return. Thus, Father Lourdel became firmly established as his exclusive European adviser. This was doubly unfortunate for the Protestants. In the first place it led to the Catholic party becoming easily the larger of the two, chiefs who had no particular loyalty to either party naturally siding with that which the King favoured. In the second place it caused Mwanga to be prejudiced against the British by Lourdel, who realized that as a result of the 1886 treaty Buganda and the country surrounding it were likely to become a British or German sphere. Of the two he preferred that it should become German, for he feared that a British occupation might mean the triumph of the Protestant mission.

The expeditions of Stanley, Jackson and Peters. While the Muslim-Christian war had been in progress three expeditions had been approaching with the alleged purpose of relieving Emin Pasha, whose province of Equatoria had been cut off from the Northern Sudan by the Mahdist revolt, leaving Emin stranded in Central Africa. The first of these three expeditions was that of Stanley, who took Emin with him to Zanzibar. But he left behind a large number of his Sudanese troops under Selim Bey, who arrived at the collecting base at Kavalli's on the south-west of Lake Albert. In July 1889 Stanley passed through Ankole, where he was asked to help the refugee Christians, but being unprepared for delay he passed on. The second expedition was that of Mr Frederick Jackson, on behalf of the I.B.E.A. Company, which had arrived at Mumia's in November 1889; not wishing to break his orders by entering Buganda Jackson had hesitated to answer Mwanga's appeal for help and had set off towards Mount Elgon in search of ivory. In February, while he was away, the third expedition arrived. This was the German one of Dr Carl Peters, who calmly searched Jackson's base camp at Mumia's, read all his letters there including those of Mwanga requesting help, and then hastened on to the Buganda capital and offered Mwanga a treaty. The Arab party had been defeated at Bulwanyi a fortnight before Peters arrived, but they were still in Bunyoro and a potential danger; Mwanga, on the advice of Lourdel, therefore signed the treaty Peters offered him. In great jubilation Peters then continued his journey to the south of the lake, having heard that Jackson had returned to Mumia's. Jackson had indeed returned to Mumia's in March and had discovered all that had happened. He was not pleased. Bristling with indignation he bore down upon Mengo in the hope of laying his hands upon the incorrigible Peters, but his bird had flown. Then, in place of the German treaty, he offered Mwanga a British one, which even the C.M.S. missionaries considered onerous. Not surprisingly it was rejected, whereupon Jackson returned to the coast for further orders. This comedy of errors played out by Peters and Jackson had one very unfortunate effect. It widened the division between the Catholic and Protestant parties. Even before either expedition arrived the Protestants had resented the way in which Father Lourdel monopolized Mwanga. When he pushed Mwanga into accepting Peters's treaty without consulting the Protestant party the friction was greatly increased, and although the Protestant, as well as the Catholic, chiefs signed the agreement they did so with great reluctance.

The Heligoland treaty. So far as political results were concerned Jackson and Peters might just as well have stayed at home, for the whole question of Buganda's future had been decided over their heads by the Heligoland treaty which definitely assigned Buganda and its neighbouring territories to Britain. Yet the British government itself had no more intention of financing the occupation and administration than it had had of financing the area acquired by the 1886 treaty. In Uganda, as well as on the coast, the I.B.E.A. Company was expected to organize and pay for the occupation. It was a task far beyond its financial resources, but it gallantly accepted the challenge, and in the next chapter we shall see the results.

CHAPTER IX

LORD LUGARD

Lugard's importance in tropical Africa. Colonization in tropical Africa began with the explorers who opened up routes to the interior of the continent. Hard on their heels came the missionaries and business men intent upon converting the heathen and developing trade. The third phase of development was chiefly concerned with the soldiers and administrators whose purpose it was to pacify and organize the regions which had been taken over. Such was the general rule although, of course, each phase overlapped the other and sometimes the order was changed if trouble necessitated the early appearance of military force. All these tasks called for men of exceptional ability and courage, and it was fortunate for Africa that at each stage, and for each task, outstanding men were found, so that the history of African colonization could almost be told through a few biographies. Dr Livingstone and Sir Henry Stanley dominated the picture so far as exploration was concerned, and Livingstone was also the greatest of many great missionaries. Sir William Mackinnon in East Africa, and Sir George Taubman Goldie in West Africa were the greatest of the business men, combining with their desire for profit an even greater desire to develop the areas concerned. Their aim, like that of Livingstone, was to 'introduce the negro family into the body corporate of nations'. But so far as military and administrative accomplishments were concerned Lord Lugard was pre-eminent.

Early career. By profession Frederick Dealtry Lugard was a soldier. In 1879, at the age of twenty-one, he was in India fighting against the Afghans; six years later he was in the Sudan campaign, and the year after he was fighting in Burma. This last campaign, which involved great strain and physical exertion in a most unhealthy climate, led to a breakdown in his health, and he therefore asked to be put on half-pay and be temporarily released from regimental duties. Never did any one choose a more extraordinary convalescence. So far from resting at home Lugard decided to find a change in visiting Africa, where he hoped he might be useful in doing something to prevent the continuance of the Arab slave trade. In 1888, at the age of thirty, and with only fifty pounds in his pocket and his rifle, he took a passage on a boat to Africa. First he offered his help to the Italians in their Abyssinian campaign; this was rejected and he continued his journey southwards towards Zanzibar. His money was getting short and he was obliged to sleep on deck among the cargo. The journey was nevertheless useful to him, for Colonel Euan Smith, the new Zanzibar consul, was travelling on the same ship and said that if the opportunity arose he would help Lugard to find employment in the East Africa Association which was to be formed. In the next year he kept that promise. Meanwhile Lugard was told that on the northern shores of Lake Nyasa the African Lakes Company was in trouble with local slave dealers and needed help. He therefore continued his journey to Mozambique on a ship swarming with rats and cockroaches and offered his services to the African Lakes Company. They gladly accepted him.

Character. Probably they would have accepted anybody. To them this rather short, strange captain with his sharp nose and long moustache was useful because he knew how to fight, but they had no more knowledge of his real worth than anyone else. For the young captain was much more than just a man with a gun. He was a born leader with immense courage and a charmed life. Where he led others would follow, whether it was storming the slavers' stockade at Kopa-Kopa's or breaching the defences at Kano. In his East and West African campaigns he gained the confidence and respect of Europeans and Africans to a quite exceptional extent. His courage was remarkable. In battle he never hesitated to attack overwhelming odds, and in 1903 set off with a force of 732 native troops and thirty-six British troops to attack the fortresses of Kano and Sokoto, which mustered well over 3000 troops behind their crenellated walls—and he succeeded. While hunting in India he once crawled through a narrow aperture into a dark cave after a wounded man-eating tiger in order to kill it—and kill it he did. In addition to the usual dangers of war there was endless malaria to be faced, and other tropical troubles which brought so many of the early European visitors to East and West Africa to the grave within a few months of arrival. There must have been a particularly vigilant providence over such a man to enable him to survive to the age of eighty-seven. Along with this leadership and courage there went a strong sense of duty and a real kindness and depth of understanding. He believed it was the duty of the white man to assist the African, and it was his desire to help to prevent the continuance of the slave trade that led him to Africa in the first place. Moreover, his ideals had a definite human warmth about them. When his caravan succeeded in freeing some slaves near Tsavo he looked after the freed African children himself, referring to them as his 'nursery' and watching over their health and games with a paternal eye. Yet he was also a strict disciplinarian and did not hesitate to punish when he considered punishment necessary. Such were the qualities which inspired affection and loyalty towards him from those who shared his campaigns. But so far as the Colonial Office was concerned he was valued for quite different qualities. They were by no means enthusiastic over hair-raising military expeditions, and sent a stern rebuke to him for not having waited for their permission to attack Kano and Sokoto. Yet the government soon came to realize that Lugard had a great gift for bringing peace and order out of chaos, and for this they valued him very highly.

Nyasaland and the African Lakes Company. In 1888 all these qualities were unknown to the African Lakes Company in Nyasaland. Nyasaland was literally a battlefield of missionary enterprise, for the Yaos who lived along the lake shore were Mohammedans and slave traders, and were aided in this work by the Zulus from the south as well as by the east coast Arabs. They were so strong that they compelled the Universities Mission to Central Africa, which had followed Livingstone's two journeys to Nyasaland, to withdraw from Nyasaland to Zanzibar in 1863. Ten years later missionaries returned to the attack when the Livingstone Free Church Mission opened a centre at Bandawe on the central west shore of the lake, and in 1876 the Church of Scotland Mission established a settlement at Blantyre in the

Shiré Highlands. Trading and transport facilities were essential if the missionaries were to hold their position, and in 1878 the African Lakes Company had been started and was managed by the Moir brothers to provide these facilities. In 1885, following Joseph Thomson's expedition from Lake Nyasa to Lake Tanganyika, the African Lakes Company succeeded in conveying a steamer from one lake to the other for work in Tanganyika, and planned to build a road connecting the two lakes. This northward expansion cut across the slave traders' route from the Upper Congo to the east coast via the northern end of Lake Nyasa, and open war began between the slave traders, led by Mlozi, and the Company. The conflict centred upon the Company's post at Karonga's on the north-west shore of the lake, which was attacked by the Arab slavers in whose hunting grounds it stood.

The campaign of Karonga's, 1888–9. When Lugard was accepted by the Company Mlozi's campaign against Karonga's had already started. Lugard's relief expedition made its way up to Blantyre and then by steamer up the lake, reaching Karonga's at the end of May 1888. The first sight of it was not encouraging. 'Karonga's', wrote Lugard, 'was a very small stockade made of upright poles forming an irregular enclosure open to the lake in the rear. Inside it was a mass of filthy native huts and huddled up among these huts were those of the white men.' Lugard immediately started cleaning up and reorganizing the stockade, and soon afterwards began to organize the forces available for an attack on Mlozi's stockade at Kopa-Kopa's. This attack was made by night on 15 June, but Kopa-Kopa's proved almost impregnable, and in attempting to storm it Lugard was shot from point-blank range; his left arm and wrist were shattered, his right arm was broken, and the bullet also passed through his chest. But although for weeks afterwards he was unable to move from his chair he continued to supervise the campaign against the slavers. Despite the failure to take the enemy's stockade, by the end of July the Karonga's garrison were sufficiently strong to be able to impede the movement of slave caravans in their vicinity, but Lugard was unable to finish the campaign; he had already overstayed his leave from his regiment, and in June he returned to England. The campaign finished temporarily in

October 1889, when an unsatisfactory treaty was made with Mlozi which failed to exact the complete surrender of the slavers, who continued slaving until Mlozi was captured and executed in 1895.

Lugard and the British East Africa Association. The campaign at Karonga's had made Lugard's reputation. Requests for his services now came from all sides. Rhodes, who had arranged to amalgamate the Lakes Company with his British South Africa Company, offered Lugard the job of commanding and organizing a permanent force for the suppression of slavery in the Nyasaland region, but this fell through when the British Central African Protectorate was formed. Another offer had come from Sir William Mackinnon for employment in the British East Africa Association. This offer Lugard decided to accept, and after five months in England, during which he tried to get help against the slavers by lectures and newspaper articles, he returned to Mombasa at the end of 1889.

Lugard's early work for the Company, 1889–90. At that moment the expeditions of Jackson and Peters were already heading for Uganda and it was fairly clear that it might be necessary for the Company to take over the region. If so, Lugard was the man the directors intended to send. Meanwhile Mackenzie allowed him to open a new route to the interior along the Sabaki river (the Athi). Lugard's idea was not merely to explore the route but also to establish a series of posts about fifty miles apart, which would be permanently manned and provide supply bases for the Company's caravans proceeding inland. In 1889 the only such inland base in existence was at Machakos, 350 miles from Mombasa. Between January and March of 1890 Lugard succeeded in establishing five more; one at Makongeni, two on the Sabaki, one at Kibwezi, and one on the Wakutukoa River. In May he was back again at Mombasa, where Mackenzie told him to prepare an expedition to go to Uganda. But in the following month Sir Francis de Winton replaced Mackenzie as the Company's administrator, and as it was his intention to make a major expedition into Uganda, which had become a British sphere by the Heligoland Treaty in July, Sir Francis thought it would be necessary to go himself. Lugard was therefore allowed to spend the next month putting into practice his schemes for making the coastal slaves work to gain their freedom, which he hoped would make them value it more than if it were simply given, besides providing their owners with some satisfaction for the loss of their property.

Lugard and the Kikuyu. Once more, however, orders were changed. Affairs at the coast made it impossible for Sir Francis to leave. At the same time it was absolutely essential that Uganda should be effectively occupied as soon as possible. Sir Francis therefore ordered Lugard to start with an expedition and to wait for him at Ngongo Bagas in Masailand, where a post was to be established. Thus, early in August Lugard set off with one of the worst-equipped expeditions ever to leave the coast, and following the Sabaki route he reached Masailand in October. As Ngongo Bagas was unsuitable for a post, Lugard built one instead at Dagoretti, a few miles from Nairobi's present site and on the edge of Kikuyu country. He got on with the Kikuyu better than any previous traveller, and regarded them as the finest tribe he had met in East Africa, maintaining that they were well able to hold their own against their Masai neighbours. But his friendly relations with them were cut short, for on 18 October instructions arrived from Mombasa that he should not wait for Sir Francis but push on himself into Uganda with all possible speed. On 1 November he left Dagoretti, and after a record march by way of Lake Naivasha, Lake Baringo, and the Nandi hills, he crossed the plains around the edge of Lake Victoria and approached the capital on 18 December.

The expedition reaches Buganda, December 1890. Mengo, on which the king's palace stood, was on one of four hills. The Roman Catholic mission had their headquarters on the hill of Rubaga to the northwest of Mengo, while the Protestant mission had its station on the hill of Namirembe due north. The eastern hill, Kampala, was the one which Lugard chose as the sight for his camp and which became the headquarters for the Company.

The difficulties in Buganda. When Lugard arrived Buganda was impoverished and still divided. The Muslim-Christian war had left many areas desolated, food was scarce, a cattle pest had taken almost all the cattle, and plague had sadly reduced the population. More serious still was the increasing friction between the Roman Catholic and Protestant parties. In fact by 1890 these parties were more commonly called the Fransa (French) and Ingleza (English) than Catholic and Protestant, for religion was far from being the only cause of division, and each party depended not so much on the European missionaries as on the Baganda leaders. Some of these leaders were genuine Christians, some were nominal Christians, but the vast majority of both sides were chiefs and followers who were not even nominal Christians and were merely out to gain what they could as the old standards collapsed. The death of Mackay in February 1890, and of Father Lourdel three months later, made no difference to the parties, for religion was not the chief consideration. For the same reason Bishop Tucker, who arrived shortly after Lugard and was dismayed to see that his congregation brought their guns even to church, failed to stop the growing rivalry by a conference with the French missionaries. The main quarrel arose over official appointments. The political organization of Buganda included certain official appointments which carried with them much influence and much land. These appointments had been equally divided after the war so that the political power of both parties was theoretically equal, and it had been agreed, so that this equality should not be upset, that a chief who changed from one party to another should give up his appointment. But on account of the king's support the Fransa were increasing their numbers more rapidly than the Ingleza; they therefore tried to amend this last provision, while the Ingleza continued to insist that appointments must be given up when a chief changed his party. During 1890, and still more in 1891, the question became acute. Other less important differences included the Ingleza claim to a part of Sese Island, which controlled the canoe transport of the lake, and charges of robbery and trespassing by both sides. Had the Mohammedans not been threatening both parties from Bunyoro it is likely that war would have occurred. Even so, the arrival of Lugard's expedition increased the tension almost to breaking point as Fransa fears and Ingleza hopes ran high. Mwanga too, with the murder of Bishop Hannington on his conscience, and his partiality to the Fransa party, was more than a little apprehensive at the arrival of this new English-man who had entered Buganda from the east and camped on one of the neighbouring hills despite every objection put in his way.

As it happened, all this excitement was unnecessary, for Lugard had been instructed to treat all parties without prejudice or favour, although it had been added that if other parties should refuse to co-operate he must consolidate the Ingleza. They were not easy orders to carry out.

Mwanga's acceptance of the treaty. The first step from Lugard's point of view was to get Mwanga to acknowledge the authority of the Company. He first visited the king the day after his arrival at the capital and then drafted a treaty which he showed to both the French and English missionaries. On 24 December this was presented to Mwanga and the chiefs in an atmosphere of extreme tension:

All came armed with loaded rifles, the Fransa to support the king against the English, and the Ingleza to defend Captain Lugard. One angry partisan actually covered Captain Lugard with his gun, but the muzzle was instantly beaten down by one of the Ingleza chiefs. The king was terrified and greatly excited as the strange Englishman, heedless of his evident disinclination, insisted that he should sign the treaty.

Such was an eye-witness report of the scene, and as Lugard felt that if he persisted war would result he temporarily withdrew. It was not until two days later that the treaty was actually signed; the chiefs agreed to accept it, and this forced Mwanga to agree also.

By this treaty of December 1890 Mwanga acknowledged the Company's supreme authority, and placed his territory under their protection to the exclusion of all other European powers, while the Company on their side agreed to protect Buganda and promote its civilization and prosperity through a Resident. In addition there were three important general points. First, the slave trade was made illegal. Secondly, traders of all nations were permitted, but they were not to trade in guns and ammunition. Thirdly, missionaries of all creeds were free to settle, provided they were only engaged in preaching the Gospel and the arts of civilization, and were to be treated with complete impartiality.

Lugard's position in Buganda early in 1891. At the time this treaty gained Lugard no new ally and no security. Mwanga still preferred the French and Germans to the British, and disliked anything which restrained his desires for independence. The Fransa were deeply suspicious of the grant of religious toleration, and the Ingleza were bitterly disappointed that Lugard did not become a partisan of their cause. To maintain his position Lugard had only fifty trained soldiers and 270 undisciplined porters, with very little ammunition and a useless worn-out Maxim gun. Fortunately his position was improved at the end of January 1891 by the arrival of Captain Williams with reinforcements and another better Maxim, but the force was still very inadequate.

The next two months were spent in consolidating the Company's position. Early in February Stokes arrived. This renegade missionary, who was now chiefly concerned with ivory trading and carrying guns between Buganda and the coast, was on this occasion bringing Bishop Tucker for the C.M.S. and a large supply of ammunition and guns for the Fransa chiefs. Had he arrived before Lugard the arms which he carried might have occasioned immediate war. As it was, Lugard, knowing that Stokes was on his way, had hurried to Buganda and was established there before Stokes arrived, so that in accordance with the December agreement he forbade the importation of the arms and ammunition. After a vain attempt to bribe Lugard Stokes withdrew. Meanwhile Lugard pressed on with the construction of a fort on Kampala hill, which was completed in March.

The Mohammedan defeat at Bugangadzi. The next step was to deal with the Mohammedans. After the defeat at Bulwanyi, the Mohammedan troops had withdrawn to Bunyoro and there, early in 1891, Kalema died. He was succeeded in the leadership of the Mohammedan party by Mwanga's uncle, Mbogo, who led a raiding expedition into Buganda and carried off a number of the inhabitants. To repel such attacks the Catholics and Protestants were ready to unite, and Lugard succeeded in raising a Buganda army under the generalship of Apolo Kagwa and recruited from both the Christian parties. In May this army defeated Mbogo and his Mohammedan party at

Bugangadzi. But to Lugard's disappointment it was unable to follow up the defeat by an advance into Bunyoro owing to the rains and the swampy country, which made the soldiers unwilling to proceed.

The expedition to Kavalli's. The defeat of the Mohammedans left the Ingleza and Fransa parties face to face once more, and without the Mohammedan menace to restrain them hostility grew rapidly. In any case it was already obvious that the Company's position in Uganda could not be held unless a strong central force was established. But where could such a force be found? The administrator had informed Lugard that no help could be sent from the coast. It was equally obvious that recruits from within Buganda itself would belong to one of the rival factions and would therefore not be prepared to fight in a neutral army. In this extremely difficult position Lugard came to the conclusion that the only possible solution was to get the support of the Sudanese troops under Selim Bey who had remained in the area of Lake Albert after the departure of Stanley and Emin Pasha. After the defeat of the Mohammedans, Lugard decided to take an expedition to Kavalli's on the south-western shore of Lake Albert where Selim Bey was supposed to be. Leaving Captain Williams in charge at Kampala the expedition set off at once. It did not head straight for Kavalli's but first travelled south into Buddu, where Lugard hoped to establish trade on the lake shore. In June, having started a trading post in Buddu, he travelled westwards to the Katwe salt lake at the northern end of Lake Edward, where another post, Fort George, was established to extract and guard the very valuable salt deposits. Then, turning northwards, the expedition kept to the eastern side of the 16,000 feet peaks of the Mountains of the Moon and succeeded in reinstating King Kasagama of Toro, whom Kabarega had previously driven out. It reached Kavalli's on 7 September 1891 and found Selim Bey settled there with 600 troops and their hordes of wives, followers, and slaves. Reports of Selim Bey vary. Stanley had said that he was given to good living and ease, and certainly his extreme corpulence would have suggested this. But on the other hand Lugard was impressed by his character, his loyalty to the khedive, and the fact that he was willing to give up his supreme command and serve the Company under the British Captain. As Selim Bey agreed to accompany Lugard the two expeditions, numbering over 8000 people, set off in October for Kampala by way of Toro and Ankole. Most of these troops were ordered to garrison a line of forts along the Toro-Bunyoro frontier to guard Toro from Kabarega's raids, and with the remaining company of about 300 soldiers and 600 rabble Lugard arrived at Kampala on the last day of 1891. He has been much criticized for bringing these Sudanese to his aid, and understandably so, for their line of forts became centres of undisciplined oppression which were the scourge of the Bunyoro border. Besides this they were destined to cause serious trouble in the future. Nevertheless, it is difficult to see where else Lugard could have acquired the force which was absolutely vital to the maintenance of peace and the Company's position.

The Fransa-Ingleza war, January–March 1892. In Lugard's absence Williams had been struggling to prevent a clash between the rival parties, and had found it extremely difficult. Despite the December agreement arms continued to be smuggled into the country hidden away in bales of calico, and the excitement in the rival armies had reached a pitch where war was certain. Lugard made a last attempt to appeal to the French bishop, Hirth, but it was in vain and the crisis approached. There has been keen argument about the blame for what followed. The French mission alleged that Lugard and the Protestant missionaries deliberately provoked the Fransa into war. Lugard and the Protestant missionaries alleged that the Fransa, who were in a majority, were determined to defy the Company's administration and thereby pave the way to driving out the British mission and establishing their own control over the country. 'I emphatically state', said Lugard later in his official reply to the charges of the French government, 'that it was the Catholic party who entirely and of purpose provoked the war.'

The storm broke on 24 January 1892. Two days previously a street fight had occurred in Mengo, during which an Ingleza was shot by a Fransa. The Fransa was tried by Mwanga and acquitted, which Lugard regarded as a clear miscarriage of justice. He assumed, rightly or wrongly, from this and from the aggressive attitude of the Fransa chiefs, that a Fransa attack was imminent, and in accordance with his instructions to consolidate the Ingleza party in case of a crisis he issued arms and ammunition to the Ingleza chiefs. Among the four hills the armies began to muster. Lugard offered protection to the missionaries of both missions in his Kampala fort—an offer which the Protestant missionaries accepted but which the Catholic priests declined. On 24 January a shot was fired and the long expected battle began between the Baganda of the rival parties. From his fort Lugard and his Sudanese watched the battle but took no part in it until the Fransa force began to swarm up Kampala hill itself. Then the one Maxim gun he had came into action. Its fire was decisive. The Fransa army retired in confusion and the Catholic mission hill of Rubaga and its fortress were overrun. Meanwhile the Ingleza troops pursued the remainder of the Fransa army, which took refuge on Bulingugwe Island, taking Mwanga with them. At that point the war might well have ended, for Lugard sent for the Catholic missionaries and offered to reinstate both the king and the Fransa chiefs if they would recognize the Company's supremacy and return Mwanga. They refused, whereupon Lugard sent his Sudanese troops to Bulingugwe to take the king by force. Meanwhile the Catholic bishop, Hirth, had himself gone to Bulingugwe, and from there he fled to Buddu with Mwanga, who was virtually his prisoner. Great movements now began, of Fransa travelling into Buddu and Ingleza fighting their way out of it, and civil war threatened to cover the whole country. Fortunately this calamity was avoided because Mwanga—worthless as a man but absolutely vital as a king—escaped from his Fransa escort, and on 30 March appeared once more at his capital, 'very dirty, with scrubby beard and unwashed garments and in an evident state of fear and trembling'. But grubby as he was Mwanga was the key of the whole war, for without him it would have been impossible to make a settlement which the Baganda would have accepted. With his return the war ended, but, brief as it had been, many lives were lost on both sides, including that of Sembera Mackay, the first Protestant convert.

The settlement after the war. A new treaty was made to mark the end of the war. Again the Company's supremacy was recognized, and again the chieftainships were allotted between the parties. But this time there were two differences. In the first place the chieftainships were not now allotted equally, for the Fransa only received those of Buddu. Secondly, to the consternation of both Catholics and Protestants, Mbogo and his Mohammedan party were now also allotted three small chiefdoms on condition that they recognized the sovereignty of Mwanga.

The proposal to withdraw from Uganda. Now that Uganda was again at peace Lugard felt able to leave affairs in the hands of Captain Williams, while he himself returned to England, where Uganda's fate was being decided. The fact was that the Company's extension into Uganda, which had been made for political reasons and not for profit, had cost about £40,000 a year, which was more than the Company, whose income was very small, could afford to pay. By the middle of 1891 it was clear that the Company could not afford to maintain Lugard in Uganda, and therefore Sir William Mackinnon, having appealed in vain to the government for financial aid, informed Lord Salisbury of the Company's decision to withdraw from Uganda and make Dagoretti their farthest outpost. But although the British government were prepared to accept this with indifference, the British public were not. A quite astonishing wave of indignation swept the country at the thought of abandoning the key point in Central Africa. On 28 September the leading article of *The Times* expressed the general feeling:

Such a withdrawal would be nothing short of a national calamity. It would mean not only the loss of a great amount of capital already expended, but the destruction of our influence and prestige throughout Central Africa, the practical defeat of our anti-slavery policy, the persecution of the numerous missionaries labouring in Uganda, and the reconquest by Mohammedan fanatics of the only African state that has shown a disposition to accept Christianity. Whether we desire it or not, the British East Africa Company must be identified for all practical purposes with national policy.

The decision to retain Uganda. The C.M.S. were as disappointed as the Company at the prospect of withdrawal, and while the government was reconsidering its decision in view of the unexpected strength of public opinion, Sir William Mackinnon and his friends subscribed £25,000 personally, and Bishop Tucker, who was on a brief visit to England, raised £15,000 by an appeal to the C.M.S. Gleaners Union. These contributions enabled the Company to stay in Uganda for another year. When Lugard arrived in England in October of 1892 and joined in the campaign to retain Uganda the Liberal government were still undecided, but in November they temporized by agreeing to send Sir Gerald Portal, the consul-general of Zanzibar, to visit Uganda and make a report; meanwhile the Company was to be given financial aid to enable it to continue its occupation until March 1893.

Sir Gerald Portal's expedition, 1893. The verdict of Sir Gerald Portal was a foregone conclusion, for the main facts of the situation were well known in Zanzibar. On 1 April 1893, soon after his arrival, he hauled down the Company's flag on Kampala hill, replaced it with the Union Jack, and proclaimed a provisional British protectorate over the region. He also made a new agreement with Mwanga, and signed a new agreement between the two Christian parties which was more favourable to the Catholics, for it arranged that there should be two Prime Ministers, two chiefs of soldiers, and two chiefs of canoes, so that both Catholics and Protestants should be represented. In addition the Catholics were given several chieftainships, including the province of Kamia and the island of Sese, in addition to those of Buddu. Portal, whose brother had died in May at Kampala, and whose own health was poor, left the capital for the coast on 30 May and on arriving at Zanzibar made out his report. This was sent to the government and emphasized again the need to protect the missions, the promise to end slave trading in the interior, and the strategic importance of Uganda in controlling the head-waters of the Nile. After much opposition Parliament confirmed the protectorate in August 1894.

The end of the I.B.E.A. Company. Thus ended the work of the Imperial British East Africa Company in Uganda. Its work throughout the rest of East Africa was almost ended, too, for during its existence it had spent £450,000 and received only a trivial revenue from the collection of duties on goods from the interior. In 1892 even this revenue came to an end when the British government imposed free trade on the coast. Thus, the East Africa Company, which—unlike the Royal Niger or South Africa Companies—was purely administrative, was left with practically no resources except its own capital. The directors therefore had no choice but to end the Company, and opened negotiations with the government for that purpose in 1893. They were forced to accept a parsimonious grant of £250,000 in compensation, a poor reward for their almost entirely philanthropic efforts. Perhaps Sir John Kirk wrote the best epitaph of the Company. 'With all its faults,' he wrote, 'it has been an honest concern, not a money-making one, and but for its work we should not now possess a footing in East Africa.'

The British East Africa Protectorate, 15 June 1895. The administration of the Company's territories was therefore taken over by the Foreign Office, and what is now Kenya became the British East Africa Protectorate on 15 June 1895.

Lugard's experience in Africa. Meanwhile Lugard, who had done more than any other man to bring Uganda into the Empire, was busy in Nigeria, which was to be the main concern of his career. But it is interesting to notice that he was employed to lead an expedition across the Kalahari in 1896, so that during the 1890's Lugard was active in South, East, and West Africa. This work, together with his participation in the Sudan campaign, illustrates the breadth of his African experience.

The masterpiece of his career, however, was Nigeria. His work there must be briefly mentioned not only for the interesting comparison it affords with East Africa but also to complete the biographical picture of tropical Africa's greatest administrator.

The condition of Nigeria. The Niger region, like East Africa, had aroused British interest in connexion with the suppression of the slave trade, but again the government had been reluctant to take over the region. Except for Lagos, which became a Crown Colony in 1861, development had been left to Sir George Taubman Goldie and his trading companies. As the Imperial British East Africa Company had been rivalled by the Germans in East Africa, so was Goldie rivalled by the French along the Niger. In 1884 he succeeded in buying out the rival French trading companies, and by the Berlin Conference and the Anglo-French Convention of 1890 the Lower and Middle Niger were recognized as a British sphere of influence. But the French continued to cast covetous eyes upon the countries within the Niger bend, and it became clear that force was needed to keep them from encroaching. For this purpose Lugard was employed.

French and British rivalry in West Africa. His first task was given him by Goldie in 1894, in connexion with the region of Borgu, which was coveted both by the French in Dahomey and by the Royal Niger Company. To secure the region a French expedition of 500 men had set out to secure a treaty from the king of Nikki, the leading chief of the area. Goldie promptly engaged Lugard to lead a rival expedition to Nikki on behalf of the British. This arrived before the French, and Borgu was secured. But French encroachment continued, and in 1897 the Colonial Secretary, Joseph Chamberlain, formed the West African Frontier Force of 2000 men, commanded by Colonel Lugard, in order to help the Company to maintain its boundaries against the French. In 1898 peace was made by another Anglo-French Convention.

The end of the Royal Niger Company. Despite this peaceful settlement, the Colonial Secretary came to the conclusion that the Niger region had become so important politically and commercially that it would be more fitting for the government rather than the Royal Niger Company to administer it. On 1 January 1900 the Company's administrative duties ceased, and it became merely a trading concern. But it had done important work in securing Nigeria for Britain, and at the end it was given more than three times as much compensation as the I.B.E.A. Company had received from the government.

Lugard's work as High Commissioner in Northern Nigeria. The withdrawal of the Company's charter was the occasion for a general tidying up of the administrative arrangements in Nigeria; the British sphere was divided into the colony of Lagos (which became part of Southern Nigeria in 1906), and the two protectorates known as Southern Nigeria, which extended upstream to Idah, and Northern Nigeria, which extended northwards to the Say-Baruwa line on the desert

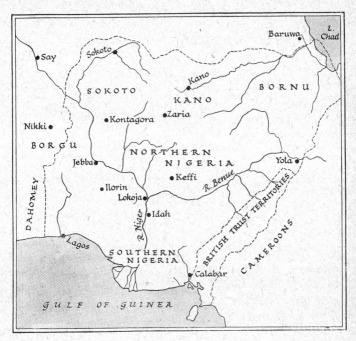

Map 12. Nigeria.

fringe. The first High Commissioner for this northern protectorate was Sir Frederick Lugard in 1900. At once he was faced with two major difficulties. The first was an acute shortage of European staff, which was due to the Boer War and the Ashanti campaign. The second was that a large proportion of the people he was in theory governing, especially the Fulani emirs of Sokoto and Kano in the north, had no intention of accepting his rule.

Indirect rule. Lugard's answer to the difficulties arising from the shortage of European staff was the system of 'indirect rule' which he explained in his first annual report:

The Government utilises and works through the native chiefs, and avails itself of their intelligence and powers of governing, but insists upon their observance of the fundamental laws of humanity and justice. Residents are appointed to promote this policy by the establishment of Native Courts. The Provincial Courts are instituted to deal with the non-native and to enforce the laws of the Protectorate, more especially those which deal with slave raiding. If an Emir proves unamenable to persuasion he is deposed and a successor recognized by the people will be installed in his place.

By this system Sir Frederick Lugard, with a mere handful of Europeans, was able to administer effectively one of the largest regions of the British Empire. So successful did the system prove that it spread beyond the boundaries of Nigeria and became accepted as the basic principle of British rule in tropical Africa, and was one of the most valuable of Lugard's contributions to the Empire. Lugard was the chief exponent of the system of indirect rule, but the same plan was worked out by Sir Harry Johnston, whose agreement with Buganda in 1900 adopted the principle.

The only answer to the problem of obtaining recognition of British sovereignty throughout the Northern Nigerian protectorate was force. The first campaign in 1901 was directed westwards and resulted in the acceptance of Lugard's authority in Kontagora, Borgu and Ilorin. The second campaign was directed eastwards, and by the end of 1902 Yola in the south and Bornu in the north had accepted British authority. But the greatest campaign was in 1903 against the emirs of Kano and Sokoto. This again was successful, and by assuring the defeated emirs that there would be no interference with their Mohammedan religion, Lugard gained their permanent loyalty.

In 1907, when Sir Frederick Lugard left Northern Nigeria to become governor of Hong Kong, the country was peaceful, slavery had been ended, and prosperity was increasing rapidly as the effects of peace and improved communications made themselves felt.

Lugard and the union of Northern and Southern Nigeria. In 1912 Lugard returned to Nigeria as governor of both the protectorates. The intention was that he should form a united Nigeria, since financial, administrative and transport problems all pointed to the need for union. By 1914 preparations were complete and Sir Frederick Lugard became the governor-general of a united Nigeria with its capital at Lagos, while the northern and southern provinces were placed under lieutenant-governors who were responsible to him. Indirect rule was maintained in the north and later was also introduced where possible in the south. Despite the difficulties brought by the World War of 1914–18, it was clear that the new arrangement was far more efficient than the old, and within the first twenty years of the union the external trade of Nigeria increased three-fold, bringing a huge increase in prosperity.

Retirement and 'The Dual Mandate'. In 1918 Sir Frederick Lugard, who had laid the foundation for this prosperity, retired. He was now sixty and had lived an extremely arduous life, but even in retirement his mind was still upon Africa, and in 1922 he published his classic work *The Dual Mandate in Tropical Africa*, stating his belief that the colonization of Africa could, and should, be beneficial to both European and African by improving the trade of the one and the standard of living of the other. 'Europe is in Africa', he wrote, 'for the mutual benefit of her own industrial classes and of the native races in their progress to a higher plane; the benefit can be made reciprocal, and it is the aim and desire of civilized administration to fulfil this dual mandate.'

Lugard's international influence. The Dual Mandate was not his only task during his retirement; he also carried on his work in the international sphere and was particularly active in pursuing the question of slavery, for in the 1920's the number of slaves in the world still ran into millions. In 1925 he was the British representative on the International Commission set up to investigate the whole problem of slavery. This commission resulted in the setting up of a new Anti-Slavery Convention which succeeded in destroying the remains of slavery in Sierra Leone, Hong Kong, northern Burma, north-east

India, and—most difficult of all—Abyssinia. In 1931 he followed this up by successfully supporting Earl Buxton's suggestion that a Permanent International Slavery Commission should be set up to ensure that slavery in all its forms should be finally ended throughout the world.

In addition, he did important work for the Mandates Commission and promoted international collaboration in research, especially in matters of anthropology and language.

In 1928 he became the first Crown Colony administrator to be made a peer, as Baron Lugard of Abinger. But in the next year came a great blow when his wife died. Before her marriage in 1902, she had herself, as Miss Flora Shaw, played an important part in colonial affairs. Lord Lugard himself died in 1945, at the age of 87.

CHAPTER X

LATER ZANZIBAR

Accession of Barghash. In 1870 Seyyid Majid was followed on the throne by his brother Seyyid Barghash, who ruled until 1888. During this period European countries began to take a much greater interest in the development of Africa. A good deal more detail is given about this in ch. VII on 'The Scramble for Africa and the First Partition of East Africa'. Here it is important to notice that England's interest in Zanzibar, which began by being limited to the suppression of the slave trade, had gradually become enlarged, under the influence no doubt of the opening of the Suez Canal in 1869, which had brought East Africa over 4000 miles nearer to the gate of Europe. Thus in Seyyid Barghash's reign the chief British representative in Zanzibar, Sir John Kirk, came to occupy the position of an unofficial Prime Minister to the Sultan. In securing this unusual position Kirk was aided by the good reputations earned by previous British consuls, but he himself was by far the most outstanding of the British representatives at Zanzibar.

Sir John Kirk. John Kirk was born in 1832. His medical and botanical qualifications caused him to be recommended to Livingstone as a useful member of his Zambezi expedition in 1858–63. Livingstone did not find it easy to get on with Europeans and he often wished that he was alone with Africans, as he had been on his first great journey across the continent. He and Kirk, however, became real friends, and it was through Livingstone's recommendation that Dr Kirk was offered the post at Zanzibar of agency surgeon and vice-consul. He accepted this in 1866. A year later he married Miss Helen Cook, who bore him a family of five daughters and one son.

Social conditions in Zanzibar. At this time there were roughly 300,000 people in the island of Zanzibar, about two-thirds of whom were African slaves. The Arabs, Indians and Europeans formed only a fraction of the population, which included also a number of the original African inhabitants. It has been estimated that there were about 4000 Arabs, together with some 6000 Indians, the great majority of whom were Muslims, and sixty Europeans, of whom twenty-two were Englishmen. These last were the members of the Universities' Mission to Central Africa, a few business-men and their families, the consul and the vice-consul, Kirk. As the filth and smell of the town of Zanzibar were what might be expected from a place in which there was no drainage system, and where the rotting bodies of dead slaves might be seen on the beach, there was plenty for a doctor to do. When cholera struck the island in 1869–70 and reduced the population by a tenth, there was even more than many doctors would have been able to cope with.

Kirk's work as consul. At the same time Kirk was kept desperately busy doing not only his own government work, but that of the consul as well, for the latter was sick. He was worried also about his inability to solve the problem of getting further supplies to Livingstone, who was cut off in the interior by a tribal war. However, with the help of his wife, he managed to deal with these difficulties, and after his appointment as consul-general (in 1873) he played a leading part in Zanzibar politics until his retirement in 1886.

Decree of 1873. The biggest problem that faced Kirk during this period was the need to get the co-operation of the Sultan in the abolition of the slave trade. When this had been largely secured by the decree of 1873, forbidding the export of slaves from East Africa and closing all slave markets under the control of the Sultan of Zanzibar, he was faced with the growing German interest in East Africa. This resulted in the delimitation treaty of 1886 dividing East Africa into British and German 'spheres of influence'. Under this treaty Zanzibar, Pemba and a narrow coastal strip were allotted to the Sultan of Zanzibar.

The importance of Kirk's influence. It was fortunate for East Africa that Kirk was acting-consul in Zanzibar when England was stirred by Livingstone's writings and actions to insist that slavery be abolished in East Africa. Only a man of exceptional character and reputation could have secured the support of the Sultan in enforcing the treaty of 1873 which, supported by the proclamation of 1876, forbade the conveyance of slaves by land under any condition. It is true that the British navy could enforce the treaty of 1873 once the consent of the Sultan, Seyyid Barghash, had been obtained, but the Sultan's active support was needed to ensure that the proclamation was obeyed. That he did give this, and was prepared to do so against the will of his subjects, reflects credit on Seyyid Barghash and on the trust which he placed in Kirk. This trust was deepened as the years went by, and from 1873–85 Kirk shared the control of the Sultan's lands. To co-operate in this way with a ruler who in theory governed as a despot demanded unusual tact, understanding and fairness. These were qualities which Kirk possessed, and it was partly due to his influence that British trade with Zanzibar increased even more rapidly than that of other nations, so that by 1878–9 it was responsible for at least one-third of the imports and more than a half of the exports. Apart from this, direct trade between India and Zanzibar amounted to £200,000.

The declaration of 1862 and German ambitions. Unfortunately Kirk was unable to convince England of the possibilities of the Anglo-Arab partnership in which he believed. English ministers were concerned with world affairs and the growing power of Germany at a time when danger threatened also from Russia. They were, therefore, prepared to conciliate Germany in East Africa (see ch. VII).

The Sultan's overlordship of much of the East African mainland had been acknowledged in the slave-trade treaties and in the 1862 declaration, signed by England and France, which stated that:

Her Majesty the Queen of the United Kingdom of Great Britain and Ireland and His Majesty the Emperor of the French, taking into consideration the importance of maintaining the independence of His Highness the Sultan of Muscat and of His Highness the Sultan of Zanzibar, have thought it right to engage reciprocally to respect the independence of these Sovereigns.

The boundaries of this land had never been defined and the danger of this was clear to Kirk. Adequate armed forces were also needed; and in 1877 Kirk suggested that Lieut. Lloyd Mathews, R.N., should be given command of a small army to see that the Sultan's proclamations were carried out. General Mathews, as he was now called, proved an ideal choice. For the rest of his life he looked on Zanzibar as his adopted home; and when Britain eventually took over the Protectorate of Zanzibar he was appointed First Minister to the Sultan. It was to the General's small army that Kirk turned when danger from German ambition threatened Zanzibar. In 1880 General Mathews was therefore instructed to set up a fortified post 120 miles from Bagamoyo on the mainland. Kirk, however, was discouraged by the British government in his efforts to show by concrete signs that the Sultan's power extended inland. When Bismarck, the great German Chancellor, gave support to the Society for German Colonization, Kirk saw the danger that threatened Seyyid Barghash, but he was helpless because England had already decided not to oppose the Germans. He could only look on helplessly when Germany followed up the Congress of Berlin of 1884 by annexing a large area opposite Zanzibar which the Sultan had always regarded as his own. When this was followed by the news that the Sultan of Witu had accepted a German protectorate, Kirk was even ordered by England to persuade Barghash to accept the situation.

Kirk's later career. The happy partnership between the Sultan and his unofficial Prime Minister had now not much longer to run, and it was a relief to Kirk to go on leave, just before the delimitation treaty of 1886 was forced on Barghash. He never returned. His last important official service was as a British representative at the Conference of Brussels in 1890, where his long experience of Africa enabled him to play a leading part. Apart from this, he was a director of the Imperial British East Africa Company and as such remained closely linked with East Africa until the break-up of the Company in 1894. Later he was vice-chairman of the Uganda Railway Committee.

European interest in Zanzibar. It has been convenient to give an outline of the career of Sir John Kirk before that of the Sultans of Zanzibar with whom he was connected. These were Seyyid Majid and Seyyid Barghash. The latter had been exiled to Bombay for his attempts to snatch the throne from Seyyid Majid, who succeeded his father Seyyid Said. On the death of Seyyid Majid in 1870, Seyyid Barghash became Sultan of Zanzibar, and it was during his reign that close links were made between the island and Europe and Asia. To a large extent this was due to the growing interest in Africa, particularly marked in the period 1870–88 during which Seyyid Barghash ruled at Zanzibar. The great period of East African explorers, which may be said to have been from 1856 to 1873, was drawing to a close, but the interest of Europe, which had been stirred by their descriptions, was now concerned with the need to stop the slave trade. For Britain this meant concentration on Zanzibar.

Development of communications. Zanzibar's commercial possibilities had been increasingly realized since the reign of that gifted businessman, Seyyid Said. During the reign of Seyyid Barghash there was a development in communications, which in East Africa has usually been the prelude to increased material prosperity, and these possibilities became even more promising.

In 1869 the Suez Canal had been completed and although the main line of communication with the East lay across the Indian Ocean, and not down the coast of Africa, the cutting of the canal made an African branch-line practical, so that the route up and down East Africa was no longer a backwater. The value of the canal to East

Africa was shown in 1871 when Seyyid Barghash was persuaded to provide a yacht to start a regular service to the Seychelles, thus linking Zanzibar with one of the mail routes. A year later this was followed up by the start of a monthly mail service between Zanzibar and Aden run by the British Steam Navigation Company (now the British India Company). This contact with Aden was a link with the rapidly improving steamship service between England and India. Then in 1879 the Eastern Telegraph Company speeded up communications further by laying a submarine cable from Aden to Zanzibar.

Barghash. Barghash's exile to Bombay had enlarged his knowledge of the world and he was quick to see the value of linking Zanzibar with the outer world. He also enjoyed the opportunities which this offered of supplying himself with European luxuries. In doing so he did not neglect the needs of his humbler subjects; he ran a line of four steamships to India, to bring food prices down in Zanzibar by importing cheaper grain. Finally in 1875 he set off to see this distant continent of Europe for himself, and paid a visit to England. He visited the Queen at Windsor, and was given the freedom of the City of London.

Domestic policy. Meanwhile in Zanzibar itself Barghash had shown himself a forceful and energetic ruler. Without his driving force the island might have suffered a worse blow in 1873 than it did, when most of its clove trees were destroyed by a cyclone. Again, his father, Seyyid Said, had originally been attracted to Zanzibar because of its sweet water. Yet there were frequent complaints of the foul drinking water which was offered in the town of Zanzibar. This was remedied by Seyyid Barghash, who arranged for a conduit to carry sweet water from the spring of Chem Chem to the town.

Suppression of the slave trade and relations with Britain. Yet to many of his subjects these benefits counted for little against the concessions he made to England in stopping the slave trade. The treaty of 1873 and the proclamations of 1876 were bitter blows at what they regarded as the main source of their prosperity, and to Seyyid Barghash at the end of his long reign it must have looked as though he had tried to secure British friendship in vain. In 1875 an unsuccessful attempt by the Egyptians to invade the northern coast of the Sultan's lands was checked by his determined attitude, supported most effectively by Kirk. But Seyyid Barghash had seen the danger to his mainland, for he well knew that Zanzibar had neither the wealth nor the population to develop the interior or to govern it effectively. If pressure should be put on him to do this, either with the object of stopping the slave trade, developing other trade, or for scientific interest, he knew that he might be forced to retire altogether from the interior. In the circumstances he decided that it was wise to risk asking the British to do what he could not do himself. In 1877, therefore, he approached Mackinnon with the offer of a trade concession under which Mackinnon and his friends were to take over the political and economic control of his mainland territories. P. 100 of ch. VII describes why this came to nothing.

Barghash's successors. Seyyid Barghash himself did not live much longer, and with his death in 1888 there followed a rapid succession of Sultans: Seyyid Khalifa 1888–90, Seyyid Ali 1890–3, Seyyid Hamed 1893–6, and Seyyid Hamoud 1896–1902. As England took over the protectorate of Zanzibar, when she signed a treaty with Germany in settlement of their territorial claims in Africa, there were a number of administrative changes during these reigns.

Anglo-German rivalry: relations in Africa. Rivalry between Germany and England had grown steadily worse in the 1890's (see ch. VII) and it was finally agreed that if England accepted some changes in the boundaries of South and West Africa and handed over Heligoland, a useful naval base off the coast of Germany, Germany would recognize a British protectorate over Zanzibar and give up her own protectorate. At the same time the boundary between the British and German spheres of influence was defined as a line beginning on the north bank of the River Umba and, skirting the northern base of Mount Kilimanjaro, drawn to a point on the eastern side of Lake Victoria Nyanza. It was explained to the Sultan that in future all his dealings with foreign governments would be under British control. However, his claim and that of his successors to rule in Zanzibar would be supported by the British and he would be allowed to choose his own successor, subject to British approval. Seyyid Ali was well aware that if he did not accept a British protectorate his kingdom would be swallowed up by the Germans, who were showing a threatening activity. He therefore signed, but struggled to secure as much money as he could in return for handing over to Germany all rights in the coastal strip between the Umba and the Rovuma.

SULTANS OF ZANZIBAR

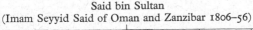

Said bin Sultan
(Imam Seyyid Said of Oman and Zanzibar 1806–56)

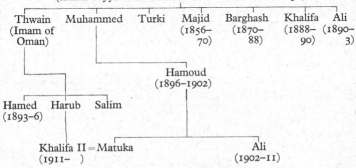

Thwain (Imam of Oman)	Muhammed	Turki	Majid (1856– 70)	Barghash (1870– 88)	Khalifa (1888– 90)	Ali (1890– 3)

Hamoud
(1896–1902)

Hamed (1893–6)   Harub   Salim

Khalifa II = Matuka
(1911–   )

Ali
(1902–11)

Reforms in Zanzibar. In taking over responsibility for the administration of Zanzibar the British government were concerned with the low standards accepted in many departments. The streets of the town itself were covered with filth, and it was often not possible to get through them because they were blocked by the remains of old buildings. The approaches to the harbour were dangerous. The provincial governors were paid such low salaries that they made them up by bribes. Nor was it easy to get the money to improve these things, for the Treasury itself was one of the worst run departments. As no proper accounts were kept and there was no attempt to draw up a budget, most of the money went to those who did very little work to deserve it. If there were to be reforms, it was clear that they would have to begin with the Treasury, and at length the consul-general succeeded in arranging that the Sultan should have a fixed Civil List, but that the rest of the revenue was to be paid into a Treasury presided over by a British official. The amount of the revenue was also increased by making Zanzibar a free port, to enable it to compete successfully with Dar es Salaam. This had been developed by Seyyid Majid so that he could retire to this 'harbour of peace' if things became too difficult in Zanzibar. After this the British consul-general turned to other urgently needed reforms, some of which were to take many years to complete. A start was made, for instance, with a reform of the legal system, the harbour was improved, port regulations were issued, and the smell of Zanzibar became less unpleasant when a gang of scavengers was employed to sweep the streets.

The choice of a successor to Seyyid Ali. Only a beginning had been made with reforms when Seyyid Ali died, but the British were now able to use a weapon they had taken when the Treaty was signed which gave them the protectorate of Zanzibar. This was the clause which said that, while the successor to the throne could be named by the reigning Sultan, he was to be appointed only if the British approved the choice. When Seyyid Ali died, Hamed bin Thwain was informed that he would receive support from the British government, provided that he was guided by the consul-general in the question of slavery and in the internal administration of Zanzibar. He had also to take an oath of allegiance to the Queen of England and to accept a further reduction in the amount of the revenue which he was allowed to keep for his personal use; nor would it be possible for him to circumvent this last restriction, for the Treasury was to remain under British control. Hamed bin Thwain was quick to accept these terms. Seyyid Barghash had once said that the law of succession in Oman and Zanzibar was that he who had the longest sword succeeded. The new Sultan knew that that person in his day was the British consul-general, who had the power of the British Empire behind him.

Arab discontent. Although Seyyid Hamed bin Thwain had been eager to accept the throne on these terms, he soon became very discontented when he realized how much power was possessed by his

British chief ministers. Many of the Arabs around him were eager to work on his resentment, for they hated the British attitude to slavery: it was clearly aimed at eventual abolition, and, in their opinion, at the destruction of their prosperity. Seyyid Ali had been forced to sign an anti-slavery decree which took one more step in this direction, and if the British were not turned out the future was clear. Meanwhile the restriction on the amount of the revenue which the Sultan might retain for his own use hit at all the hangers-on who reckoned to be kept in idleness by the Sultan.

The problem of compensation for I.B.E.A. In 1895 Seyyid Hamed's grievances were greatly increased. In the previous year I.B.E.A. had finally retired from Uganda, a British protectorate had been declared, and it was proposed to declare a similar protectorate over the area now known as Kenya. I.B.E.A. was asking for compensation for the Company's expenses in developing the British sphere of influence. Much against the will of General Mathews and the British consul-general the government proposed to find the money for this by making the Sultan of Zanzibar pay over the £200,000 he had received from the Germans when he signed an agreement giving them full control of the coastline of German East Africa previously ruled by the Sultans of Zanzibar. The Sultan was told that he was to pay this sum of money to I.B.E.A., because the Company was giving up the concessions which he had previously granted to it on the coast. It was further explained that one-quarter of the money was to be paid to the Company to compensate it for the improvements it had made. Naturally enough the Sultan and the British consul-general assumed that the coastal area would now be administered by Zanzibar, but even this consolation was denied. The British considered that it would be sufficient if they paid to the Sultan the same rent which had been given by I.B.E.A. and in addition paid interest on the money that had been used to buy out the Company. The coastal area would be administered as a whole with the mainland.

The attitude in England. There was less criticism in England of this scheme than one would have expected, largely because of the slavery question. This made Zanzibar so unpopular that some of the abolitionists wanted Zanzibar itself to be annexed; the government, too, feared that the end of slavery would mean the beginning of financial assistance to Zanzibar, and were anxious to save money before this should happen. Moreover it was, of course, more efficient to administer the coast and the mainland together.

Rebellion on the coast. The transfer of the coast from the Company to the British government was therefore marked by a rebellion, due partly to the causes given above and partly to the zest of members of the Church Missionary Society who no longer had their energies fully absorbed by converting the heathen tribes of the interior and looking after freed slaves. Encouraged by the establishment of European administration on the coast, the missionaries were working hard to convert the Muslims to Christianity. This increase of their activities to include Muslims, as well as heathen, among those to be converted was very much resented by the followers of Islam.

A disputed succession. No sooner was this rebellion suppressed, than the death in 1896 of the Sultan caused a second crisis. The eldest male member of the royal family of Zanzibar was Seyyid Hamoud, who was a good deal more acceptable to the British as a ruler than Seyyid Khaled, the son of Barghash. This did not appeal to Seyyid Khaled, who considered his claim was the better and tried to establish it by entering the palace and there proclaiming himself Sultan. Unfortunately he had no real understanding of the damage which could be done by the naval guns that he was told would be turned on him if he refused to surrender. After the bombardment Seyyid Khaled was rescued by the Germans, who took him down to Dar es Salaam, and Seyyid Hamoud became Sultan. He was succeeded in 1902 by his son Seyyid Ali bin Hamoud who abdicated, on grounds of ill health, in 1911. This long succession of short reigns was followed by that of Seyyid Khalifa who has reigned through two world wars, and has celebrated his silver jubilee.

Economic progress. By far the most important event in the reign of Seyyid Hamoud was the end of the legal status of slavery in 1897, of which details are given in ch. IV. This caused very little disturbance in the economic condition of the protectorate, largely owing to the wise manner in which it was carried out. Zanzibar at this time was still dependent on the growing of cloves and coconuts which, even today, are the main cash crops produced by the island. In 1947, for instance, their combined exports sold for nearly a million pounds. In the reign of Seyyid Hamoud, however, efforts were made by the new Department of Agriculture to find fresh crops suitable for a tropical climate. These efforts were successful in that it was shown that it would pay the people of Zanzibar to experiment with a far larger variety of crops, such as coffee, tea, cocoa, cinnamon and nutmeg, but the inhabitants were not convinced that the new crops would pay them better than their old favourites, cloves and coconuts. The British consul-general felt that nothing could be done with the older generation of Arabs, and that the best hope for the future lay in the education of the young. In 1907, therefore, it was decided to start a Department of Education, and primary schools were set up in Zanzibar town and some of the chief villages. Despite this the Zanzibaris continued to concentrate on their two main crops, reckoning to import foodstuffs. The Second World War shook them free from their prejudices, and they saw the need for subsistence farming.

The development of internal communications. In the reign of Seyyid Hamoud's son, Seyyid Ali, economic development was helped also by the improvement of communications. Not only were so many new roads built that the island had seventy-five miles of good roads by 1913, but the first electric telegraph was also opened. This linked Zanzibar town and Chake Chake. These towns had also the advantage of the good telephone system which was introduced into both Zanzibar and Pemba.

Measures of hygiene. Nor could the nickname which Livingstone gave it of 'Stinkibar' any longer be given to Zanzibar. The streets were swept regularly, precautions were taken against malaria, thousands of rats were killed every year as a check on bubonic plague, and efforts were made to secure clean milk as a step in the fight against tuberculosis which, in 1909, killed 183 people in Zanzibar town alone. The result was a considerable improvement in the health of the population.

Constitutional changes. With regard to the constitution, important changes were made at the beginning of Seyyid Hamoud's reign. The British consular court was replaced by a judge and assistant judge appointed by the Crown. These formed Her Britannic Majesty's Court for Zanzibar, and under this came subordinate courts. In all of these courts the Indian code of civil and criminal procedure was used. A number of cases were not, however, affected by this change. The Sultan's own Arab and African subjects, for instance, were still tried in his own courts, until in 1899 a regular system of native courts was set up to deal with these people, and in 1908 British judges were appointed to sit in the Sultan's courts.

Transfer to the Colonial Office. In 1913 there was a further very important change when the administration of Zanzibar passed from the Foreign Office to the Colonial Office. At the same time a Protectorate Council was set up, to enable the Sultan to take a more active part in public affairs. The posts of British Consul-General and First Minister were combined and given to one man called the British Resident in Zanzibar, under the control of the Governor of British East Africa.

Legislative Council set up and the post of High Commissioner abolished. Although it had been a wise step to transfer the administration of Zanzibar from the Foreign Office to the Colonial Office, which was better able to deal with its problems, a few years' experience showed that this also was not entirely satisfactory. For one thing, too much delay was caused by referring matters from Zanzibar to the High Commissioner who, as Governor of East Africa, was resident in Nairobi. In 1925, therefore, the post of High Commissioner was abolished. At the same time the Protectorate Council was also abolished, largely because it was out of touch with the unofficial community. In its place a Legislative Council was set up, with an official majority, but containing also unofficial members who were to be nominated after the advice of leading unofficial bodies had been secured.

Limitations on the Sultan's power. Before this change could be introduced, the Sultan's consent had to be obtained, because it meant that his power of legislating by issuing decrees would be limited. As the Sultan was anxious that his subjects should have a greater share in the work of government he agreed. At the same time a small Executive Council was set up to advise him and to discuss what measures the government should introduce into the Legislative Council.

Executive Council. It was then decided that the Executive Council should consist of the following *ex officio* members (that is, members who are present because of their office): His Highness the Sultan, the British Resident, the Chief Secretary to the government, the Attorney-General and the Financial Secretary. In addition to these members, three other senior officials were usually to be appointed by the Sultan. In 1942 the Senior Commissioner was also appointed as an extra *ex officio* member, and at the same time he became a member of the Legislative Council.

Composition of the Legislative Council. The British Resident, the Chief Secretary to the government, the Attorney-General and the Financial Secretary were also members of the Legislative Council, which had in addition five official and six unofficial members appointed by the Sultan. The six last have since been increased to eight in number.

As the British government, the Sultan and his subjects all wish Zanzibar to advance by suitable stages to self-government within the Commonwealth, further constitutional changes were announced in 1955 and became law in 1956.

A Privy Council is to be set up to advise the Sultan. At first this will consist of only six people, the British Resident, the Chief Secretary, the Attorney-General, and three others to be nominated by the Sultan. In addition both the Executive and the Legislative Councils are to be enlarged so as to give further weight to the views of the community as a whole.

The Executive Council is to be increased by three unofficial members, to be called representative members, that is, one African, one Arab and one Indian. These members will be nominated by the Sultan on the advice of the British Resident.

On the Legislative Council the number of unofficial members will be increased from eight to twelve. These twelve will represent the general public of Zanzibar and Pemba. For this purpose four Arabs, four Africans, three Indians and probably one European will be chosen. The method of appointing these members is under review. At the same time four additional official members will be appointed, so that there will be thirteen members on the government side; the official majority will be four, even if the British Resident does not vote.

As regards local government, Zanzibar is now divided into three districts, Pemba Island, Urban Zanzibar and Rural Zanzibar. Each district is in charge of a district commissioner under the general direction of the senior commissioner, and is sub-divided into mudirias and further sub-divided into shehias. Local Councils exist in both islands, and the Zanzibar Township Council is in process of elevation to a Municipality.

CHAPTER XI

THE RAILWAY AND THE ECONOMIC DEVELOPMENT OF KENYA

Brussels Conference. In 1890 the Brussels Conference at last stated its conclusions, the most important of which were directed against the slave trade. They declared that the participants intended:

The gradual establishment in the interior, by the powers to which the territories are subject, of strongly occupied stations, in such a way as to make their protective or repressive action effectively felt in the territories devastated by slave hunting.

The construction of roads and, in particular, of railways, connecting the advanced stations with the coast, and permitting easy access to the inland waters, and to such of the upper courses of the rivers and streams as are broken by rapids and cataracts, in view of substituting economical and rapid means of transport for the present means of carriage by men.

The need for railways. The conference had stressed the need for railways, knowing that once these were built caravans would no more be used. It cost two or three hundred times as much to bring goods by caravan as it would cost to bring them by railway; moreover, if there were no caravans it would not be possible to carry slaves from the interior to the coast. In addition the Imperial British East Africa Company knew that the construction of a railway to the coast would make the development of Uganda and its administration much easier. They had in fact already laid down some seven miles of a very light railway from Mombasa as a gesture of good will. They could not do more because the construction of a railway is very expensive, and the Company, owing to the cost of Lugard's administration in Uganda, was already desperately short of money. They had already tried to cut down expenses in what is now Kenya. In spite of this need for economy Sir William Mackinnon, the chairman of the Company, could show that it had fought hard against the slave trade and released over 4000 slaves in less than three years. He was also able to point out that Germany's aggressive policy under Carl Peters's leadership had forced the Company, in the interests of the empire, to attempt the effective occupation of some 750,000 square miles, and this had cost them a great deal of money.

The withdrawal of I.B.E.A. from Uganda. Despite this, it came as a shock to the British when the Company announced in 1891 that it was making arrangements for the withdrawal of Captain Lugard and his entire force from Uganda. Fortunately, arrangements for the survey of the proposed railway had already begun, and the English friends of the Protestant mission in Uganda were able to collect enough money to enable Lugard to stay on in Uganda until the British government was prepared to take over.

Difficulties of construction. It had not been easy for the government to decide to construct a railway from Mombasa to Victoria Nyanza running through land that was known to very few people in England. No engineer, for instance, had any detailed information about the escarpments flanking the Rift Valley, although these steep rises were serious obstacles in the way of the railway. There were also the long stretches without water between Mombasa and Mtito Andei, the tsetse-fly country, and the dense bush and rock through which a way had to be hacked. To these difficulties must be added the problem of labour, for the Africans in this area had no experience which would enable them to build a railway and had not even used a pick and spade.

It was not long before another difficulty appeared, the danger from wild animals. The House of Lords was told of a party of man-eating lions which had halted the work for three weeks, during which time two of them had killed twenty-eight Indian coolies and scores of Africans. The two lions were killed by Colonel Patterson who described his adventures in *The Man-eaters of Tsavo*. It is not surprising that many of the Africans believed these lions were possessed by the spirits of their dead chiefs, who had come back to warn them against the railway. Nor did the lions flee when the railway was completed: they would still occasionally stroll on to the platform and set the station master a problem.

By now, however, the Foreign Office was determined that the line should run through to Victoria Nyanza. They knew that the Germans would construct a railway to the lake if the British did not, and that communications must be improved if England was going to be responsible for Uganda. Nor was the strategical importance of the country overlooked. It was realized that it dominated the northern and western shores of Lake Victoria and held almost the only exit to Lakes Albert and Edward, thus controlling the head-waters of the Nile. One by one the obstacles in the way of its construction were cleared. Parliament agreed to meet its cost, and coolie labour was imported from India. The interests of the coolies were carefully guarded by the British government of India. It was stipulated that, if a coolie wished to remain in East Africa at the end of his contract, he could do so, provided he forfeited his right to a return passage. In this way the number of Indians in what is now Kenya rose to just over 13,000 in 1898. By the next year the rails had reached Nairobi, the headquarters of the railway being moved there from Mombasa. No one in that year had thought of Nairobi as the site of the future capital; it was merely regarded as the last stretch of flat land on which to prepare for the long climb to the top of the Rift Valley escarpment; and it took its name from the Masai word for the cold stream which ran there.

The next step was to run steamers on the lake. These had to be brought from England in sections which were assembled at Kisumu.

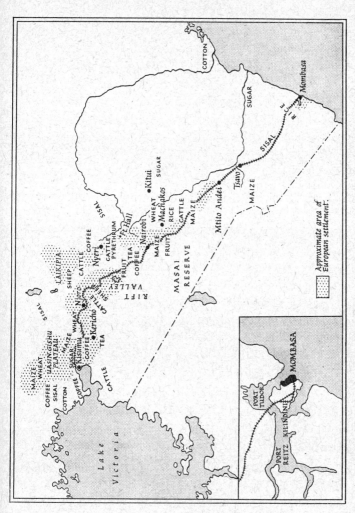

Map 13. The Railway, European Settlement, and Agricultural Products of Kenya.

The first steamship, the 'William McKinnon', was launched two years before the railway opened, having been carried up from the coast on the backs of porters. Before the lake was reached further obstacles had to be overcome. The Kikuyu escarpment was one of these. There was trouble, too, with the Nandi who first saw in the railway a free supply of iron for making weapons and wire for bracelets, and later ambushed the escorts of railway survey parties. But in 1901 all these difficulties were past and the 572 miles of railway line from Kilindini to Kisumu carried the first train on its triumphant passage, festooned as though for a party.

Costs. The railway had cost Great Britain £9500 a mile and it ran at a loss of nearly £50,000 a year, excluding interest on the capital cost. At the time this cost seemed overwhelming, yet before the railway reached Nairobi it had saved countless lives and made the 'famine of the rice' the last great famine in the history of the Akamba people. In 1898–9 famine due to an evil trinity of locusts, drought and rinderpest had struck the Akamba. It was halted by the free distribution of rice brought up from the coast by the railway to the starving people round Machakos.

In 1897, the year in which the Uganda railway, as it was then called, was begun on the mainland of East Africa, slavery was finally abolished throughout British East Africa, and with the construction of the line the last threat of the slave trade was silenced. The cost of carriage had also dropped from 7s. 6d. per ton per mile (the old charge by caravan) to 2½d. per ton per mile. It has been said that Kenya was conquered by a railway, and its modern history may well be said to have begun in 1901; for the railway has been the basis for subsequent development.

Extension of the railway. To those responsible for the development of the new colony it seemed to have been weighed down by a load of debt before it had a chance to succeed; and the critics of the railway felt justified in their prophecies that it would never pay its way. Yet not only did it make a working profit in 1905, its later profits eventually helped the Treasury to pay the general expenses of government. Moreover, by 1936 the original 572 miles of railway had grown to 1625 miles, which included major extensions, as well as several branch lines. In Uganda a line was built to Namasagali which linked up Lake Victoria with Lake Albert via Lake Kyoga, using 'bus and steamer. Another major extension concerned Tanganyika where the Germans had constructed a line from Dar es Salaam to Lakes Victoria and Tanganyika, and from Tanga to Moshi. At the end of the First World War, when the country fell under British control, a link was made between Moshi and what was in 1924 known as the Kenya–Uganda railway.

Indian traders. Today the story of this development is impressive. In 1901 it would have been described as impossible; and those who had the task of making the railway pay looked out bleakly on a land in which the native inhabitants had never seen a wheel, used a plough or exchanged goods for money. Along the coast were to be found Indian traders who had been established there for centuries, for the link with India was an ancient one and the Indians had helped to finance and organize the trade caravans in the days of the Arabs. With the coming of the railway the Indians penetrated inland into the present-day Kenya for the first time, although Alidina Visram, the leading Indian merchant, had extended their business up to Uganda more than twenty years before the coming of the railway. They had used bullock-carts and porters to carry supplies and had set up small centres of trade. Two other Indian traders, Adamjee Alibhoy and M. G. Puri, were also established at Machakos before the coming of the railway, but with these exceptions it is generally true to say that it was not until about 1900 that the Indians effectively spread into the interior. They then practically had a monopoly of the trade in the small township of Nairobi. Although the Indian community was active in developing the early trade of Kenya, they were not so concerned about developing the natural resources of East Africa. Sir Charles Eliot, the Commissioner for the East Africa Protectorate, considered that, if these were to be developed, European settlers would have to be encouraged to take up land in East Africa.

The land problem and the Akikuyu. The British government was anxious that this should not mean that any Africans were dispossessed of their land, but the settlers came at a time when four disasters had struck the land—smallpox, rinderpest, drought and locusts. In Kitui the rinderpest epidemic struck with such speed that the Akamba stockments were surrounded by thousands of rotting carcases, and as the full force of the disasters developed the Akamba population dwindled until, at a place like Nazi, it is believed that about half the population died or moved to other parts. There was a similar fall in the population of Kikuyuland, and this at a time when the Akikuyu had been expanding across the Chania into the lands occupied by the Wanderobo. This was a tribe of hunters who supplemented their livelihood by collecting honey. Numerically they were inferior to the Akikuyu, who could therefore have driven them out if they had felt that this would have secured for themselves an undisturbed title to the land. According to Dr Leakey in his book *Mau Mau and the Kikuyu*, the Akikuyu believed that this was not possible, because 'The Spirits of the owners would make it impossible for the new occupiers to carry out their agricultural activities with any hope of success, or with any hope of the blessing of Ngai, the god of the Kikuyu'. For this reason negotiations had to be carried on between individual Kikuyu and Wanderobo with a view to 'mutual' adoption before the actual transfer of property rights. In this way the goodwill of the departed Wanderobo spirits would be secured for the Akikuyu who took over the land. A religious ceremony would then be held to mark the boundaries. In this manner the Akikuyu had been steadily advancing across the Chania river from about the middle of the sixteenth century. At the same time they retained a fringe of forest, secured by fortified villages against attack from their neighbours the Masai. The disastrous close of the nineteenth century put an end to these interesting developments, and many Akikuyu moved back to the Nyeri and Fort Hall districts. By tribal custom these people still retained their claim to the land they had vacated.

Friction over land. Complicated by this background, the land question was from the beginning fraught with difficulties for the new government of the East Africa Protectorate. One more example was added to the list of countries for which Britain reluctantly accepted responsibility, only to find that her hesitation could be justified by the problems they set her people. Friction inevitably arose over land claims. Difficulties of this kind were not restricted to East Africa. In South Africa, too, there was a wide gap between the Bantu and the European ideas of land ownership. The latter believed in the personal and private ownership of land, while the former believed that all the members of a tribe had a right to the use of such fundamentals as the grass, water and timber on the tribal lands. In East Africa the difference between African and European ideas of procedure in acquiring land has been indicated by the reference to the Kikuyu advance across the Chania. Land disputes, however, cannot usually be set out fairly unless they are given in considerable detail; this is not possible in a book of this size, which can only aim at a bare outline of the issues involved.

The need for European settlers. The difficulties began with the need for European settlers, if the railway was to pay. The British taxpayer had invested millions in building a railway on which every train ran at a loss. This could not go on for ever: somehow the railway must be made to pay for itself. Yet the Africans would never be able to supply enough traffic without assistance. Sir Charles Eliot, the new Commissioner for the East Africa Protectorate, thought the answer was to attract European settlers. If settlers were to be attracted, it was necessary to place the alienation of land on a sound basis. With this object the East Africa (Lands) Order in Council was issued in 1901 and defined Crown land as 'all public lands which for the time being are subject to the control of His Majesty by virtue of any treaty, convention or agreement, or of His Majesty's Protectorate, and all lands which have been or may hereafter be acquired by His Majesty under the Lands Acquisition Act'. The Order in Council then went on to arrange for the disposition of such lands, but, as Mr M. F. Hill in his book *The Permanent Way* rightly points out, it was unfortunate that the order did not make it sufficiently clear what was meant by 'public lands'.

The coming of South Africans. The next step after the issue of the Order in Council was to secure the settlers, and Sir Charles Eliot arranged for the attractions of East Africa to be made known in South

Africa, where he hoped that the unsettled, poverty-stricken state of the country at the end of the Anglo-Boer War might mean that South Africans would be tempted by the opportunities offered in East Africa. This proved to be true, and a number of South Africans were eventually allocated land in the Uasin Gishu Plateau. 'At this time', the Foreign Secretary declared, 'there were no indications of any desire on the part of white settlers to colonize the East Africa Protectorate', and he apparently thought settlers might be obtained more quickly if they were not drawn only from British stock. After one or two suggestions had had to be put aside, the Colonial Secretary's suggestion was followed up, that 5000 square miles of the highlands of East Africa should be allotted to Polish and Russian Jews who were refugees from persecution in Europe. These people did not, however, feel that land in East Africa would solve their problems, and firmly declined the offer, much to the relief of the handful of British settlers already established in East Africa.

The Masai agreement of 1904. Linked with the coming of the early settlers was the problem of the Masai. According to a rough estimate, in 1904 they owned 50,000 head of cattle and 600,000 sheep, they themselves being about 45,000 strong. They roamed over a vast stretch of country which included the land north and south of the new railway line. In view of the danger of clashes between the Masai warriors and the white settlers, it was suggested that the Masai be moved into two reserves linked by a corridor, half a mile wide. The northern reserve was Laikipia and consisted of some 4500 square miles, and the southern, which was of about 4350 square miles, ran down to the border of German East Africa. The area provided was, therefore, generous, but the Masai were given no alternative, and there is some evidence that the tribe were rather unwilling to abandon their claims to the grazing grounds in the Rift Valley.

The Masai agreement of 1911. The agreement covering this move was made in 1904. In a few years it was seen to be working badly: the presence of tick-borne disease in the corridor resulted, for example, in the tribe becoming split into two. Lenana, the great Laibon of the Masai, suggested, therefore, that the tribe should be reunited in one reserve. If the Masai moved from the northern reserve it would mean that Laikipia would be freed for European settlement. Hence the tribe were offered an increase of the reserve in the south to 15,177 square miles, or approximately one and a half square miles of land for each Masai household, which averaged five people. There were complications, however, in carrying out the move, and during this time Lenana sent the following message from his death-bed: 'Tell my people to obey the government as they have done during my life. Tell the Laikipia Masai to move with their cattle to the Loieta plains.' This message had considerable influence, and the northern Masai expressed their wish to move south. In 1911 a new agreement was drawn up and orders were given a year later for the move to be completed, but when the time came some of the northern Masai changed their minds and asked for the move to be cancelled. Eventually, after considerable further agitation, it was completed in 1913. The manner in which the move was carried out has been strongly criticized. Sir Frederick Jackson, for instance, after saying that he was at first against the move wrote, in *Early Days in East Africa*, 'I then, in the interests of the Masai themselves, changed my view, and was in favour of the move. I am, however, thankful that I had nothing whatsoever to do with the negotiations that led to it, nor with the move itself.'

The Carter Land Commission. The Masai were not the only tribe for whom reserves were suggested. There was even a recommendation from the Land Committee that a European reserve should be made. This was not done, but after 1904 native reserves were set aside. In 1915 the government declared that the reserves were Crown Lands and their boundaries were defined by the Crown Lands Ordinance of 1926. Afterwards it was claimed that some of the land which had been included in certain of the native reserves had later been taken for European settlement. Although only relatively small portions of land were involved, it was felt that steps should be taken to remove the grievances felt by the Africans. The boundaries of the reserves were therefore formally proclaimed in 1926, and in 1932 the government appointed a Royal Commission, known as the Carter Land

Commission, to investigate the question of native lands. The report of this commission led to adjustments in land which were accepted by the government as the final settlement of claims based on past injustice. A substantial area of land was also added to the native reserves to meet permanent economic needs. The native areas were then transferred from the Crown to the Africans themselves. Their rights to these lands were guaranteed for ever and a Native Lands Trust Board was set up to watch over them. The boundaries of the Highlands area, in which Europeans were to have a privileged position, were also defined and safeguarded by a Highlands Board. These changes created native areas of 52,097 square miles. By comparison the extent of the Highlands in 1950 was 16,173 square miles including 3979 square miles of forest reserve, which is not considered to be available for settlement. The difference between these figures and the total area of Kenya is largely made up of the Turkana and Northern Frontier districts, which are inhabited by nomad tribes observing no fixed boundaries.

Lord Delamere. When the dust raised by the arguments over land has blown away, it will be seen that the coming of the European settlers changed the country as profoundly as Peter the Great changed Russia, for democracies may administer a land, but under their rule profound economic changes have to be initiated by the individual. Initiative, self-reliance, determination, courage, all these were called for and possessed in some measure by the settlers who came up from the south or from Great Britain. Even a short history cannot overlook one man in particular: Lord Delamere, who lived from 1870 to 1931. His colourful career cannot be compressed adequately into the limited space which is all it can be given here. Only the main outline of the story is indicated, leaving the details to be filled in by subsequent reading, and argued over both by those who admired and by those who hated him. Few would deny that he was a man of intense vitality and volcanic temper; as such he came in for a great deal of criticism, which was not lessened by his high-handed procedure on occasion. There was the time, for instance, when two Indian policemen arrived at his farm when he was away, and had to spend the night there. Seeing an empty tent pitched conveniently, they went to sleep on the camp bed inside. Unfortunately Lord Delamere returned late that night and went to look for Sammy McCall, to whom the tent belonged. Finding the police inside he sent for some Masai to make threatening noises behind the tent, and when the police shot out he hit them on the head with a heavy African club which he had borrowed from the Masai.

Early career and contribution to stock farming. By the time he was twenty-one Hugh Cholmondely had become the third Baron Delamere and inherited Vale Royal, Cheshire, the estate whose finances were to be drained to provide the money for his East African ventures. He soon decided that hunting in the winter and shooting in the autumn did not provide him with sufficient excitement, and went off big-game hunting in Somaliland. After this he returned there every year until 1896, when he extended his journey into the Northern Frontier District, and so into Kenya, where he was entranced by the country. He returned to England, married and tried to settle down at home, but it was no good, his heart was in East Africa. Finally, in 1903 when he was wondering whether to live there permanently, he met with his third serious accident. By the time he was able to get up he had thought things over. Lying on his back for nearly a year in Nairobi he had decided that the Highlands were potentially good farming land, well suited for white settlement. First, however, someone had to prove that first-class stock could be bred there and give good returns, and that crops could be grown which would lift the land from the level of subsistence farming. Even for a wealthy man this would mean risking all his capital, but Delamere was prepared to take the gamble to show that East Africa was a place where the English way of life could flourish. His first venture emphasized the price he would have to pay, for the concession of 100,000 acres which he obtained at Njoro cost him several thousand pounds in capital before he proved that sheep could not be run there successfully. This was land over which the Masai had never grazed their flocks, and because it was totally unoccupied the government had been ready to rent it to Lord Delamere for £200 a year, provided he spent £5000 on developing it within the next five years. When four-fifths of his flock of imported ewes died, owing to a mineral deficiency in the soil, Delamere turned to cattle, but here again his imported stock was doomed, for the tick which carries East Coast fever abounded in his land and in those days no one dipped cattle to safeguard them from the disease.

Wheat. Equator Ranch, as Lord Delamere called his home, had proved a failure as a stock farm; it remained to be seen whether wheat could be grown there. First the land had to be ploughed, and there were no trained oxen or horses available. Next, fences had to be put up to keep out the wild animals. These tasks finished, Delamere looked forward to the first big crop of wheat on which he had staked so much money, but the wheat was riddled with rust. With this third failure Lord Delamere would have been ruined if he had not been able to raise a mortgage on his estate in England. Even so, his life for the next six years was a bleak one in a windowless, mud-floored shack. The money he was able to raise went on tracking down the remedy for rust. To do this he called in the help of a scientist, for whom he built a simple laboratory. Here research was done on the breeding of a rust-resistant variety of wheat. Three years later Lord Delamere harvested his first successful crop.

Summary of achievement by 1914. Now Delamere could give his mind to his stock, the remnants of which he had transferred to a farm, 'Soysambu', which he had bought near Gilgil. By 1914 he had proved that stock could be graded up in Kenya and the land improved. The years of struggle were over. That they had been hard can be read in Lord Delamere's own words. He summed up his experience at Equator Ranch as follows:

I had 3000 acres under cultivation—mostly wheat—on the Njoro farm alone.

The result after a few years working was that sheep had proved a failure and big losses had been incurred; that the land had been proved unsuitable for improved cattle until the East Coast fever menace was dealt with; the wheat was proved to have come to stay. That the possibility of ploughing large acreages in a country where the plough had never been seen was proved to be an economic proposition; that large numbers of natives had been taught ploughing and working with other implements; and that I had managed to get rid of £40,000 in cash which I had invested in the country.

Leader of the white settlers. By now Lord Delamere was looked on as a leader by the other settlers, who felt the need of a spokesman in a land where the government was in the unique position of having preceded the settlers, and therefore claimed, in the words of Huxley's *White Man's Country*, that 'All actual or potential sources of wealth —land, minerals, forests, rivers, lakes—belonged to the state'. All forms of transport—railways, roads, lake steamers and accessories such as wharves and harbours—were state-built and state-owned. Private trading in the most important commodity in the country, land, was prohibited. This position was peculiarly irksome to the many settlers who had hoped for a freer life overseas and who relied on their own initiative to carve out a future which should be beneficial to themselves and the country of their adoption. In other parts of the empire, such as the New England and plantation colonies, England had only taken over responsibility for the administration when there were already settlers there who had begun to develop the land and organize themselves. In East Africa, however, the government was there first, and it was primarily concerned with political administration, and not economic development. There was, therefore, a good deal of friction between the government and the settlers, which could not result in official discussions until the first Legislative Council was authorized in 1907. Lord Delamere was appointed to this body, and suspended a year later, in 1908, for unruly behaviour over the labour question. Reference to this problem will be made in discussion of East African crops.

Agitation for elections. It was not long before Lord Delamere became convinced that the unofficial members of the Legislative Council should be elected, and not nominated, as a step towards ultimate self-government for the Europeans, and he was working to secure this when the First World War broke out.

Services, 1914–18. British East Africa was now faced with the Germans along the whole of its southern frontier, which lay right through the middle of Masailand. Delamere, quick to see that his knowledge of the Masai was the best gift he could give his country, offered to organize the Masai warriors for intelligence duties along the German border. This was to be at his own expense. It was a hard life and eventually the strain proved too much for his strength and he collapsed. His war service, however, was not over, for in 1917 he was elected to the War Council and was in office when the German General von Lettow was driven out of German East Africa.

Elections to the Legislative Council. In both England and East Africa the end of the war brought an extension of the franchise to those on whose support their country had relied, and in 1920 the first election was held to the Legislative Council, which was now to include eleven unofficial members chosen by the European community. Two Europeans were also chosen as unofficial members of the Executive Council, one of whom was Lord Delamere. In this position he was to have a degree of influence which often surprised those who did not realize the value of his experience in a land where officials were not permanent residents.

Devonshire White Paper. The grant of elected representatives to the Europeans alone did not long go unchallenged, and in 1920 the Indians demanded the vote on the same terms. With this they linked the rights to acquire land in the Highlands and to have an unchecked entry into East Africa. Both these claims were strongly opposed by the European settlers, who looked to Lord Delamere to lead them. He accepted this responsibility and led a deputation to England to lay their case before the Secretary of State for the Colonies. A settlement was finally reached in 1923; details of this and of the struggle which preceded it are given on pp. 194-5 of the following chapter. The White Paper which was issued in 1923 by the Colonial Secretary, the Duke of Devonshire, to cover the terms of the settlement contained also the following important statement:

Primarily, Kenya is an African territory, and H.M. Government think it necessary definitely to record their considered opinion that the interests of the African native must be paramount, and that if and when those interests and the interests of the immigrant races should conflict, the former should prevail.

This was qualified by the further statement that:

Obviously the interests of the other communities, European, Indian and Arab, must generally be safeguarded. Whatever the circumstances in which members of these communities have entered Kenya, there will be no drastic action or reversal of measures already introduced.

Dairy farming. After the publication of the Devonshire White Paper, Delamere developed a third branch of farming. Before the war he had shown that stock and wheat could be profitable assets to Kenya. Now he concentrated on dairying, and in addition to building up his own herds established a co-operative creamery in 1925. The next year saw the export of the first butter from Kenya, and in 1930 the Kenya Co-operative Creameries were formed. This was followed by the establishment of the Kenya Farmers Association.

Staple commodities. Agriculture is the basis of Kenya's economy, and Lord Delamere had played the leading part in its early development. The search for staple commodities, the development of coffee, sisal, wattle, tea, and pyrethrum, the growth of African production, and the start of secondary industries, have still to be described. At the close of the last century the first fast-growing wheat, passion fruit, tomatoes, Cape gooseberries and potatoes to be grown in the hinterland of East Africa were planted at Machakos by a missionary, Stuart Watt, in an effort to make the little mission station he had established there self-supporting. He also experimented with eucalyptus and wattle trees. Experience has shown that Ukambani is well fitted for fruit growing, and from this tiny beginning it has developed to a point where a fruit and vegetable canning plant has been set up which exports throughout the world.

Coffee. Missionaries were also responsible for the introduction of coffee into Kenya, for the French Fathers of St Austin's mission planted the first coffee near Nairobi in 1896. It throve there and was developed by many of the early settlers to such an extent that in 1947 coffee was being grown on over 64,000 acres in Kenya, and of late, as a cash crop, it has brought in good returns to Africans also.

Tea and Sisal. Two other valuable Kenya crops were introduced early in the twentieth century—tea and sisal. The former was first started at Limuru in 1904, and three years later an enterprising district commissioner raised one plant in the prison garden at Kericho. It was not, however, until two planting companies came from India in 1925 that any real progress was made. Sisal found its way to Kenya from Tanganyika, where it had been introduced by the Germans in 1893.

Pyrethrum. Probably the most valuable crop to be introduced since the beginning of the century has been pyrethrum. The fact that it was not grown in the country until 1930, although today Kenya leads the world in first-class products of this plant, tempts one to encouraging forecasts about the agricultural potentialities of East Africa. On the other hand, soil erosion throws a menacing shadow.

The Soil. Erosion is a threat to other parts of Africa, where the earth is baked by the sun and trodden hard by the stock who occupy a special place in the lives of Africans. The heavy rains then wash away the unprotected soil, with deep channels. When the rains have gone these can be seen as big dry ditches, a sign that the land is being destroyed by erosion. In East Africa this menace was made worse by the rapid growth of population, together with the weakening of the soil through excessive planting of maize. The introduction of European medicine and veterinary skills, together with the ending of tribal wars, was responsible for the rapid growth of population and stock. Meanwhile heavy planting of maize took place in the depression which followed on the First World War and was encouraged by official recommendation of maize. It was not only considered a suitable crop, both for the Highlands and for the African areas, but it was also to provide bulk for the railway to carry to Mombasa. Unfortunately it was not then realized how much goodness maize took out of the soil. The lesson was learnt, but the problem of eroded and weakened soil in Kenya is one for serious thought.

Scientific farming. If a country makes use of science, it becomes easier to plan its farming wisely. Much can be done for livestock, for instance, through the veterinary department. The first veterinary officer to come to the mainland was Captain Haslam, who was posted to Ukambani at the time of the great rinderpest plague at the end of the nineteenth century. Although he himself was murdered when he went to Kikuyuland to deal with the rinderpest there, his work was continued, and since the Second World War scientific research into the problems of farming has increased considerably. Much of it now covers the whole of East Africa, not only one territory.

Labour problems. Changes of the size that have been described in this chapter always disturb the pattern of the ordinary man's life, and this was true of British East Africa. Before the coming of the Europeans, a man's work was to protect the tribe by fighting and to look after the cattle. Women had to look after the home and till the ground. If East Africa was to shake herself free from the sleep of centuries, her people had to be given the chances offered by education and brought into touch with the rest of the world. This meant that the old pattern of life would have to be disturbed. It had begun to change when the railway was built and brought East Africa into closer touch with the outside world and ended the evils of the slave trade. By the beginning of the twentieth century, too, the first schools, hospitals and 'vets' had appeared on the mainland of East Africa. Development had begun. It could only go on if the wealth of East Africa could be increased. Here the European settlers were an asset; but they could not run their farms without labour and the Africans were reluctant to change the habits of centuries. The old way of life provided most of them with what they wanted and they saw no reason to alter it. Many of the Europeans were shocked, for they came from lands where food was much harder to get and clothing was essential. They took it for granted, therefore, that most men must earn their living by work, and felt that it was not unreasonable that they should expect the government to tell the Africans that the young men must find work on the settlers' farms, and generally to help in recruiting labour. The governor would have preferred to let things alone; this led to the attempt, referred to earlier in this chapter, which Lord Delamere made to put pressure on the governor, which led to his suspension from the Legislative Council. A board was appointed to go into the question and suggest ways of easing the situation. The crisis was solved when they recommended the removal of some of the restrictions on African movements to which the settlers had objected, together with certain improvements in the labourer's living conditions.

Economic development, 1895–1914. It remains to look at the effect of world affairs on events in the East Africa Protectorate. In Britain the period 1895 to 1914 was one both of material prosperity and of strain due to the growing friction between Britain and Germany and Austria. In the East Africa Protectorate it was a period of economic development during which the country passed from the stage of receiving a grant-in-aid to that of financial balance.

Taxation. Until the railway was built the government considered that its work was to administer the country and not to develop it. Departments of Agriculture, Forestry, Public Works, Customs, Land, Education, Medical Services, a Treasury and a railway were, therefore, all started early in the twentieth century, and naturally they cost a good deal of money. Yet the country was not sufficiently developed for the government to be able to collect large sums in taxation. In 1902, for instance, it cost over £200,000 more to govern Kenya than was collected from the country. Nor was it easy to see how Kenya could quickly make more money, because her exports were worth less than half her imports. It was clear that the protectorate would have to receive help from England, and it was given a grant-in-aid of some £250,000 a year. It received this until 1912, when the increasing prosperity of the country in general and of the railway in particular, enabled it to do without it. Since that time the country cost the British taxpayer nothing, until a state of emergency was declared in 1952.

Problems caused by the First World War. In the 1914–18 war a very great strain was put on a country which had only just begun to develop on new lines. In 1914 the total European population of the East Africa Protectorate was about 3000. Of these, 1987 joined up during the war, leaving a bare minimum to carry on the government and run the farms. A vast army of African porters was also required to supply the troops in the field. Nearly 60,000 were recruited in Uganda and the great majority of the rest came from the East Africa Protectorate. Losses in both groups were heavy; and the end of the war saw a sadly impoverished country.

The veterinary services had been too busy keeping transport animals alive to be able to spare much time for producers' troubles; African stock had been shifted about according to military needs, and without due regard to quarantine restrictions. Disease had, therefore, spread and in 1916 rinderpest reappeared. Nor was this all: weeds and grass had spread over the ploughed land and through the coffee plantations. For many men, years of hard work had been wiped out by four years' absence. There was hunger, too, for in 1918 there had been a drought and a bad famine. Finally, the administration of the country, the roads and the railway had all been seriously weakened by the war.

The soldier settlement scheme. In 1919 a new governor, Sir Edward Northey, arrived to deal with these difficulties. During his period of office a number of important steps were taken. These included the reorganization of the railway by placing it on a business footing under an inter-colonial council with its finances separated from those of the protectorate, and the introduction of the soldier settlement scheme. The latter had been suggested during the war, when it was feared that Africans might return from fighting with an idea that the shooting of white men was a lighter matter than they had previously thought. A good safeguard against this view was felt to be an increased European population, and when it was realized how many thousands of men would be jobless and restless after the war, the arguments for a scheme to settle some of them on the land in East Africa were strengthened. So began the second large flow of settlers to East Africa. They were allotted 257 small farms free of purchase price, and in addition 1053 larger farms were offered for purchase on favourable terms. To carry out this scheme $17\frac{1}{2}$ square miles were taken from the Nandi reserve, and this grievance was not remedied until the Carter Land Commission's Report in 1933.

Shortage of labour. By 1919 the European population of Kenya had increased by 300 per cent to some 9000. The African population, for which there are no exact figures available, had been reduced by war, famine and the influenza epidemic which swept through East Africa as well as England. The demands on the labour supply by both private employers and the government were, therefore, difficult to satisfy, especially as the damage done by the war had to be repaired and the population fed. The problem was acute and there was much bitter discussion in England and East Africa over the degree of pressure which might be justly put on Africans to persuade them to leave the reserves and work outside. Eventually a further amendment was made to the Native Authority Ordinance, to the effect that the consent of the Secretary of State must be obtained before any compulsory labour was called out.

Currency crisis. No sooner had Kenya steered her way past these difficulties than she was involved in the currency crisis of 1920. The original token for exchange in East Africa had been cowrie shells, provided they were not offered on the coast, for there they could be picked up on the shore. Some of the up-country missions had even developed their use further, and used to type out primitive stamps marked as worth so many cowrie shells, and in this way pay for the porterage of goods with the caravans. With the gradual increase of trade cowrie shells were no longer adequate, and I.B.E.A. had issued its own rupees which were current together with those of India. When the British government took over the protectorate of East Africa it was natural that the Indian rupee should become the standard coin, for at first there were closer trade links with India than with the West. In time, however, trade with Britain developed and there was a growing desire to deal in pounds. After the war, the difficulty was that the value of the pound, in terms of rupees, was increasing for reasons outside the control of East African authorities, and a rupee was no longer worth only 1s. 4d. In 1920 it was decided that the protectorate must change from the Indian to the British currency. The difficulty was to fix the value of the pound in terms of rupees. After much discussion it was decided that the value of the rupee used in East Africa should be stabilized at 2s. Therefore wages, which had previously consisted of a fixed number of rupees each worth 1s. 4d., now consisted of the same number of coins each worth not 1s. 4d. but 2s. This increased the cost of production. A little later an effort was made to reduce these internal costs by the introduction of a new coin, the shilling.

Depression. In Europe the end of the First World War was followed by a slump. The same thing happened in Kenya, where the problems described above added to the difficulties. This was followed from 1925 to 1929 by years of expansion and lavish expenditure. In the 1930's depression again set in. The world prices for primary products were steadily falling, and Kenya was an agricultural country, and as such badly hit when the forward-on-rail value of maize fell from Shs. 11/10 a bag to Shs. 3/20 a bag and coffee from Shs. 89/50 a hundredweight to Shs. 46/50. All over the world the mid-1930's were a time of falling prices, unemployment and general distress. In Kenya, where this was made worse by locusts and droughts, it is not surprising that the budget could not be balanced. A new source of revenue had to be found and in 1937 income tax was introduced. This was a tax which fell particularly heavily on the European community—Africans in practice were exempt—and for that reason was much criticized.

Outbreak of war. From this point onwards things began to improve, although over in Europe men were growing increasingly concerned about the plans of Hitler for world domination. Knowing the close understanding between Hitler and Mussolini, men assumed when war with Germany came on 3 September 1939 that Italy would attempt to invade Kenya from her base in Abyssinia. Fortunately Italy did not declare war until May 1940, by which time East Africa was assured of support from South Africa. As in 1914, a high proportion of the population enlisted to serve their country; in addition the East African Railway's Nairobi workshop was the centre from which motor ambulances, mortars, lorries, stretchers, etc. came to help in equipping the East Africa Command.

Conduct of the war. Once Italy entered the war, fighting began in the Northern Frontier district and British Somaliland. By the autumn of 1940 the position had improved to such an extent that it was possible to move from the defence of Kenya to the attack on Italian Somaliland. South African, Nigerian, Northern Rhodesian and Gold Coast brigades were now serving with the East African forces, and after the successful attack on Italian Somaliland these forces pushed on into Abyssinia. Here their progress, once they had begun to use the roads the Italians had built, was extraordinarily rapid, and with the fall of Abyssinia British arms secured their first complete success on land.

East Africa's contribution. The nature of East Africa's contribution to the war effort then changed. Guards for prisoner-of-war camps and garrisons for the conquered lands had to be provided. Troops were sent also to help in the defence of Ceylon and India and to other theatres of war. East Africa was also a training base and a place of asylum for refugees from the Middle East and Poland. All this meant that greater emphasis had to be placed on agricultural production.

Post-war development. As a country producing vitally needed foodstuffs, Kenya flourished at the end of the war, especially as she could now draw on people and capital who turned, with the withdrawal of Britain from India, to Kenya. The resources of the land itself were also increased through the extension of scientific research into its agricultural problems.

Kenya, moreover, is ceasing to be entirely a farming community. Tobacco, matches, brewing, bricks, plastics, metal boxes and clothing of all kinds are among its developing secondary industries. So far the Africans are in these trades only as employees. Their progress in agriculture, however, has been marked, and it is estimated that in 1951 the value of African subsistence farming was £22,100,000 and the net value of African grown and marketed produce £4,700,000.

CHAPTER XII

THE CONSTITUTIONAL DEVELOPMENT OF KENYA

Introduction. This chapter deals with the development of the government of Kenya, which controls a multi-racial community. The task of designing a form of government which will allow each section of the community to play its due part in the development of the country is a complex one. This makes it difficult to pick one's way through the labyrinth which is the story of the constitutional development of Kenya. The chief stages are, therefore, summarized in the table below.

CHIEF STAGES IN CONSTITUTIONAL DEVELOPMENT OF KENYA

Period	Non-African local government	African local government	Central government
Before the British came	None	Local tribal custom	None
I.B.E.A.	Forts and out-posts	Local tribal custom	Semi-military and commercial
Foreign Office	Forts and out-posts	Local tribal custom	Over-all attempt to raise standards
1900	Soldiers, settlers and traders form communities. Nairobi has a township committee	Local tribal custom	
1902		Village headmen	Departments of Agriculture, Forestry, Medical Services, Judicature, etc. had been set up
1903	Township Ordinance	Hut tax	
Colonial Office takes over from Foreign Office			
1905			Executive Council set up
1907			Legislative Council set up
1912	Headmen given extended powers		
First World War			

CHIEF STAGES IN CONSTITUTIONAL DEVELOPMENT OF KENYA (*cont.*)

Period	Non-African local government	African local government	Central government
1918			Two European settlers on Executive Council. First Elections to Legislative Council. Indian on Executive Council
1923			Devonshire White Paper. Member to represent African interest on Executive Council
1924		Local Native Councils set up	
1927			Indians on Legislative Council
1928	Seven District Councils established		
1937			Reorganization of Executive Council
Second World War			
1944			First African member of Legislative Council
1948		African District Councils	Unofficial Majority on Legislative Council. Establishment of High Commission
1952	County Council Ordinance		Changes in composition of Legislative Council
1954			Council of Ministers

A distinguishing feature of Kenya local government is the existence of two different systems. In the table above these are set out under the headings 'Non-African local government' and 'African local government'. Under both, increasing responsibilities have been given to the local people; and since the 1952 County Council Ordinance it can be said that local government in Kenya is largely carried on by councils on which they are represented. In many ways this form of government is similar to that in England, but in Kenya the central government has always had more control over local affairs than the central government has had in England. Further details about the development of the Kenya system are given in the appendix.

Beginning of central government. In central government Kenya has undertaken an experiment in multi-racial rule of such importance that its development down to 1955 is given in detail. Central government began with the appointment of a Commissioner for the East Africa Protectorate. He recognized that there were a number of matters which affected the whole country; and by 1902 Departments of Agriculture, Forestry, Public Works, Trade and Customs, Land, Judicature, Medical Services, a Treasury and a Post Office had been set up. In 1905, when the Executive Council was formed, the members were chosen from the heads of these departments. This body was similar to the advisory council which governors usually had to help them in the nineteenth century.

First Legislative Council. In 1907 it was thought by the Colonial Office that the East Africa Protectorate was ready to take another step forward; and the new governor was given instructions to form a Legislative Council. There was no question at the time of any one being elected to the Council; the governor nominated eight men. Six of these were officials, that is men who were in the employment of the Colonial Office, and two were unofficials. These last two included Lord Delamere who hoped that his appointment meant that the settlers' opinions would be seriously considered. He soon found that its meetings were only to give formal consent to laws, estimates and supplies, and he sent in the first of his many resignations.

Introduction of the franchise. After the 1914 war the loyal support which had been given by British East Africa was rewarded by several constitutional changes. In 1918 it was announced that two European unofficials would be placed on the Executive Council. In the following year it was also announced that the long-awaited franchise would be granted to the Europeans, eleven of whom were to be elected to the Legislative Council. Eleven electoral areas were defined and the first elections to be held in the country took place the following year. In addition, it was planned that there should be five nominated Indian members, one member elected by the Arabs, and one European nominated to represent the Africans. The Indians were already resentful of the fact that land grants in the Highlands were not made to men of their race; and the proviso that Indian members should be nominated, and not elected, made them determined not to co-operate. In practice, therefore, there were no Indian members of the Legislative Council for another seven years.

The status of the Indian community. During these years prolonged and bitter discussions went on between the British government and the European and Indian communities in Kenya. The end of the war had meant for India, as well as Kenya, an advance in self-government. Indians everywhere were proudly aware of the aid their country had given to the imperial cause during the war. At the same time the Dominions had refused India's request for the removal of restrictions on immigration and there was friction in South Africa over the treatment of Indians. In Kenya the Indians were demanding equal representation with the Europeans on the Legislative Council, the end of segregation in the townships, and the right to hold land in the Highlands. They also asked for promotion on merit, not race, to the highest posts in the police, army and civil service. The Chief Secretary replied that 'His Excellency has no hesitation in affirming that universal suffrage for the Asiatics in this Protectorate on equality with the whites is out of the question.'

Devonshire White Paper. The Indians had no intention of accepting this and sent a deputation to England, which was soon followed by one from the settlers putting the opposite view. This position was further complicated by the close link, stressed in the earlier pages of this book, between East Africa and India. The Indian government, therefore, was particularly sensitive to events in East Africa which it felt might further disturb the troubled relations that already existed between England and India. For a time it looked as if it would be impossible to find a compromise, but, after a stormy interlude, the Devonshire White Paper of 1923 was issued. The terms of this settlement may be summarized as follows: Five Indian members were to be elected to the Legislative Council on a communal roll and there were also to be elections to the Nairobi Town Council on a communal basis. In practice the reservation of alienated land for Europeans in the Highlands was to be continued. Indian immigration was to be restricted in the economic interests of the Africans. A few years later the Indians took their seats in the Legislative Council, when it was made more fully representative in 1927. There was now an official majority of two. In this respect there were no further changes of importance until after the outbreak of the Second World War.

Changes in the Executive Council. There was, however, an important change affecting the Executive Council. This had existed from the start of British rule in East Africa. Roughly speaking it was a council consisting of advisers chosen by the governor, two of whom had, since 1919, been selected from the European settlers. This represented an advance towards self-government, although the Europeans felt that they still did not have very much say about the way in which the laws were carried out. An Indian was added in 1921; in 1923 an unofficial member was appointed to represent native interests, and in 1952 an African was appointed for this purpose. This still did not alter the fact that the Executive Council was almost entirely composed of officials.

Then in 1937 income tax was introduced, much against the will of the Europeans. In return for their acceptance of this, they were promised that the Executive Council should be reorganized. Henceforth it would consist of four members as apart from heads of departments; and the two European unofficial members would be appointed for a fixed period.

7-2

The relationship between the Legislative and the Executive Councils. The Council, therefore, now consisted of certain officials and unofficials. Out of this has grown a feature of the government of Kenya which is unique; and that is the appointment of the leader of the Europeans in the Legislative Council to one of the seats in the Executive Council, together with one of the members for Nairobi. As these two members are not bound to support the government, it sometimes happens that there are men who oppose the government present at its confidential discussions. It is important, however, to realize that this does not mean that the Legislative Council can control the Executive Council; it cannot. Even if the members of the Legislative Council are strongly opposed to the policy of the Executive Council, they cannot force the members of the latter to resign: the Executive Council is responsible to the governor and not to the Legislative Council; Kenya, therefore, is rightly described as not yet having full self-government.

Advances in self-government. The First World War had been followed by the grant of representative government to Kenya. The second was followed by a great advance in self-government in many parts of the British Commonwealth of Nations. India and Pakistan at last achieved this status in 1947. A year later Ceylon followed. A major change came also to the continent of Africa, when the Gold Coast and Nigeria were granted self-government. In East Africa the war was not over when the first advances were made, for in 1944 the first African took his seat in the Legislative Council. There were now two representatives of African interests. When this number was increased in 1948 to four, all of whom were Africans, there was for the first time an unofficial majority in the Legislative Council. Nor were these changes regarded as final. In 1952 there were further alterations in the composition of the Legislative Council, designed to fill the gap while discussions were held about the future constitution of the colony. The outbreak of Mau Mau terrorism has led, however, to these discussions being postponed and the composition of the Legislative Council in 1955 was as follows:

Official or government		Unofficial	
His Excellency as President		Europeans elected	14
Vice-President and Speaker		Asians elected	6
Ex officio	8	Africans nominated	6
Nominated	8	Arabs nominated	1
An additional number of nominated members who may be chosen from within or without the public service, but who are expected to vote for the government on matters the government considers of great importance	10	Arabs elected	1
	26		28

'*Ex officio*' means members who are present because of their office, for example the Minister for Finance. As they are helping to carry out the government's policy, these men will vote for it.

Council of Ministers. The power reserved for the Secretary of State for the Colonies (Mr Lyttleton) was well illustrated when he announced a proposal to alter the constitution by setting up a Council of Ministers which will be the chief instrument of government in the Colony. He stated that this body will have a collective responsibility for decisions on government policy. The members of the Council of Ministers will be:

The Governor.
The Chief Secretary.
The Minister for Legal Affairs.
The Minister for Finance and Development.
The Minister for African Affairs.
The Minister for Agriculture, Animal Husbandry and Water Resources.
The Minister for Internal Security and Defence.
The Minister for Local Government, Health and Housing.
The Minister for Education, Labour and Lands.
The Minister for Forest Development, Game and Fisheries.
The Minister for Commerce and Industries.
The Minister for Works.
The Minister for Community Development.
A European Minister without Portfolio.
An Asian Minister without Portfolio.

Of the six unofficial members, three will be European elected members, two will be Asian and one will be an African.

Allotment of posts. Mr Lyttleton then announced which posts were to be held by the official and nominated members. Greater interest, however, was taken in the allotting of responsibilities to the unofficial members, who had not previously taken any responsibility for the actions of the government, for it was realized that Kenya had now taken a long step forward on the road to multi-racial self-government. The posts given to the unofficial members were distributed on a racial basis as follows:

Minister without Portfolio (European).
Minister for Local Government, Health and Housing (European).
Minister with Agricultural Portfolio (European).
Minister of Works (Asian).
Minister without Portfolio (Asian).
Minister for Community Development (African).

At first sight it looked as though the Council of Ministers would take over the functions of the Executive Council. However, the Secretary of State was careful to add that this Council would remain and deal with such tasks as the approval of draft legislation. All members of the Council of Ministers would, however, be members of the Executive Council.

Under-secretaries. Another change introduced at this time was the appointment of a maximum of five Under-secretaries, one of whom will be an Arab, and two others Africans. These men will be able to gain valuable experience in governing.

The Lyttleton proposals did not meet with unqualified approval, many Africans considering that they should be allowed to choose their representatives by direct election. In 1956 this demand was met by the Coutts proposals, under which an African qualifies for the vote on a points system: points are awarded for age, education, property, etc.

Outline of central government. At this point it is possible to give an outline of the central government of Kenya. At the head is the governor, who represents the sovereign and has his power of veto. He is, however, controlled in his turn by the Secretary of State for the Colonies, who holds Cabinet rank in England. Immediately under the governor comes the secretariat. This is divided into sections, each of which deals with different branches of the administration. Out in the country its officers are Provincial Commissioners having District Commissioners below them, under whom again come the District Officers.

At the same time the governor is assisted by the Council of Ministers, whose functions were briefly described on p. 197 of this chapter, and by the Executive Council. Until 1954 this was a kind of 'steering committee', deciding the orders and importance of matters of policy to be submitted to the Legislative Council by the governor through his ministers. Since 1954 this function has been taken over by the Council of Ministers. The Secretary of State has, however, stated that the Executive Council will continue to deal with draft legislation. When 'bills' have been drafted by the various ministers they are submitted to the Executive Council before being presented to the Legislative Council. Bills when passed are called Ordinances—in Britain a Bill is called an Act when it has passed through Parliament. The Executive also has to approve the orders and rules which are made to carry out the Ordinances passed by the Legislative Council. The third function of the Executive Council is to deal with all disciplinary questions belonging to the Colonial Service.

The function of making laws belongs, as its name suggests, to the Legislative Council, and for a Bill to become an Ordinance it has to pass through the same stages as it goes through in the House of Commons. Apart from its composition, it should be noted that there are two important differences between the Legislative Council of Kenya and the Houses of Parliament in England. The first is that the Legislative Council cannot control the Executive Council in the way in which the House of Commons can control the Cabinet, whose members will be expected to resign if they are out-voted in the House of Commons on an important matter. In Kenya, however, let us suppose that the Minister of Finance, who is a permanent official and a member both of the Executive Council and the Council of Ministers, has introduced a bill which is out-voted in the Legislative Council.

The Minister of Finance does not have to resign, nor does the Executive Council or the Council of Ministers have to resign as a body, nor is the governor obliged to agree to the majority's decision in the Legislative Council.

In Kenya, as in England, there are Ministers who are responsible for the different departments. There is, for instance, a Minister of Finance, who is comparable with the Chancellor of the Exchequer, and whose task it is to introduce the Budget into the Legislative Council. He is, however, chosen by the governor, and, as has been shown above, is not subject to direct control by the Legislative Council. The second important difference between the Legislative Council and the Houses of Parliament is that the latter can, if it should be necessary, legislate on behalf of a Colonial Council.

The composition of the Legislative Council was given on p. 197 of this chapter. It remains to add that each Legislative Council lasts four years and meets about four times each year in Nairobi; and that its laws cannot be vetoed by the Executive Council. This power is reserved for the governor alone.

The chief qualifications for the franchise are that you should be a British subject, either a male Arab, or of European or Indian origin, twenty-one years of age, and have resided in the colony for a year. You must also have lived in the area in which you wish to vote for at least three months. (You can be disqualified on certain grounds, such as insanity.) Similar qualifications are needed for election to the Legislative Council, but they are a little stricter.

Inter-territorial co-operation. It has been shown that local government bodies have expanded to cover much wider areas than the ridges which the tribal councils ruled before the coming of the British government. In a similar way the powers of the central government developed; and it became necessary to consider how common problems should be solved by the protectorate of Uganda, the mandated territory of Tanganyika, and the colony and protectorate of Kenya.

Before the Second World War there had been talk of federation, but it was felt that this was premature. At the same time the three countries shared many problems which it was wasteful to consider separately. From 1926 onwards, therefore, there was always a conference twice a year between the governors of the three lands, together with the British Resident of Zanzibar. It had no authority and its decisions could be carried out only after they had been referred to the various governments. During the Second World War the need for this co-operation was seen even more clearly; and it was finally agreed that an East African High Commission should be set up, consisting of the governors of Kenya, Tanganyika and Uganda. At the same time, in 1948, the East African Central Legislative Assembly was created to provide a means of discussion of the common interests of the three territories.

Composition of the East African Central Legislative Assembly. On the official side there are seven *ex officio* members who are officers in the service of the High Commission and three others, one being nominated from each territory by the governor. The Speaker is appointed by the High Commission. The thirteen unofficial members are chosen as follows: one is elected by the unofficial members of the Legislative Council of each territory, making a total of three; one European, one Indian and one African member are appointed by the governor of each territory (in Kenya the European and Indian members are elected by the European and Indian members respectively of the Legislative Council) and one Arab member appointed by the High Commission.

Services. Because it concerned all three territories, and was best dealt with by the newly created High Commission, the Kenya–Uganda railway and harbours fell under the High Commission and became known as the East African Railways and Harbours. Other services which fall under the High Commission are the Posts and Telecommunications, Customs, Research and Income Tax. These were selected because their separate functioning had been shown to be wasteful of time and money. There is no advantage, for instance, in having three different sets of stamps; and there are things to be gained by post-office workers sharing each others' training schools. The three territories also have sufficient similar research problems for it to be an economy of effort to share the same research stations in medicine and agriculture.

The services of the High Commission can be divided today into two groups. The first are 'self-contained' and include the services that pay for themselves, such as Customs, Posts and Telegraphs, Railways. The second are the services that require financial assistance, such as the Desert Locust Survey and the East African Literature Bureau; many of these are partly financed by the Colonial Development and Welfare Fund.

GOVERNMENT OF KENYA, 1955

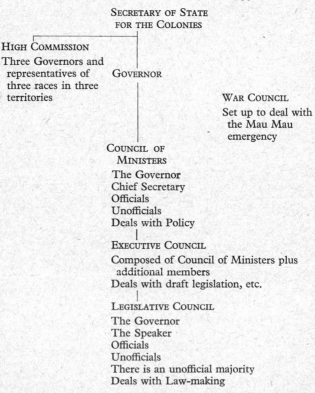

SECRETARY OF STATE
FOR THE COLONIES

HIGH COMMISSION
Three Governors and
representatives of
three races in three
territories

GOVERNOR

WAR COUNCIL
Set up to deal with
the Mau Mau
emergency

COUNCIL OF
MINISTERS
The Governor
Chief Secretary
Officials
Unofficials
Deals with Policy

EXECUTIVE COUNCIL
Composed of Council of Ministers plus
additional members
Deals with draft legislation, etc.

LEGISLATIVE COUNCIL
The Governor
The Speaker
Officials
Unofficials
There is an unofficial majority
Deals with Law-making

CHAPTER XIII

THE LATER HISTORY OF UGANDA

When Sir Gerald Portal hastened from Kampala in 1893 he left Captain Macdonald to act as commissioner in his place. The problems of Uganda had now begun to change, for the hostility between the political-religious groups was subsiding, and with the arrival of Bishop Hanlon in 1895 to take over the new Roman Catholic diocese which had been allotted to the Mill Hill Fathers, hostility between the two factions practically ceased and the number of Christian converts multiplied at a remarkable speed.

The Mohammedan rising of 1893. But during Macdonald's brief period as acting commissioner one of the old parties revived and made its last effort. This was the Mohammedan party which, in 1893, began to demand a greater share of territory than the three small chieftainships allotted to them in the previous year. What made this agitation a particular danger was the fact that the Sudanese troops under Selim Bey, who had been introduced by Lugard from Kavalli's, were openly sympathetic, for they too were Mohammedans—and it was feared that there would be a general rising of the Mohammedan party supported by the Sudanese. This was prevented by the defeat of the Mohammedans by the Baganda Protestants, the disarming of the Sudanese garrison at Port Alice (now Entebbe), and the arrest of Selim Bey. Macdonald's prompt action almost certainly prevented another civil war.

The Invasion of Bunyoro. The next trouble came from Bunyoro. The line of forts left along the Toro-Bunyoro border by Lugard rapidly became centres from which the Sudanese garrisons raided the surrounding country, and Sir Gerald Portal had accordingly moved these garrisons into Buganda, where they could be effectively supervised. No sooner had they been withdrawn than Kabarega of Bunyoro took the chance of resuming his raids into Toro and drove Kasagama, whom Lugard had reinstated, back into the Ruwenzori Mountains.

For this reason, and also because Bunyoro had long been regarded as a refuge for revolutionaries from Buganda, the new commissioner, Colonel Colvile, decided that Bunyoro must be taken if there was to be peace. The invasion of Bunyoro was launched on the last day of 1893 when Baganda and Sudanese troops crossed the Kafu River and overran the country. To make the occupation more effective a line of forts was built from Kibiro on Lake Albert southwards to Hoima and Baranwa. Kabarega, for all his faults, was a courageous leader; he withdrew northwards into the forests and a series of campaigns was necessary before he was finally captured five years later. The southern portion of his kingdom was divided in 1894 between the Protestant and Catholic Baganda chiefs, while Kasagama returned to Toro.

The years of peace, 1894–7. With the subjugation of Bunyoro and the Mohammedan party, and with the old Protestant and Catholic feud dead and buried, the next three years were unusually peaceful and prosperous ones for Uganda. Apart from guerilla warfare against Kabarega, the only cause for apprehension was the approach of the Belgians from the west. This was settled by the Anglo-Belgian agreement of 1894, by which the boundary between the British and Belgian spheres was fixed at 30° E. and along the Nile-Congo watershed. Meanwhile Portal's report had been considered by Parliament, and on 18 June 1894 the British government officially accepted the protectorate of Buganda. And although it did not yet officially accept responsibility for Bunyoro, Toro, and Ankole, the British maintained garrisons in the first two and the commissioner agreed to protect Ankole.

The rising of the chiefs, 1897. The formal acceptance of the protectorate in 1894 came as a great relief to both Catholic and Protestant missions. It did not, however, to Mwanga. He did not like the restrictions on his power which the protectorate involved, or the high standard of conduct advocated by the missions. He was not alone in these dislikes. Several of his chiefs also wanted a return to the bad old days. In 1897, therefore, these chiefs, probably aided by Mwanga, planned a revolt, which was fortunately discovered. The chiefs con-

cerned were arrested and Mwanga fled across the lake to Buddu,
where he raised a large army to support him. The acting commissioner,
Major Ternan, had just led a punitive expedition against the Nandi,
who were raiding along the caravan route. He marched out to meet

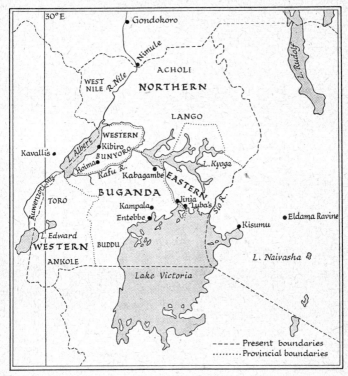

Map 14. Uganda.

Mwanga with Baganda and Sudanese troops. After a sharp battle
ending in a bayonet charge the rebels were defeated, and Mwanga fled.
The rebel troops did not give up so easily, however, for they went to
Marongo on the Ankole frontier, which was notorious as a hideout
for criminals from Buganda, known as the 'colony of bhang smokers'.

Together with these criminals they made a second stand against Major Ternan, but were again defeated, and by August the rebellion was over. Meanwhile, in place of Mwanga, Daudi Chwa, his infant son, was proclaimed Kabaka, with a regency of three leading chiefs.

The Sudanese mutiny, the causes. No sooner had Mwanga's rebellion been dealt with than a mutiny broke out among the Sudanese troops. In view of the trouble these troops caused it would be easy to get too evil a picture of them. As their behaviour in the Toro forts showed, they were certainly not angels; on the other hand they had many good qualities—their courage was beyond question—and in 1897 their grievances were very real. Having fought against Kabarega in Bunyoro they had been marched several hundred miles east against the Nandi. As soon as the Nandi campaign was over they had been marched west again to Buddu to deal with Mwanga, and immediately that rebellion was crushed they were ordered to march back east again to Eldama Ravine. This time it was for an expedition under Major Macdonald to explore the headwaters of the Juba River and also to be ready to give assistance against French expeditions from the Congo and Abyssinia, and against Mahdists in the southern Sudan as General Kitchener advanced upon Omdurman. Had the Sudanese been well led they might have accompanied the expedition loyally, but in fact their European officers, who were good and popular, were continually changing, and this unsettled the troops. Above all, their pay was far less than that of Sudanese troops at Machakos or in German East Africa, and even so it was six months in arrears. On the other side of the picture there is little doubt that some of the leaders, such as Mabruk Effendi, wanted to create trouble in order to gain control of Uganda for the Sudanese, and that they used the very genuine grievances of the soldiers simply as a means to achieve this end.

The events of the mutiny, 1897–8. The mutiny started on 23 September 1897 near Eldama Ravine, which was the collecting centre for Macdonald's expedition. Macdonald and Jackson who was with him were in no position to grant all the Sudanese requests, as they themselves had strict orders from Britain concerning the expedition. When the troops did not receive satisfaction they marched back towards

Buganda, killing and looting as they went, and finally took up their position in Luba's fort. Major Thruston, who was in military charge of Uganda, went to Luba's to negotiate with them, but while there he was imprisoned with two other Europeans and later all three were killed. Meanwhile Macdonald, with Swahili and Baganda troops, besieged Luba's, which held out determinedly from October 1897 to January 1898. Constant attacks were made upon it and in one Macdonald's brother was killed with G. L. Pilkington of the C.M.S., whose translation of the Bible into Luganda had made him one of the most popular missionaries in the country. The situation was now critical. Indian troops had been sent for from Jubaland and from Bombay but could not arrive without considerable delay. Meanwhile it was feared that the other Sudanese garrisons in Bunyoro, Toro, Buddu, and Kampala might join the mutiny. To make matters worse Mwanga reappeared in Buddu in January declaring himself a Mohammedan, and raised 2000 armed troops. Macdonald had to take part of the force besieging Luba's in order to deal with Mwanga, who was quickly defeated. But while Macdonald was away the mutineers took the opportunity to escape from Luba's, and began to march towards Bunyoro, where the Sudanese garrisons were showing signs of joining the mutineers. The immediate danger was averted by the arrival of Lieut. Scott with Indian and Swahili troops, who marched sixty-five miles in three days, disarmed the Sudanese garrisons in Bunyoro, and prevented the mutineers from joining them. The last major stand of the Sudanese was at Kabagambe on the central part of the southern shore of Lake Kyoga, where they were successfully attacked in February 1898. A number of them fled across Lake Kyoga and carried on local skirmishes until the last were dispersed by the Lango expedition of 1901, but the real danger had ended with the storming of Kabagambe.

The exile of Kabarega and Mwanga. Meanwhile two royal trouble-makers had at last been caught—Kabarega and Mwanga. Mwanga had fled to Kabarega after being defeated by Macdonald. When captured in 1899 the two prisoners presented a remarkable contrast. Mwanga was despondent in the extreme, but Kabarega was a proud monarch to the end. While in hospital he kicked a European doctor's bottom for attending to a sick man of humble origin before himself. Both kings were exiled to the Seychelles, where Mwanga died in 1903, and although Kabarega returned to Jinja twenty years later he died of influenza almost at once.

The need for reorganization in Buganda. Throughout the Uganda mutiny the three regent chiefs of Buganda had shown remarkable loyalty and good sense, and had been supported by the great majority of the Baganda people. But the country was exhausted, disorganized, and full of troops. This led to difficulties between the military and civil authorities, and the home government decided to send out a Special Commission to reorganize the administration.

Size and condition of the protectorate in 1900. The man selected as Special Commissioner was Sir Harry Johnston, whose period of office was the turning point in Uganda's history. In 1894, as we have seen, the British had assumed a protectorate over Buganda (known as the Kingdom of Uganda until 1908 when it was changed to the current word Buganda) but by the end of the nineteenth century the protectorate of Uganda had come to include a much greater area than just the Kabaka's kingdom. In fact the area which comprised the protectorate of Uganda when Johnston arrived was about double the present size of the protectorate. Its boundary extended from Gondokoro eastwards to Lake Rudolf and then southwards through Naivasha to the northern border of German East Africa, which extended from Kilimanjaro to Lake Victoria at 1° S. and then was continued westwards to the 30th meridian of longitude. This marked the western boundary, following the Congo-Nile watershed. The only non-Africans were the Protestant and Catholic missionaries, apart from a very few European, Indian, and Arab traders. The only external trade which could pay for the enormous cost of porterage to the coast was ivory, and until the arrival of the railway at Port Florence (Kisumu) at the end of 1901 communication was difficult and extremely slow.

Sir Harry Johnston. Johnston already had a very wide experience of African affairs when he arrived. Besides being a doctor of science, an author, and a painter, he also was a great administrator and traveller. In 1882 he had visited the Congo area; two years later he led an expedition to Kilimanjaro; in 1887 he was in the consular service in West Africa, and two years later he was appointed consul-general for Portuguese South-East Africa, where he followed up Lugard's work in stopping the slave trade in Nyasaland and establishing a settled administration there. From 1897 to 1899 he was consul-general in Tunis. He left this post to take up his appointment in Uganda.

The 1900 agreement: the land settlement. The three main questions he was called upon to deal with were concerned with land ownership, taxation, and government. As Buganda was the most advanced of the provinces under his jurisdiction, it was with Buganda that he made the first, and most important, agreement on these points. The land question was the one which aroused the greatest controversy and which had the deepest effects. Before 1900 all land had been regarded as belonging to the Kabaka, who had the power to turn a chief out of office and out of his land at a moment's notice. After discussions with the three regents, the leading chiefs, and the missions, Johnston put forward the suggestion that assuming the area of Buganda to be about 19,000 square miles—which was actually an over-estimate—about 10,000 square miles were to be Crown land, 1000 square miles were to be allocated to the royal family and principal chiefs, and the remaining 8000 square miles were to be divided between all existing landowners. The 9000 square miles which were not allocated to the Crown were known as the 'mailo' lands (from the English square mile), and the division of them was a gigantic task, which Johnston wisely left the Buganda Council (Lukiko) to settle. The effect of this land arrangement was to break down the old feudal organization, and the security given by the new system of absolute ownership provided a great incentive to increase production.

The financial settlement. The second question to be decided by the agreement was that of finance. The cost of administration had hitherto been paid by Britain through Parliament, and during the previous three years had cost a million pounds. By the agreement of 1900 the Baganda were asked to help to pay for the administration by a hut tax of three rupees a year. As they had paid tribute to the Kabaka from time immemorial, this was accepted without difficulty, although at first the people did not find it easy to raise the money. This was chiefly due to the shortage of rupees. Many of the population had never seen one. For a while the government accepted 2400 cowrie shells instead, and wild animals were also accepted, if brought to Entebbe alive, at the rate of 1000 huts for an elephant, 100 huts for a hippopotamus and so on, until the streets of the little township became so like a zoo that the government insisted again on rupees. The effect of the tax upon Baganda life was startling, for it made the earning of wages a necessity and spurred even the slothful into taking some sort of work. Unfortunately, however, it also led to overcrowding, and in 1909 was replaced by a native poll tax, which is now the chief source of revenue.

The constitutional settlement. The assumption on which Johnston based his proposals concerning the government of Buganda was that the old forms of government should be retained and modified under the supervision of the British administration. In was, in fact, the principle of indirect rule, which was particularly suitable to Buganda, where native government was already strong. By the 1900 agreement the Kabaka, assisted by the Lukiko, was to continue to rule in Buganda over the Baganda, his decisions being subject to the approval of the commissioner or governor. Daudi Chwa was recognized as Kabaka, the succession to the throne being confined to the family of Mutesa. The Parliament was to contain the Prime Minister (Katikiro), the Chief Justice (Omulamuzi), the Treasurer (Omuwanika), twenty county or saza chiefs, three important men from each county, and six other important people. All were to be appointed by the Kabaka and approved by the British government. In addition a committee of the Lukiko was appointed to act as a court of appeal. Besides having its central government, Buganda was divided into counties supervised by a saza chief, each county was divided into gombololas according to its population and size, and in each gombolola were villages, also with chiefs.

Such were the essentials of the 1900 agreement with Buganda. No other kingdom in the protectorate was given such extensive control of its affairs, but agreements were also made with Toro in 1900, with Ankole in 1901, and much later with Bunyoro in 1933.

Boundary alterations in the twentieth century. Johnston left Uganda in 1901, having laid the foundations on which the protectorate developed. In the twenty-five years which followed his Commission the size of the Uganda protectorate was practically halved. The first portion to be lost was the eastern area, lying between the Sio River and Naivasha, which was ceded to the East Africa Protectorate in 1902. In 1914 the Gondokoro and Nimule districts were also ceded —to the Anglo-Egyptian Sudan—but at the same time the present West Nile district was acquired by Uganda. In 1926 yet a third adjustment was made, by which the Rudolf Province, lying between the Turkana escarpment and Lake Rudolf, passed to Kenya. But although Uganda's size has been halved, there still remains a compact and fairly well-populated territory, which has been brought under organized administration so peacefully that the Foreign Office was able to transfer control of the protectorate to the Colonial Office as early as 1905.

The development of the central government, 1900–54. The government, as well as the boundary, of Uganda has changed since Johnston's time. The agreement of 1900 was followed in 1902 by the Uganda Order in Council which established the constitution of the protectorate. By this Order the administration of the whole of Uganda was put into the hands of a commissioner, whose title was changed in 1907 to that of governor; he was the direct representative of the British sovereign. The next major step in political development came in 1921 when the first Executive and Legislative Councils sat in Uganda. When this first Legislative Council was constituted it was a comparatively small affair with four government members and two European unofficial members. It was not until 1926 that the first Asian member was appointed. In the 1930's the attention of the country was absorbed by the world economic crisis, but in the 1940's there was a definite increase in political interest among Africans in the protectorate, especially after the Second World War. Since then

African representation in the central government has grown rapidly. In 1945 Africans were represented for the first time on the Legislative Council, which was reorganized with seven government members and seven unofficial members (two Europeans, two Asians, and three Africans) besides the governor, whose vote gave the government side a majority. Membership of the Council was further increased in 1947, 1948, and in 1950, when African representation was made equal to that of the European and Asian unofficial members combined. An even bigger change came in 1954 when the Council was reconstituted and enlarged with twenty-eight official members (this included eleven cross-bench members—six Africans, four Europeans, one Asian—who were drawn from the public and could vote and speak as they wished except on matters of confidence, when they were obliged to support the government), and twenty-eight representative, or unofficial, members (fourteen Africans, seven Europeans, seven Asians).

Provincial administration. As well as this Central Administration, the protectorate is divided into four provinces—Buganda Province, Northern Province, Eastern Province and Western Province. The Northern, Eastern and Western Provinces are each supervised by a Provincial Commissioner who is generally responsible for public affairs in his province. Each province is divided into districts, each of which is supervised by a District Commissioner (aided by Assistant District Commissioners) who is responsible to the Provincial Commissioner, and who consults with representatives of the African local governments on local affairs. In Buganda the administrative hierarchy is: Resident, Senior Assistant Resident (who may or may not be Protectorate Agent in addition) and Assistant Resident.

Local government. The relationship of Buganda to the central government is different from that of the other provinces on account of the 1900 agreement. Subject to the governor's consent, the Kabaka and the Lukiko have power to make laws for all natives of Buganda. In the other provinces are African local governments at different stages of development. There are African rulers in the Ankole, Toro, and Bunyoro districts of the Western Province and each of these has appointed ministers and councils. In other districts, where there is no ruler, the African local government consists of senior executive officers and chiefs exercising executive authority, assisted by local councils. There are also District Councils (consisting of chiefs, elected members and nominated persons) which give the people as a whole some experience of local government on democratic lines by allowing them, through their representatives, to express their opinions on matters of local or tribal interest. The Buganda and the African local governments have their own treasuries.

It is not within the scope of this book to trace the development of each province of the protectorate, and it must suffice to say that in the provinces as well as in the central government, an increasing amount of administrative responsibility has been given to the African population. This is in accordance with the government's long-term aim of building Uganda into a self-governing state with the government of the country mainly in the hands of Africans.

Buganda and the 1953 crisis. The importance, however, of the kingdom of Buganda calls for an outline of its development, especially in connexion with the constitutional crisis of 1953. For about forty years following the 1900 agreement, the relations between the Buganda and protectorate governments were, generally speaking, good. In the 1940's, following the Second World War, unrest came in the shape of strikes and riots in 1945 and 1949, in which economic discontent was mixed with political agitation for a more democratic Lukiko. But it was not until the 1950's that a major crisis occurred. Two factors played a major part. One was the desire of the Baganda to preserve and improve the status and institutions of their kingdom. This desire had already shown itself, amongst other things, in the determination of the Baganda to resist all suggestions concerning East African federation lest it might decrease their control over Buganda. The second factor was the political condition of Buganda in relation to the protectorate government. The Lukiko had been democratized a few years after the 1949 rebellion; this had decreased the Kabaka's influence on the council, but he was still virtually the sole link between it and the governor. In 1953 this link was severely strained when an occasion of difference was unintentionally provoked by a remark of the Colonial Secretary which was regarded as raising again the issue of East African federation.

It was unfortunate that circumstances should have forced two such men as the governor and the Kabaka into political collision, for both were sincerely anxious to promote the interests of the African people. Sir Andrew Cohen had come to Uganda as governor in 1952, when his achievements as head of the African Department of the Colonial Office had already made him famous. He had been closely associated with the rapid progress of the West African territories towards self-government, and he came to Uganda with the aim of democratizing not only the government of Buganda but also the government of the protectorate; he aimed also at a great expansion in education and industry. His faith in the ability of Africans to develop self-government was beyond question. The Kabaka Mutesa II, who had succeeded Daudi Chwa in 1942 at the age of eighteen, had been one of the first to welcome the appointment of Sir Andrew, for they were old friends. Frederick Mutesa himself was no illiterate despot but a man of education faced with a powerful Lukiko. Educated at King's College, Budo; Makerere College, Kampala; and at Cambridge University; and serving for a time with the Grenadier Guards (becoming a Captain), the Kabaka was a man with European as well as African attachments. Nevertheless, when the fears of an East African federation were revived in 1953 he decided to support his ministers and the Lukiko in demanding, among other things, that the federation issue should be dropped, and that Buganda should become independent within 'a short, stated space of time'. Sir Andrew, after consultation with the Colonial Secretary, gave a speedy assurance that a policy of federation would not be followed, but he refused to grant the request for immediate independence, which was considered impractical, for Uganda had always been developed as a united territory whose main centres— Kampala and Entebbe—were situated in Buganda. The Kabaka, in accordance with the 1900 agreement, was expected by the governor to support these views in the Lukiko. The Lukiko stated later that 'If he had chosen to do the Governor's bidding, we, the Lukiko would have expelled him'. As it was, the Kabaka refused to comply and announced his intention to oppose the governor's decisions publicly and to advise the Lukiko to reject them. After persistent attempts at compromise had failed, recognition was withdrawn from him by the British government in November 1953 and he was deported to Britain.

The Namirembe recommendations. To end the political deadlock the Colonial Secretary invited Professor Sir Keith Hancock to visit Uganda and make proposals in connexion with the Buganda constitution. These proposals, which were made at the Namirembe Conference (1954) where he acted as independent chairman, included the suggestion that while the kingdom of Buganda should remain an integral part of the protectorate of Uganda, certain constitutional changes were desirable. It was proposed that the conduct of public affairs in Buganda should be in the hands of ministers, and that to implement this proposal the Buganda ministerial system should be broadened to include a Minister of Health, a Minister of Education, and a Minister of Natural Resources, as well as the existing Katikiro, Omulamuzi, and Omuwanika. These six ministers, who together would constitute the Ministry, were to be elected by the Lukiko, approved by the governor, and appointed by the Kabaka. At the same time it was proposed that responsibility for important social services, including education and health, should be transferred to the Buganda government. In addition it was suggested that consultative committees should be set up to promote understanding and to settle future points of difference between the protectorate and the Buganda governments, so that the Kabaka would no longer be virtually the sole link between them. The Kabaka himself was to become a constitutional monarch; all his traditional titles and dignities were to be retained; all laws passed by the Lukiko were to be signed by him; but ministers, and not the Kabaka, were to be responsible for every act and were to take the blame for all mistakes, and through them formal communications with the protectorate government were to be made. To these proposals the Constitutional Committee, which the Lukiko had elected to negotiate on its behalf, unanimously agreed. So also did the governor. However, as the Kabaka had been deported, he could not give his consent to the proposals, and without his consent they could not become authoritative. With this difficulty unsolved unrest in Buganda continued.

A ministerial system of government for the protectorate, 1955. While the proposals were being considered, further changes were proposed by the governor and were introduced in the constitution of the central government, with effect from July 1955. Their main purpose was to associate the people of Uganda more closely with the executive side of the government, and a ministerial system of government was introduced. Seven members of the public (five being Africans) were invited by the governor to sit on the government side of the Legislative Council. Five of these (three being Africans) also became members of the Executive Council with the status of Ministers. In addition two African Parliamentary Under-secretaries were appointed. The structure of the Legislative Council was not drastically altered, in view of the major alterations which had already been made in 1954, but there were adjustments to increase the representation of Buganda and the two other most heavily populated districts outside Buganda —Busoga and Ankole. These adjustments increased the total membership of the Council from fifty-six to sixty (thirty officials, including a government back-bench, and thirty unofficials) and brought the proportion of African members to half the total. In order to secure stability the governor proposed that no further revisions should be made until 1961.

The new Buganda agreement, 1955. During 1955 the constitutional difficulties of Buganda were also settled. A delegation from the Lukiko negotiated with the British government a transitional agreement which ran until the main agreement was signed by the Kabaka when he returned to Buganda—amid tremendous enthusiasm —in October. This agreement was unanimously accepted by the Lukiko and followed in the main the recommendations of the Namirembe Conference. However, an important new feature was that direct elections for the Baganda members of the Legislative Council were promised in 1961, and possibly in 1957 if the Baganda government could produce a workable scheme by then. In the unravelling of this political knot, it is interesting to notice that the Baganda appealed to reason and not to violence, and that the British were willing to consider and, in some cases, to grant, the requests of the Baganda people.

Economic development: cotton. The economic history of the Uganda Protectorate is one of steadily increasing prosperity. Sir Harry Johnston had found a country where ivory was the only export, and he anticipated that the most likely method of increasing prosperity would be the encouragement of plantations of rubber, coffee, and cocoa under European management. It was Sir Hesketh Bell, who was commissioner, and later governor from 1905–9, who was mainly responsible for the decision that Uganda should be developed as an African state. A major factor leading to this decision was the astonishing success of African farmers in growing American upland cotton. This had been introduced into Uganda almost simultaneously by Mr Borup of the C.M.S. and by the protectorate government in 1903–4. After 1915 the output of cotton had grown sufficiently to enable the protectorate to dispense with the assistance of a grant-in-aid. In the early 1950's cotton exports alone brought in £15–30 million annually, making cotton easily the greatest single product. It did, in fact, bring in more than all the other exports put together. This great development during the last fifty years has been steadily encouraged by the government, which has carefully controlled the type of seed used, supplied it free to African growers, and generally supervised and assisted the industry throughout. The area now occupied by cotton is over a million acres, and all of it is grown by Africans on plots which range from the size of a tablecloth to fields of several acres where hired or communal labour is necessary. Preparation of the plots begins in April and planting is done between May and September. Harvesting usually begins in November or December and is followed by a definite limited buying season. The buying is now restricted to ginneries and stores at established centres, and the price is fixed by the Governor-in-Council after consultation with the Lint Marketing Board, which controls the marketing, processing, and disposal of cotton. Most of the 140–150 ginneries in Uganda are owned by Asians, but Ordinances passed in 1952 have enabled Africans to share in the ginning industry, and by 1954 seven working ginneries had been acquired by the government for sale or lease to African co-operative societies. The world importance of Uganda's cotton production lies in its quality rather than in its quantity, for its production is only 1 per cent of the world's total. Its price depends mainly on the cotton markets of Egypt, the Mississippi Delta, South Carolina, Peru, and Brazil, whose staple is of similar length.

Coffee. The crop next in economic importance is coffee. As early as 1903 coffee was exported from Uganda, but it was during the slump following the 1914–18 war that the Agricultural Department began to encourage Africans to grow coffee as an alternative cash crop. During the early 1950's the crop brought in £11–12 million annually, and today Uganda is the greatest coffee producer in the Empire. By far the greater part of the crop is grown by Africans and is of the Robusta variety. Again, production is encouraged and controlled by the government. The raw coffee is processed either at a hullery or at a curing works, and marketing is the responsibility of the Coffee Industry Board. Other important agricultural exports include tobacco, tea, hides and skins, sugar, fish, and ground-nuts.

Mining. The mining possibilities of Uganda were not seriously considered until after the 1914–18 war, and minerals still do not provide a major part of Uganda's exports. Those of value are located mainly in the Western Province, and at present tin and wolfram are of chief importance. However, the copper deposits which were discovered at Kilembe in 1927 became important when the railway extension from Kampala reached Kasese in 1956.

The development of transport. In connexion with the economic development of Uganda, two other factors should be mentioned. The first is the railway, on which all development has depended. Without it transport costs would have made profitable production impossible. For example, before the railway was built the cost of head porterage from Uganda to Mombasa might be as much as £300 per ton, whereas the rail freight on cotton lint for that distance is now less than £5 per ton. At first the cotton-growing regions of Uganda were linked to the railhead at Kisumu by steamers across Lake Victoria. In 1912 the Busoga railway, joining Jinja and Kakindu, was completed and later extended to Namasagali. In 1927 it was joined to the main line from Kenya. However, it was not until the Nile bridge was built at Jinja in 1931 that the main line reached from Kampala to the coast. In the early 1950's the Western Uganda extension carried the railway still further into the interior, and by 1955 it reached Nkonge, almost exactly 1000 miles by rail from the coast. In 1956 the extension was completed to the railhead near Kilembe. With this development of the railway has gone a remarkable extension of road transport to feed the railheads, and today Uganda's road system has made possible the production of cotton in all parts of the protectorate where the climate is suitable. The steamer services on the lakes also provide an essential link in Uganda's communications.

Hydro-electric power. The second factor which should be mentioned is the Owen Falls Hydro-electric Scheme. It was Sir Winston Churchill who wrote in 1907 that 'it would be perfectly easy to let the Nile begin its long and beneficent journey to the sea by leaping through a turbine'. In 1954 his statement became a reality when the Queen opened the great dam thrown across the Nile at Jinja. The electrical power from Owen Falls will have the very important effect of raising the standard of living by making possible the establishment of further industries. Moreover, it will affect not only Uganda but other territories as well, and in 1955 negotiations were completed for the supply of electricity from the Owen Falls to Kenya.

Setbacks to development. The chief setback to Uganda's economic development was the appalling outbreak of sleeping sickness which was first noticed at the C.M.S. hospital at Namirembe in 1901. Fortunately it did not spread over the whole protectorate but was confined to certain areas of Buganda, Busoga, and the islands of Lake Victoria, but in these regions two out of every three people died of it. In 1903 the disease was traced to a trypanosome carried by the tsetse fly, but this was only the beginning. From 1906 the drastic step was taken of evacuating all the affected areas, and this, together with constant medical attention, had a definite effect. By 1910 the worst of the epidemic was over, but in the meantime nearly a quarter of a million people had died. But apart from this, and the effects of the two world wars, Uganda's economic development has been rapid, and the annual value of her exports is generally more than that of Kenya.

Social development. The African population. The social history of Uganda during the first half of the twentieth century is a happy one, with no serious clash of race or class. The British government has consistently emphasized that its purpose is to promote the interests of the African people of the protectorate, and in this it has undoubtedly succeeded. The African population, which in 1900 was concerned chiefly in producing enough food for itself and measured its wealth mainly by head of cattle, has generally readjusted itself to a money economy based on the export of agricultural products, and the mutually hostile tribes which once comprised the protectorate now live at peace under an administration which they share and modify according to local custom. So much has changed and yet much that was good still remains. The family is still the chief unit in African society, and although home life varies with the climate and vegetation of the different regions of Uganda, most homesteads consist of perhaps eight acres and are largely self-supporting, with their land allocated partly to cotton and coffee, and partly to food crops such as plantains, millets, and sweet potatoes. As the profits from cotton and coffee provide what monetary wealth is required, and as there is generally no shortage of land, the African population has shown no sign of moving into the chief towns in large numbers, most of them preferring to remain close to the soil. With cultivation and economic progress has gone the vital development of education. In this the missionary societies have, as always, played a leading part. Educational facilities, on which expenditure increased five-fold between 1950–55, include not only schools but also Makerere College, which is the University College for the whole of the East African territories.

The European and Asian populations. The Asians and Europeans are a very small proportion of the total population of Uganda. Nevertheless, they play extremely important parts in the country's life—the Europeans in the administration of the protectorate, in missionary work, in commerce, and in the professions, and the Asians in trade, replacing the Arabs who were the chief traders early in the century. The Asians have also recently provided a most successful mayor for Kampala.

CHAPTER XIV

THE LATER HISTORY OF TANGANYIKA

General outline of development. The area comprising German East Africa, according to the 1886 and 1890 Partition Treaties, was substantially the same as that of Tanganyika today, except that German East Africa included the Ruanda and Urundi areas, which are now under Belgian trusteeship. Its history since 1886 may be divided into four main periods. The first lasted until 1907 and was chiefly occupied in suppressing the numerous rebellions which occurred; the second period lasted until 1914 and was characterized by a sincere, but only partially successful, attempt by the German government to develop the country by paying particular attention to the African population and to communications; the third period was that of the First World War from 1914 to 1918, during which the present Tanganyika suffered more than any other part of Africa; the fourth, and happiest, period is that of British administration shaped by the outstanding governorships of Sir Donald Cameron and Sir Edward Twining. We shall look at each period in turn.

The Germans and colonization. It was unfortunate for Germany, and still more unfortunate for East Africa, that the man who set the pattern of early colonization there was Carl Peters, generally known by the Africans as 'Mkono-wa-damu' or 'the man with the blood-stained hands'. But the Germans were not all like Peters, and the achievements of Germany in East Africa have not all been military. The first missionary to East Africa was Krapf, who was a German; the most thorough early agricultural research was done by Germans, whose research station at Amani was a model; and the greatest early advances in African education were made by Germans. When all its achievements are reckoned Germany has much to its credit. The disastrous early period, which was largely due to Peters's influence, should not lead us to the conclusion that the Germans and their administration were wholly evil. There was good as well as bad.

Aims and methods of British and German companies. As we have already seen, the development of German East Africa after the 1886 Partition treaty was undertaken not by the German government but by the German East Africa Company, started in 1888; like the British Company it received from the Sultan a concession to administer the mainland opposite its sphere of influence, but the aims and methods of the British and German companies were in sharp contrast. The British had accepted their sphere of influence reluctantly as a political and moral necessity, and were mainly concerned with developing the trade of the region, stopping the slave trade, and encouraging the missions; no major alterations were made in administration, nor at first was there any alienation of land for European settlement. The general result was that in the British sphere the Africans and Arabs accepted the Company peacefully. To the south the story was different. The Germans had acquired their region partly in the hope that an empire in Africa would bring them prestige, political power and wealth, and partly to provide an outlet for the large number of German emigrants without losing their attachment to the fatherland. The Company came, therefore, with the intention of making sweeping changes, and the clear aim of establishing German plantations. It is not surprising that their arrival met with opposition, while that of the British Company did not.

The end of the Company's administration. The first opposition came from the Arabs, whose trade and administrative functions the German Company intended to replace. Bushiri's rebellion and its suppression by Captain Wissman have already been described. In East Africa the effect was to create widespread anti-European feeling, in Germany to convince the government that the Company was incapable of administering the region; in 1891, accordingly, the Company handed over its administrative powers to the imperial government. But the situation did not improve, for the simple reason that the same officials with the same ideas still remained, including Carl Peters, who became Imperial High Commissioner for the Kilimanjaro district. In 1892 he was indicted by a German judge for excessive cruelty to natives, but it was not until 1897 that he was officially dismissed from the German colonial service for 'misuse of official power'. He died in 1918. It is a sad commentary on the Nazi regime that Hitler spoke of him as a 'model, if stern, Colonial administrator'.

The German method of administration. The imperial administration was similar in many ways to the earlier Arab system. Only in three areas—Ruanda, Urundi and Bukoba—did the Germans consider that tribal authority was strong enough to be worth preserving. In these three they allowed the native chiefs to retain their administrative authority under the supervision of a German Resident. These, however, were exceptions; elsewhere they considered that tribal institutions were too weak to be useful, and a system of direct rule was set up. The whole country, apart from the three Residencies, was divided into nineteen civil and two military districts, each under a district administrator or 'Bezirksamtmann'. Each district was then divided into groups of villages, consisting of twenty to thirty thousand people, in charge of which were officials known as 'Akida', and in charge of each village was an official known as a 'Jumbe'. The system was never satisfactory. There were only about seventy German officials, many of very poor quality, to administer the population of perhaps seven million, so that the actual working of the administration depended chiefly on the Akidas, who were usually Arab or Swahili. They were neither liked nor respected by the Africans whom they governed, and generally their only qualifications were that they could read and write and therefore obey orders. They had both executive and judicial powers and were responsible for the collection of taxes, but they were not properly supervised, and an official German report later admitted that 'the Akidas were in the habit of resorting to oppression and fraud, which made the administration detested by the people'. The general effect of the system was to further the breakdown of tribal institutions and to create a state of suspicion and enmity between the administration and the people. The bomas in which the Bezirksamtmänner lived at each provincial capital tell their own story. They were not built as civil dwellings. They were forts, with thick, square walls, windowless lower storeys, and machine-gun emplacements commanding fields of fire cleared in case of attack.

The German land policy. Meanwhile settlers were arriving: for the Germans, like the British later, assumed that the best chance of prosperity lay in the encouragement of European plantations. By 1888 about thirty such plantations had been started, and the number rose as colonists took up land in the North-east Highlands around Moshi and Arusha, and on the coast at Tanga and Pangani. In view of this colonization Germany declared its land policy in the Land Law of 1896, by which the whole of Tanganyika became Crown land except for the areas already claimed by chiefs, native communities, and individual landholders. It was also realized that most of the land was poor, and that its cultivators depended on a shifting cultivation; the *Land-Kommission* which marked out the reserves therefore reckoned to keep free from native cultivation four times the amount of land already cultivated. Unfortunately the boundaries were not strictly observed. Unfortunately also, time proved that the size of the reserves meant serious congestion, especially in the Meru and Kilimanjaro areas. This, combined with the constant demands for forced labour by the planters, and by the government for public works, seriously increased the discontent.

Early rebellions. It is not suprising, therefore, to find that the early history is marked by a series of rebellions and punitive expeditions, mostly originating in the south. The Arab rebellion on the coast was scarcely over before war began with the Hehe of the Southern Highlands, who resented German intrusion into their area. In 1891 they killed a quarter of a German column of 1000 men which had penetrated into their territory. Vengeance followed. In 1894 the walls of Kuirengu, the court town of the Hehe, 12 ft. wide, eight miles long, and built of stone, were stormed by the Germans. But Mkwawa the chief escaped. For four years the Germans tracked him. They offered a reward of

5000 rupees for his head, but so great was his influence that his followers refused to desert or betray him. When at last he was caught he had apparently died by his own hand rather than be taken alive. Trouble also occurred with the Chagga, the Nyamwezi, and the Gogo.

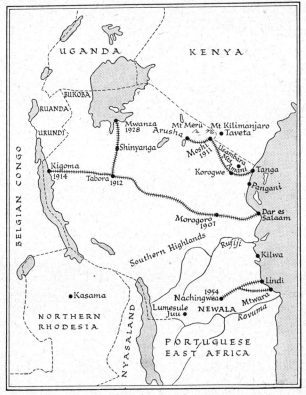

Map 15. Tanganyika.

The Maji-Maji rebellion, 1905–7. The bloodiest rising of all, known as the Maji-Maji rebellion, was still to come. There were tribes south of the Rufiji River who remained warlike and hostile despite the German attempts at pacification. They hated the Akidas, they hated the demands for forced labour, and they particularly hated the hut tax of three rupees which was imposed on the African population. Encouraged by witch doctors, who scattered water mixed with millet and maize over the warriors and assured them that this was proof against all bullets, nearly all the tribes between North Nyasa and the Kilwa coast rose in 1905, in a last great attempt to drive out the Germans. It was the most widespread revolt East Africa has ever seen. Mau Mau in comparison is a local affair concerning mainly one tribe. The Maji-Maji rebellion began with the murder of all Europeans in the area, and officials, missionaries, planters, and traders were killed almost to a man, so complete was the surprise. The revenge was equally horrible, for the Germans, finding themselves unable to end the rebellion simply by force of arms, decided to destroy the villages and crops of the affected area. By 1907 the entire south of German East Africa had been devastated, 120,000 Africans were dead, mainly from starvation, and the region was again at peace—the peace of complete exhaustion.

The reform of German colonial affairs. This rebellion was the end of the first phase of German colonization. Missionaries had sent home to Germany reports of atrocities, and the Social Democrats had supported them in the Reichstag. In 1906 their exposures shattered the happy dreams of empire which the German people had treasured. They exposed corruption and cruelty in every colony, and they gave facts to show that all colonies ran at a heavy loss to the fatherland. The Maji-Maji rebellion of 1905–7, a rising in the Cameroons in 1904–5, and the Herero War in South-west Africa drove home their arguments. Reform now became the order of the day. A separate Colonial Office was created and Dr Dernburg was appointed as the first Secretary for the Colonies.

Changed official attitude to African population. The change of policy, for which Dernburg was largely responsible, was especially noticeable in two respects. The first was the change of attitude towards the Africans. During the old regime little importance had been attached to the economic possibilities of the African population. The chief hope had been placed in the development of European plantations, and the Africans were regarded chiefly as useful labour for these. Dr Dernburg took a different view. He saw the colonies as a source of raw material for German industries, and the African population as the most valuable asset of the colonies whose economic development should be encouraged and whose rights should be guaranteed. Learning from Uganda, he encouraged cotton growing among the Africans and by 1914 the export of cotton from German East Africa was ten times greater than in 1902. In addition, the granting of lands to companies and settlers was tightened and forced labour was made illegal except for public works. Such measures were not popular with the settlers, however, and their influence not only made Dernburg's reforms largely ineffective, but also drove him from office in 1910.

Extension of the railway system. The second change in policy which coincided with the reform period was the increased attention given to communications. By 1900 the only railway in German East Africa was a 25-mile stretch of the Usambara railway which had been built in 1893 and was later extended. It was originally intended to run from Tanga to Lake Victoria, but the completion of the Uganda railway forestalled this plan. The next plan had been to build a trunk line from Dar es Salaam to Lake Tanganyika; this was actually started in 1905, but by 1907 had only reached as far as Morogoro. From that date railway construction went ahead at a much quicker pace. In the north the Usambara railway was extended to Moshi by 1911; this provided transport for the European plantations there, and was also of strategic value by reason of its position near the boundary of British East Africa. More important still was the extension of the Central Line which was pushed forward to Tabora by 1912 and to Kigoma on Lake Tanganyika by 1914, the previous arrival of the Lukuga railway through the Belgian Congo to Lake Tanganyika having acted as a strong incentive. Further plans were interrupted by war.

Economic condition in 1914. By 1914 the European population was about 5000, mainly Germans, and was concentrated chiefly in the North-east Highlands. The most important European crop was sisal, which had been introduced in 1893. Other crops which had been

8-2

found profitable were coffee, cotton, rubber and groundnuts. Much assistance had been given by the Agricultural Institute founded at Amani in the Usambara Mountains in 1902, and much by the extension of the railway system. Nevertheless, at the outbreak of war German East Africa was not a profitable concern, for her exports totalled only £1½ million and subsidies from Germany were necessary.

Education. In many ways the German administration may be criticized, but in one respect the Germans fulfilled their obligations to the African population very fully. This was in education. The government, and more especially the missions, provided education for well over 100,000 Africans, which was more than in any other German colony and was an example to the British after the war.

The World War, 1914–18. The world war of 1914–18 affected Tanganyika more than any other part of Africa, for elsewhere in the continent fighting had ceased by the end of 1915, while in Tanganyika it lasted until the armistice. It was tragically unnecessary. When Germany invaded Belgium in 1914, and Britain declared war on Germany, it was hoped that all areas in Africa might be 'permanently neutral' like the Belgian Congo. But it was not to be. The German commander, von Lettow-Vorbeck, with the aim of capturing the Uganda Railway, desired war on British East Africa. In August British ships shelled Dar es Salaam and a German patrol attacked Taveta. A few days later the German government suggested that possessions in East Africa should be considered neutral. But it was too late; the fighting had begun.

In British East Africa there was an immediate rush of settlers to Nairobi anxious to volunteer for the forces. Farms were left, families were left, and a disorganized medley of units tried to sort themselves out in the camps formed on Nairobi race-course, in the grounds of Government House, and at the other available spots. There was at first plenty of cause for worry, for the Germans had an overwhelming superiority of soldiers, arms and ammunition. But this superiority was of limited duration; for, as the British had complete naval supremacy, the Germans could receive no fresh supplies and were dependent on the land over which they fought. In fact there was no major attack by von Lettow-Vorbeck, and until 1916 most of the activity consisted of raids and patrols by both sides along the border. The British also made an attack on Tanga, but von Lettow-Vorbeck was given time to bring up reinforcements and the attack was repulsed. An interesting feature of the Tanga attack was the German use of a rather unexpected weapon in the shape of swarms of bees which were released against the British troops. There was some naval excitement also in 1915 when the German cruiser *Koenigsberg*, which had been raiding British shipping, was driven up the Rufiji River—where her hulk still lies—and put out of action. But it was in 1916 that the main assault began on German East Africa. From British East Africa a force led by General Smuts, who had just finished a successful campaign against the Germans in South-west Africa, advanced across the frontier, defeated the Germans near Kilimanjaro and in March occupied Moshi. Meanwhile an army from the Belgian Congo advanced into Ruanda and by September had reached Tabora, while a Uganda force had crossed the Kagera River and in July occupied Mwanza. By the end of 1916 British and Belgian troops had occupied the northern part of German East Africa and established a provisional administration there, while von Lettow-Vorbeck and his forces were confined to the area south of the Central railway. General Northey, advancing from the south, drove them from the Northern Rhodesian frontier, and in November 1917 the little German army was driven over the Rovuma River into Portuguese territory. From there they were pressed northwards again by British troops from Nyasaland, but von Lettow-Vorbeck, harassed and without supplies, still had sufficient genius and determination to turn to the offensive and actually advanced into Northern Rhodesia and captured Kasama in November 1918. At that point the armistice was declared.

The effects of the war on Tanganyika. No armistice, however, can turn the wasteland into productivity nor restore the sacrifice of lives which war demands. In 1918 Tanganyika looked as though it could never recover. The military campaign which had cost Britain £72 million had cost Tanganyika misery such as no other East African territory experienced. Most of the campaign did not take place on the green and pleasant highlands of the country but in its waterless and fly-infested scrubland, where the army sickened and the Africans of the porter corps died of malaria and dysentery by tens of thousands. Disease and famine followed the army across Tanganyika, reducing the population, reducing production, breaking to pieces the whole economic pattern as effectively as the retreating German army broke to pieces the Central railway. And as the war ended the influenza epidemic of 1918–19 also claimed its tens of thousands. 'Chiefs,' wrote Cameron later, 'were without people, and people without chiefs. Thirty thousand natives were said to have died of famine.... Amongst those remaining great numbers had pawned their children for food, husbands had left their wives, mothers had deserted their children, family life had very nearly ceased to exist.'

The 'Mandates' system. By the Treaty of Versailles Germany renounced all her claims to overseas possessions, but they were not handed over to the victors in full sovereignty. Instead, it was decided that the territories previously owned by Germany should be classed as 'mandates', and that the country responsible for their administration should be responsible to the Permanent Mandates Commission of the League of Nations, to whom annual reports were to be made of progress in each territory. In all mandated territories slavery was to be abolished entirely, and forced labour was forbidden except for public works, in which case adequate payment was to be made. The mandatory power was also obliged to 'promote to the utmost the material and moral well-being of its inhabitants'.

The work of Sir Horace Byatt. Britain was given the mandate to administer the former German East Africa except for the areas of Ruanda and Urundi, which were given to Belgium. Tanganyika, as the British area was renamed, was given a governor and an Executive Council in 1920. The governor appointed was Sir Horace Byatt. His task was to restore order and restore trade and, despite the after-effects of war and the world slump of the early 1920's, he did both. When he left in 1925 Tanganyika was exporting twice as much as she had exported before the war, and from 1923 no longer needed

British grants-in-aid. It was a remarkable achievement and provided a firm foundation on which Sir Donald Cameron could build.

The policy of Sir Donald Cameron. Sir Donald Cameron, who had been Chief Secretary in Nigeria, succeeded Byatt in 1925. He was the architect of modern Tanganyika and the administrative policy which he adopted was the exact opposite of that of the Germans. They had ruled mainly through alien administrators, which had encouraged the disintegration of tribal authority. Cameron's policy was to revive that authority and allow it to rule. There were two main considerations on which he based his policy. The first was that he had too few European officials to set up an efficient administration dependent on them alone. The second was that the mandate itself implied that the aim of government should be to enable the people of Tanganyika to stand by themselves, however distant the time might be when they would be able to do so. Sometimes Cameron's administration has been described as indirect rule; he himself preferred to call it native administration.

The reorganization of administration. Tanganyika, as he organized it, was divided into eleven provinces, each under a provincial commissioner whose area was divided into districts under district commissioners. In this there was nothing unusual, except Cameron's insistence on obtaining frank opinions from his subordinates and co-ordination of policy. The striking change was his deliberate revival of African institutions. In each district he sought to discover not who claimed to rule but who in fact was accepted by the tribe—or group of tribes—as the rightful ruler. The only cases where he failed to choose a satisfactory authority were in the coastal districts of the extreme south, where Angoni invasions, the disruptions caused by the Arab slave traders, and the Maji-Maji rebellion had broken tribal life into smaller fragments than elsewhere. But throughout the rest of Tanganyika, except the Bukoba District where the chiefs' authority had never been destroyed, Cameron chose his authorities so well that the system rapidly proved a success. Generally the native authority was made responsible for the maintenance of good order and government among the Africans in its area. To enable it to enforce its powers it was given a native court with limited powers of punishment and imprisonment. In addition the native authorities were made responsible for the collection of taxes under the supervision of the District Commissioner; with very few exceptions this was done efficiently and honestly, saving a great deal of expense which official tax collectors would have necessitated. There are now eight provinces instead of eleven, and larger grouping and federations of the native authorities are encouraged. Development has been supervised and backward tendencies have been checked, but Tanganyika has widely differing conditions and the speed and form of development among native administrations of different districts have varied greatly.

The Legislative Council and local government. It was to Cameron also, who always valued criticism very highly, that the early introduction of a Legislative Council in 1926 was due. It is with the advice and consent of this Council that the governor makes laws for the territory. In 1953 it was composed of fifteen official members and fourteen unofficial members. All these unofficial members were nominated by the governor, seven being Europeans, four being Africans and three being Asians. In 1954, however, it was announced that the Legislative Council was to be reconstituted. By the new arrangement there were to be thirty-one official members and thirty nominated unofficial members. Of these unofficial members ten were to be Africans, ten Asians, and ten Europeans. The ten members of each race were to be nominated on the basis of one from each of the eight provinces, one from Dar es Salaam, and one to represent special interests. The first meeting of the reconstituted Council was in 1955. In 1954 and 1955 reforms were also made in local government. Dar es Salaam was already a municipality, but Tanga, Arusha, Mwanza, and Lindi received Town Councils on an inter-racial basis, while in Newala District an inter-racial District Council was set up, with the District Commissioner as chairman. This Council included women.

Tanganyika and the United Nations Assembly. After the Second World War the status of Tanganyika was changed in name, and the basis of the administration of the territory in international constitutional law was laid down in the Trusteeship Agreement approved by the General Assembly of the United Nations in 1946. In fact, however, the general policy and procedure have remained unchanged, and the United Nations Assembly has simply replaced the League of Nations; the Trusteeship Council, to whom the reports are now sent, has replaced the Mandates Commission.

Economic development. The economic development of Tanganyika under British administration has been remarkable. By far the most important export since the beginning of the century has been sisal, which was introduced by the Germans, and whose value in 1952 was almost equal to that of all other products combined. Since before the Second World War Tanganyika has been the world's greatest producer, and the binder twine which ties the harvest of the American wheatlands comes almost entirely from Tanganyika's sisal. It is a plantation crop requiring a heavy outlay of capital and depends upon easy access to communications. It is therefore grown chiefly by Asians and Europeans and keeps close to the railway routes or the sea. The next most profitable product is coffee, grown by both the Europeans and Africans, while the third main product, cotton, is almost entirely African grown. Hides, skins and groundnuts also occupy an important position in Tanganyika's exports, and again these are chiefly African produced. Unfortunately the groundnuts scheme, run by the United Africa Company and later the Overseas Food Corporation on behalf of the British government in 1946, which was intended to encourage African production and prosperity while providing raw material for margarine and cattle food in Britain, was not a success. Apart from agriculture, Tanganyika also has the most valuable mineral resources of any of the East African territories. Until the 1930's these were not seriously developed, but since then they have come to take fourth place in the export list. At first gold was the most valuable mineral, but in 1940 Dr Williamson, a Canadian geologist, discovered an extremely rich diamond pipe near Shinyanga. By 1951 diamonds were bringing in eight times the profits of gold. The most valuable stone yet discovered in the Shinyanga mine, valued at over £10,000, Dr Williamson gave to Princess Elizabeth as a wedding present.

Transport. Together with increased production have gone improved methods of transport. In 1928 a branch line from Tabora to Mwanza was completed, which opened up the valuable producing areas around Lake Victoria and provided closer links with Kenya and Uganda through the lake steamers. In order to facilitate economic development in the south, especially in connexion with the groundnuts scheme, the Southern Province railway was constructed and by 1954 had been opened as far as Nachingwea. Originally the railway began from near Lindi, but since the new port of Mtwara was opened in 1954 the latter has become the main outlet. As in other parts of East Africa, road services have developed as feeders to the railway.

General economic difficulties. Although Tanganyika's prosperity has been rapid, it has not been without difficulties. Apart from setbacks caused by rebellions and the 1914–18 war Tanganyika's ambition to become self-supporting in foodstuffs is made difficult by lack of water and the need for a still more comprehensive system of communications. The tsetse fly is also a problem and in certain areas this pest is advancing; generally speaking, however, the tsetse tend to be fairly static and many of the large areas infested by them are in any case waterless. These difficulties are not easily or quickly solved, but advances are being made. Swynnerton led the attack on the tsetse, and investigations were made in 1954 concerning the possibility of using the Rufiji River for irrigation purposes.

General economic policy. The general economic policy of the British administration has been to increase the wealth of the country for the benefit of all. The great increase in the exports of cotton and of native-grown coffee are a measure of their success in promoting the wealth of the African producer. But there has been no rigid exclusion of settlers. Where there is land available, and where the money and skill of the settler has seemed likely to help the general prosperity of the territory, he has been allowed to enter, and his sisal plantations in particular have been of vital importance. Nevertheless, the vast majority of Tanganyika's cultivated areas are farmed by Africans and it is the increase in productivity on these farms which seems to offer the surest road to an improved standard of living for the bulk of the people.

Social development. African population. Since the commencement of British administration the African population of Tanganyika has increased steadily, and in 1953 was estimated at about eight million which, as one might expect from its greater size, is considerably more than that of either Kenya or Uganda. The Sukuma are the largest of the 120 tribes in the territory, the next largest being the Nyamwezi, Ha, Makonde, Gogo, Haya, and Chagga, and most of them live on the highlands, the lakeside, and the coastal plain. In these regions most of them graze their cattle, cultivate their land, and hope to produce enough food for themselves besides a small cash crop of cotton, coffee, or groundnuts. Some tribes, like the Masai, are purely pastoral. Great importance has been attached by the government and missions to the development of better farming methods, and experimental farms and training centres have been set up, but in general agriculture is still primitive. The religion of most of the African population is still some form of ancestor worship, often with a vague idea of a disinterested 'Supreme Being'. On the coast, however, and along the old trade routes where Arab influence has been greatest, Mohammedanism is very strong. During the last half century the Christian missions, half of which are Roman Catholic and half Protestant, have spread through much of the territory with increasing success, and the total number of converts claimed by 1953 was about one and a quarter million. The missions and government have also paid particular attention to African education. The 10-year plan prepared in 1947, and revised in 1950, provides for a considerable increase in the number of pupils attending schools, including girls.

European population. The European population of Tanganyika by 1954 was about 18,000, composed of government officials, missionaries, business men, and settlers. Under German administration most of the Europeans were Germans, but after the 1914–18 war all Germans were forced to leave and their properties were sold. Most of their mission stations, however, were taken over by missionaries of the same, or similar, denominations. In 1925 German settlers were allowed to return. Most of them were financed by the Usugara Company, which was in practice, although not in name, an instrument of the German government, and almost all of the settlers were Nazis. During the Second World War they were interned; later, most of them were repatriated and the Germans are now far less numerous than either the Greeks or British.

Asian population. As in other parts of East Africa the Asians are more numerous than the Europeans and number about 60,000. The part they play in the economic life of the country is outstanding, for not only have they controlled the petty trade of Tanganyika for many years, but recently they have also taken a large share in major commercial undertakings. In addition they are considerable landowners, much of the land having been purchased from the Germans who were forced to sell after the First and Second World Wars. Today not only is much of the town property, especially in Dar es Salaam, owned by Asians, but Asians are also among the greatest sisal producers.

POSTSCRIPT

Tanganyika, Zanzibar, Uganda, and Kenya together form the political patchwork which is East Africa. It is typical of the British Commonwealth of Nations, for in it there is unity but not uniformity. Each territory is linked with Britain, but no two links are identical, and while each territory is aiming at self-government their methods vary as local conditions vary. Tanganyika's status is that of a protectorate under the United Nations Organization, yet its administration is in British hands. As a stepping-stone towards self-government it is trying the constitutional expedient of racial parity. Zanzibar is a protectorate governed by the Sultan with the advice of a British Resident. Uganda is a protectorate ruled by a governor and composed of various African kingdoms, of which Buganda is outstanding; and the problem of regulating the speed of constitutional advances to suit each part of the protectorate is one of extreme delicacy, as the recent constitutional crisis showed. Kenya is different again, for, apart from the coastal strip which is a protectorate, it is a

Crown colony and its Highlands have attracted a much larger European population than elsewhere; racial and social problems, therefore, are particularly complex, and in Kenya the constitutional experiment of a multi-racial government is being made.

While the political status and organization of the East African territories differ amongst themselves, they differ also from those of other African members of the British Commonwealth. In West Africa the recent policy has been a short, quick passage to self-government. In Central Africa a federation has been established. In South Africa the 'apartheid' policy of racial segregation appears to be gaining ground. The East African territories have chosen different courses which they consider more appropriate to their own particular aims and difficulties, and after the recent far-reaching constitutional changes a stable settling-down period seems likely.

But constitutional and social problems are not the only questions confronting East Africa, for one of the features of the Report of the Royal Commission on East Africa (1953–5) was the emphasis on the importance of economic considerations. It pointed out that East Africa, apart from the great deserts, was at once one of the physically poorest parts of Africa and the latest to be brought into touch with the outside world. Moreover, while European standards have encouraged Africans towards a higher standard of living, the peace and improved health services which those standards have involved have resulted in a larger population and therefore less land per head. How far these facts can be offset by improved methods of cultivation and the development of industries remains to be seen, but it is certain that the progress of East Africa will be determined quite as much by its economic problems as by its political ones.

It is hoped that this book, by giving the background of the peoples and territories of East Africa, may help towards the solution of those problems by assisting the harmonious understanding on which a wise advance must depend. It is also hoped that by showing how much has been achieved in the past it may give some reasonable hope for the future.

LOCAL GOVERNMENT IN KENYA

Before the coming of the British there was no central government in Kenya; that is, no one person or body controlled the whole country and could give orders which had to be obeyed throughout the land. There were, however, local governments which could make themselves obeyed within limited areas, and the tribes who shared the land had their own customs for their particular areas. These were usually enforced by Councils of Elders, but were effective only in the nearby settlements from which members were drawn. It is not possible to describe in this book the different forms these councils took, so those of one tribe, the Akamba, have been taken as an example. This particular tribe has been chosen because the headquarters of the British government on the mainland of East Africa was originally at Machakos and the Commissioner there was probably influenced by the organization of the Akamba.

This tribe did not have chiefs, but was broken up into a number of small groups in even the largest of which the members lived within easy walking distance of each other. They were presided over by the Nzama ya Ndua (Council of Elders) which was made up of the chief elders of the group, each of whom had to pay for admission to it. The chief function of this council was to act as a court of law, but it was also responsible for religious observances. That is why these councils usually centred round places of sacrifice. Nowadays a council like this might be expected to pass new laws, but the Akamba did not think this was necessary. This was partly because laws only come in with change. If there are no big changes, men will expect their neighbours to be guided by the established customs of the tribe or group. This is particularly true if a man is interested only in a small area, and most of the tribes in Kenya occupied only comparatively small areas. Again, in the early days of many countries laws were really better described as the orders of some one person; and in the early days of Kenya there were very few people in a position to give orders to the whole tribe. None of the tribes now included in Kenya, except perhaps those in North Nyanza, had chiefs, although the Masai had their Laibon. Even these really held their position because they were the witch doctors of the tribe. Nor did the coming of the first Europeans make much difference. Those who penetrated inland were for the most part either explorers, who had no intention of staying, or missionaries who had their hands full teaching the people the laws of God. Then came the Imperial British East Africa Company, which was anxious to develop East Africa but lacked the resources to do so.

Policy of the British government. In 1895, therefore, the British government took over from I.B.E.A. the responsibility for the government of the area between the Tana and the Umba, stretching as far to the west as a line drawn from Lake Rudolf to the east of Lakes Baringo and Naivasha, down to the German East Africa border, and including in 1902 the territory to the east of the lake. This whole area was henceforth to be known as the East Africa Protectorate. The very name showed that England was thinking of the country as a whole and not as a collection of entirely separate tribes. It had therefore to be administered as a whole. To do this, communications had to be improved and order kept over a wide area. The government also aimed at raising the standard of the people as a whole. Recurrent famine had therefore to be checked, health improved and education started. When this was done the number of Africans greatly increased, because fewer were killed in battle or died of disease or famine. Apart from anything else, this increase in population had made it essential to develop the country more than in the days before the coming of the British. Development of the country meant that money had to be collected, and the fairest way to do this was thought to be a hut tax of 2s. per annum, which was introduced in 1903. The amount collected by this in the province of Ukamba in 1903–4 was £3400. It has gone up considerably since then, but has remained the same proportion of the money which a man could earn in a month's work. Change also meant laws. The British tried to enlist the help of the local councils in carrying out these laws, although Ainsworth, who was the first Sub-Commissioner of the Ukamba Province, thought that the areas over which these Councils had control were too small and that the elders themselves were not sufficiently respected by the younger men. He suggested, therefore, that headmen should be appointed by the government, and in 1902 the Village Headman's Ordinance became law. This ordinance applied to the whole of the East Africa Protectorate, but in showing the changes it led to, one particular district, the Ukamba Province, has again been taken as an example. Under this law headmen were appointed to look after the maintenance of roads and to check criminals. It was difficult at first for the government to choose headmen wisely, and cases were reported of the oppression of the African people by headmen and police. The government was shocked. It had not been realized that there were few Africans who could be trusted to deal fairly with their subordinates under these laws, which were outside their idea of government.

Native Authority Ordinance. After six years, therefore, there had to be a change, and in 1908 the more reliable government servants were appointed as chiefs and given authority over wider areas. In 1912 the Native Authority Ordinance, which applied to the country as a whole, gave the chiefs much wider powers—they were allowed to give orders, for instance, on such subjects as water-pollution.

Local Native Councils. In 1924 a further big step forward was taken when Local Native Councils were started. These may be said to have grown out of such bodies as the Nzama of the Akamba, which has already been described, for the Akamba were not the only tribe with these forms of government. These Local Native Councils, or as they are called today African District Councils, consist of the District Commissioner, the District Officer if there is one, and the local chiefs. Very often there are people on the Council who are not chiefs, but before they are appointed the local Africans can send to the District Commissioner a list of the men they would like to see chosen. As the Africans also have a say in the appointment of chiefs, which are usually made in a 'baraza' by the Provincial Commissioner, they are gradually taking over the responsibility of a good deal of the local government. This provides good training; for a citizen learns about liberty, rights and duties by being a citizen. Local government is in fact the foundation of good government, and many great statesmen have served an apprenticeship in local politics. At the same time local councils cannot be allowed to neglect important services, such as roads; they are subject, therefore, to control by the Minister for Local Government, who is an official sitting on the Executive Council. There is a link also with the central government through the District Commissioner, who in his turn is under the Provincial Commissioner. The Provincial Commissioner is in charge of one of the six provinces into which Kenya is divided, and is himself under the Minister for African Affairs.

Link with the central government. It will be noticed that there is a far closer link between the local government and the central government than there is in England. Another difference between England and Kenya is that in Kenya two rather different systems of local government have grown up side by side: the African Local Government and the European Local Government. In African areas there have been Local Native Councils, or African District Councils, since 1924; and in the Highlands, District Councils, on which all the members were Europeans, were established in 1928. Among these were the District Councils for the Trans-Nzoia, Kisumu-Londiani, and Laikipia.

Development of urban government. So far only rural local government has been described, but the coming of the railway led to economic development in the East Africa Protectorate, and ordinances for local government had to deal with the problem of urban areas. In 1903 the East African Townships Ordinance was issued. This stated that certain areas were to rank as townships. Rules were made for their health and good administration, and their cleaning, lighting and policing were declared to be the responsibility of the District Commissioner. At the same time it was stated that a rate could be levied to supply the money needed. Nairobi, however, was declared to be in a special position, as it was the only town of any size in the interior, and its affairs have been managed since 1900 by a committee. Nevertheless, the fact that Nairobi had a committee did not mean that its citizens had full control over its affairs. That was to come later. Until 1917 a government officer was always the chairman of the committee, and there was a majority of officials. It was not until 1919 that the first local government election was held in Nairobi, and the first mayor was elected three years later.

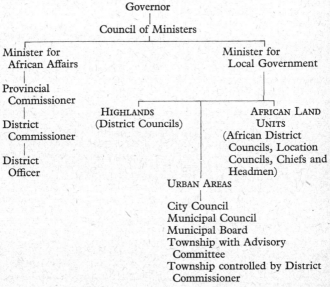

Municipalities. Nairobi became a city by royal charter in 1950. It had led the group of developing townships ever since the railway head-quarters had been transferred to it as the growing capital of the colony.

241

Townships. There are smaller urban areas than these municipalities, for the most part entirely administered by the District Commissioner responsible for the township. Some of these are rather more advanced, having committees of inhabitants who advise the District Commissioner. He is not, of course, obliged to agree to their suggestions. Members of all races are elected to these township committees, for members of all races live in the urban areas. When the town becomes sufficiently important it is called a municipality and has a municipal council—Nakuru, for instance, has a municipal council.

The system of government so far described is illustrated by the diagram on p. 241.

Introduction of County Councils. In 1952 an effort was made to fill an important gap in this system. The European District Councils did not cover as wide an area as the African District Councils; nor did they charge a local rate until 1946, and even then only one District Council had a rating system. In fact they have been described as little more than glorified road boards. In 1952, therefore, an ordinance was passed which allowed districts in the White Highlands to present schemes setting up County Councils. These would correspond roughly to the African District Councils, whose position in the African Reserves would be unaffected. They would be in authority over the District Councils (Councils divided into Urban and Rural Districts in much the same way as they are in England).

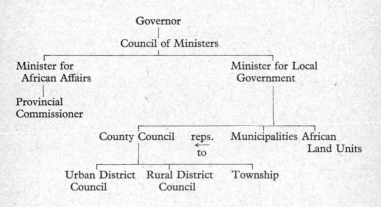

The six municipalities in Kenya are also to be included. They are Nairobi, a city by royal charter, Nakuru, which has a municipal council,

Mombasa (the old capital of the colony), Kisumu, Kitale, and Eldoret, which all have municipal Boards at different levels of development. All these municipalities are controlled by multi-racial Councils or Boards, and they will be able to keep these and to send representatives to the County Council in whose area they are to be found. The present picture of local government is therefore shown by the diagram on p. 242.

In addition, a typical County Council is shown in the figure below:

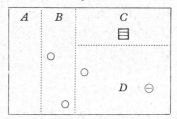

County Council

All the area enclosed in the large rectangle is controlled by a County Council except for ▤, which represents a municipality;
⊖ represents an Urban District Council;
○ are townships.

The small rectangles within the large rectangle represent four different Rural District Councils—*A*, *B*, *C*, *D*.

Composition of County Councils. The County Councils will consist of Europeans, Asians and African councillors, but not more than two-thirds will be elected Europeans. The number of councillors will vary according to the interests of the different communities they represent.

Functions. They will have the general control of all county roads and of bridges, fords, drifts, culverts and drains. They may also appoint a Medical Officer of Health, make grants of money towards the establishment and maintenance of hospitals, build, maintain and manage schools, libraries, museums and art galleries; license shops in rural areas; deal with welfare centres, trees and outspans. On undertaking any, or all, of these tasks the County Councils are allowed to draw up by-laws which have the effect of local regulations. In order to carry out these functions the County Councils are instructed to levy rates. Lastly they may delegate these functions to the Urban and Rural District Councils and townships which fall under them.

243

Composition of Rural and Urban District Councils. The members of the Rural District Councils will continue to be elected Europeans because the area which they cover will be predominantly European. The position is different in urban areas, because there are a number of Asians living in townships. In Urban District Councils, or townships, therefore, the Councils will be wholly, or partly, nominated, and will include non-Europeans.

Qualifications for election to a Council. The qualifications for election to a Council are similar to those in England. You must be twenty-one, and either own property in the area, or have lived there for twelve months. In addition you must live in premises of a given minimum annual value, or have earned £10 a month for six months in the previous year.

Comparison with English local government. Both the European and the African District Councils function as in England, the members doing a good deal of their work through committees. Their work is, however, more limited in scope, although it is hoped that it will increase with the introduction of the County Councils Ordinance. This is partly because the country is not yet fully developed and there are fewer services available. In England, for instance, an Urban District Council will be expected, among its other duties, to deal with the provision of allotments, swimming baths, washhouses, libraries, museums and parks.

APPENDIX II

SUGGESTIONS FOR FURTHER READING

The titles given are of books recommended for schools that are building a reference library. Those marked with a dagger (†) are out of print and can only be purchased second-hand at the current market value, which in the case of some of the earlier works may be considerable.

Books which appear more than once are starred (*) in the later entries.

GENERAL

L. W. HOLLINGSWORTH, *A Short History of the East Coast of Africa.* (Clear and simple outline. Easily obtainable.)

† SIR R. COUPLAND, *East Africa and its Invaders.* (Detailed standard authority on early history.)

SIR R. COUPLAND, *The Exploitation of East Africa.* (Detailed authority following on *East Africa and its Invaders.*)

S. COLE, *The Pre-history of East Africa*. (Penguin book. Easily obtainable.)

I. F. EVANS, *The British in Tropical Africa*. (General outline of development.)

A. PIM, *Economic History of Tropical Africa*. (General outline of economic development.)

†K. INGHAM, *Europe and Africa*. (Outline of S. C. syllabus on Tropical Africa.)

C. G. SELIGMAN, *Races of Africa*. (Authoritative and easily obtainable in Home University Library series.)

LORD HAILEY, *An African Survey*. (Very detailed and authoritative survey of African affairs.)

†T. R. BATTEN, *Tropical Africa in World History*. (Useful, simple school book in four cheap volumes.)

R. REUSCH, *History of East Africa*. (This gives valuable and interesting detail, particularly in connexion with the Arabs and early settlement on the coast.)

CHAPTER I. EARLY HISTORY OF EAST AFRICA

*SIR R. COUPLAND, *East Africa and its Invaders*.

*L. W. HOLLINGSWORTH, *A Short History of the East Coast of Africa*.

J. H. PARRY, *Europe and a Wider World*. (Outline of European discovery and settlement up to 1715. Hutchinson's University Library, No. 31.)

E. PRESTAGE, *Portuguese Pioneers*. (Authoritative detailed account of Portuguese discovery.)

LEY, *Portuguese Voyages*. (Useful source book. Everyman series.)

HART, *Sea Road to the Indies*. (An interesting account of the Portuguese maritime explorers.)

GENESTA HAMILTON, *In the Wake of da Gama*. (Colourful account of the Portuguese pioneers in East Africa.)

Apart from *Akamba*—Lindblom, *Akikuyu*—Father Cagnolo and *The Social Institutions of the Kipsigis*—Peristiany, most of the detailed studies of tribes are out of print and very scarce. There is, however, a new series of detailed East African Tribal studies by the International African Institute. In addition the East African Literature Bureau has produced two cheap, useful series: (1) 'The Peoples of Kenya' (titles still in print are *The Kamba* and *The Nandi*). (2) 'Custom and Tradition in East Africa' (titles still in print are *Nandi Customs and Law*, *Kamba Customs and Law*, *Home life in Kikuyuland*, *The Ntemi*).

Chapters II and X. Earlier and Later Zanzibar

*Sir R. Coupland, *East Africa and its Invaders*.
*Sir R. Coupland, *The Exploitation of East Africa*.
*L. W. Hollingsworth, *A Short History of the East Coast of Africa*.
L. W. Hollingsworth, *Zanzibar under the Foreign Office*. (Standard book on the period.)
R. H. Crofton, *Zanzibar Affairs 1914–1933*. (Contains specialized source material.)
G. E. Tidbury, *The Clove Tree*. (General account of clove industry.)

Chapters III and IV. Slavery, the Slave Trade and Abolition

Sir R. Coupland, *The British Anti-Slavery Movement*. (A general outline of the movement. Home University Library series.)
*Sir R. Coupland, *East Africa and its Invaders*.
*Sir R. Coupland, *The Exploitation of East Africa*.
†W. E. Ward, *Africa and European Trade*. (Longman's African Histories, Bk. 2. Cheap and simple outline.)
J. D. Fage, *An Introduction to the History of West Africa*. (Contains the best available account of the West African slave trade.)
E. A. Loftus, *Elton and the East African Coast Slave Trade*. (Cheap abridged version of Part I of *Travels and Researches among the Lakes and Mountains of Central Africa, 1879*.)
J. A. Williamson, *Builders of the Empire*. (Contains useful biography of Wilberforce.)
J. Mbotela, *The Freeing of the Slaves in East Africa*. (A translation from the Swahili account by the son of one of the slaves freed by the British.)

Chapter V. Exploration

J. I. Macnair, *Livingstone's Travels*. (An account of Livingstone's travels in his own words, with a brief explanation.)
J. I. Macnair. *Livingstone the Liberator*. (Collins' pocket series biography.)
D. Middleton, *Baker of the Nile*. (Draws largely on Baker's own account.)
J. M. Synge, *Book of Discovery*. (Interesting detail for school work.)
M. Perham and J. Simmons, *African Discovery*. (Extracts from explorers' accounts, with brief explanations.)

'Early Travellers in East Africa'. This series of cheap, useful books includes:

> *Early Travellers in Acholi.*
> *Thomson, through Masai Land.*
> *Charles New.*
> *Johnston on Kilimanjaro.*
> *Gregory: the Great Rift Valley.*
> *Speke.*
> *Baker.*

(These books cover explorers whose work it was not possible to treat in ch. v.)

VERE HODGE and P. COLLISTER, *Pioneers of East Africa*. (A short book providing useful background.)

J. A. HUNTER and D. MANNIX, *African Bush Adventures*. (This includes an account of Tippoo Tib and some of the early East African settlers.)

The works of some explorers themselves are listed below but may not be easily obtainable:

L. KRAPF, *Travels and Missionary Labours in East Africa.*

J. H. SPEKE, *Journal of the Discovery of the Source of the Nile.*

SIR R. F. BURTON, *First Footsteps in East Africa.*

D. LIVINGSTONE, *Missionary Travels and Researches in South Africa.*

D. LIVINGSTONE, *Narrative of an Expedition to the Zambezi and its Tributaries.*

H. M. STANLEY, *Autobiography.*

H. M. STANLEY, *Through the Dark Continent.*

H. M. STANLEY, *In Darkest Africa.*

J. THOMSON, *Through Masai Land.*

J. THOMSON, *To the Central African Lakes and Back.*

CHAPTER VI. MISSIONS

R. OLIVER, *The Missionary Factor in East Africa*. (Detailed authoritative account of missionary development.)

A. R. TUCKER, *Eighteen Years in Uganda and East Africa*. (Bishop Tucker's work in East Africa.)

H. R. A. PHILP, *A New Day in Kenya*. (Account of Protestant missionary effort up to 1935.)

*L. KRAPF, *Travels and Missionary Labours in East Africa.*

FORBES, *Planting the Faith in Darkest Africa*. (An account of the work of Père Lourdel.)

BOUNIOL, *The White Fathers and their Missions.*

CHAPTER VII. SCRAMBLE AND PARTITION

★SIR R. COUPLAND, *The Exploitation of East Africa.*

P. L. McDERMOTT, *British East Africa or I.B.E.A.* (An account of I.B.E.A. and its work.)

F. JACKSON, *Early Days in East Africa.* (Jackson's travels and work in East Africa.)

E. LEWIN, *The Germans and Africa.* (An account of the German Colonial Movement.)

CHAPTER VIII. UGANDA TO 1890

H. B. THOMAS AND R. SCOTT, *Uganda.* (Standard work on Uganda giving history and general survey.)

†H. B. THOMAS, *The Story of Uganda.* (Small, simple school history.)

R. P. ASHE, *Two Kings of Uganda.* (Account of events by early missionary. Not easily obtainable.)

C. W. HATTERSLEY, *The Baganda at Home.* (Account of the Baganda. Not easily obtainable.)

C. NORTHCOTT and J. REASON, *Living Names. Six Missionaries in Africa.* (Small, cheap book giving useful outline of Mackay. Fuller biographies are not easily obtainable.)

CHAPTER IX. LORD LUGARD

F. D. LUGARD, *The Rise of our Empire in East Africa.* (Account of work in East Africa.)

★H. B. THOMAS and R. SCOTT, *Uganda.*

†★H. B. THOMAS, *The Story of Uganda.*

★R. OLIVER, *The Missionary Factor in East Africa.*

★A. R. TUCKER, *Eighteen Years in Uganda and East Africa.*

J. V. WILD, *The Story of the Uganda Agreement.* (Cheap, useful account in the series 'A Treasury of East African History' published by the East African Literature Bureau.)

CHAPTER X. (See Chapter II)

CHAPTER XI. RAILWAY AND ECONOMIC DEVELOPMENT OF KENYA

E. HUXLEY, *White Man's Country.* (Lord Delamere's biography, with background history of Kenya's early development.)

M. F. HILL, *Permanent Way*. (Detailed account of the Uganda Railway with fairly full historical background. There is a very much smaller version by Patrick Pringle, *The Story of a Railway*, published by the East African Literature Bureau.)

*F. JACKSON, *Early Days in East Africa*.

J. H. PATTERSON, *The Man-Eaters of Tsavo*. (An exciting account of difficulties caused by lions in the building of the railway.)

Settlers of Kenya. (A condensation of *White Man's Country*.)

M. F. HILL, *Kenya, Land of Endeavour*. (Easily obtained booklet written for the Bulawayo Exhibition.)

F. H. GOLDSMITH, *Ainsworth, Pioneer Administrator*. (Provides interesting local background.)

CHAPTER XII. CONSTITUTIONAL DEVELOPMENT OF KENYA

Books giving relevant detail further to that included in this chapter are not easy to obtain.

CHAPTER XIII. THE LATER HISTORY OF UGANDA

*H. B. THOMAS and R. SCOTT, *Uganda*.

†*H. B. THOMAS, *The Story of Uganda*.

J. V. WILD, *The Uganda Mutiny*. (Cheap, useful account in the series 'A Treasury of East African History' published by the East African Literature Bureau.)

*M. F. HILL, *Permanent Way*.

SEMPA, *The Buganda Government and its Constitutional Functions*. (Cheap small book in English and Luganda published through the East African Literature Bureau.)

CHAPTER XIV. THE LATER HISTORY OF TANGANYIKA

STEER, *Judgement on German Africa*. (Contains very readable account of Tanganyika's background and development for the general reader.)

V. L. CAMERON, *Across Africa*. (One of the few books available on Tanganyika.)

R. HINDEN, *Local Government and the Colonies*. (One of the few easily obtainable books on Tanganyika's local government.)

INDEX

Chief references in italics

INDEX

Thin
29.iii.57